TECHNICAL TRAINING MANAGEMENT

BCS, THE CHARTERED INSTITUTE FOR IT

BCS, The Chartered Institute for IT, is committed to making IT good for society. We use the power of our network to bring about positive, tangible change. We champion the global IT profession and the interests of individuals, engaged in that profession, for the benefit of all.

Exchanging IT expertise and knowledge
The Institute fosters links between experts from industry, academia and business to promote new thinking, education and knowledge sharing.

Supporting practitioners
Through continuing professional development and a series of respected IT qualifications, the Institute seeks to promote professional practice tuned to the demands of business. It provides practical support and information services to its members and volunteer communities around the world.

Setting standards and frameworks
The Institute collaborates with government, industry and relevant bodies to establish good working practices, codes of conduct, skills frameworks and common standards. It also offers a range of consultancy services to employers to help them adopt best practice.

Become a member
Over 70,000 people including students, teachers, professionals and practitioners enjoy the benefits of BCS membership. These include access to an international community, invitations to a roster of local and national events, career development tools and a quarterly thought-leadership magazine. Visit www.bcs.org/membership to find out more.

Further Information
BCS, The Chartered Institute for IT,
First Floor, Block D,
North Star House, North Star Avenue,
Swindon, SN2 1FA, United Kingdom.
T +44 (0) 1793 417 424
F +44 (0) 1793 417 444
(Monday to Friday, 09:00 to 17:00 UK time)
www.bcs.org/contact
http://shop.bcs.org/

TECHNICAL TRAINING MANAGEMENT

Commercial skills aligned to the provision of successful training outcomes

CEdMA Europe

Published by BCS Learning and Development Ltd, a wholly owned subsidiary of BCS, The Chartered Institute for IT, First Floor, Block D, North Star House, North Star Avenue, Swindon, SN2 1FA, UK.
www.bcs.org

ISBN: 978-1-78017-480-8
Hardback ISBN: 978-1-78017-496-9
PDF ISBN: 978-1-78017-481-5
ePUB ISBN: 978-1-78017-482-2
Kindle ISBN: 978-1-78017-483-9

British Cataloguing in Publication Data.
A CIP catalogue record for this book is available at the British Library.

Disclaimer:
The views expressed in this book are of the authors and do not necessarily reflect the views of the Institute or BCS Learning and Development Ltd except where explicitly stated as such. Although every care has been taken by the authors and BCS Learning and Development Ltd in the preparation of the publication, no warranty is given by the authors or BCS Learning and Development Ltd as publisher as to the accuracy or completeness of the information contained within it and neither the authors nor BCS Learning and Development Ltd shall be responsible or liable for any loss or damage whatsoever arising by virtue of such information or any instructions or advice contained within this publication or by any of the aforementioned.

Publisher's acknowledgements
Reviewer: Jeremy Green
Publisher: Ian Borthwick
Commissioning editor: Rebecca Youé
Production manager: Florence Leroy
Project manager: Sunrise Setting Ltd
Copy-editor: Mary Hobbins
Proofreader: Barbara Eastman
Indexer: John Silvester
Cover design: Alex Wright
Typeset by Lapiz Digital Services, Chennai, India.

CONTENTS

LIST OF FIGURES AND TABLES

AUTHOR

This book was written on behalf of CEdMA by **Philip Bourne**. Philip has 30 years of proven management and directorship skills within the computer and education/training industry. He has continually achieved annualised business growth and high gross profits, while striving for optimum outcomes in a results-orientated environment, without compromising quality of service or standards. He has developed and maintained global business relationships, and people from varying multicultural backgrounds, for companies such as Lotus Development, IBM and Symantec. Key to his success has been his ability to provide and develop innovative solutions to broad-based business and training challenges.

Philip has held positions as board chairman with CEdMA, vice president for BCS and non-executive director for BCS Learning & Development Ltd.

CEdMA Europe (Computer Education Management Association – Europe) is the premier organisation for training executives, managers, and professionals on a management path within the vendor Information Communication Technology (ICT) arena, covering hardware, software, cloud and learning technology-related companies.

CEdMA Europe was founded in September 1993, following a successful launch of CEdMA in the USA in January 1991, when training development managers from Intel, Interactive, Hewlett Packard, Novell, Santa Cruz Operations, Sun Microsystems, and Wang Laboratories met to discuss the creation of a consortium that focused on the training needs in the computer industry, where it was decided that the computer industry could benefit from an organisation that would provide leadership and direction in establishing standards for training.

Through its 200 members that represent over 50 global technology companies, CEdMA Europe provides access to a vast level of experience and resources who share a passion for providing high-quality training on technology and certification products, while running efficient and successful commercial business units.

For commercially based training professionals who are actively employed in an ICT company, membership provides a niche opportunity to really understand the education business through the years of hard-earned experience of fellow CEdMA members and:

- receive timely insight into the pulse of the technology training industry;
- gain access to useful data points on industry benchmarks and standards;
- gain access to a forum for colleagues to exchange data and ideas on education projects;
- learn from others what it took to successfully drive specific types of projects.

For more information contact info@cedma-europe.org, or visit http://www.cedma.org/cedma-europe.

PREFACE
The accelerated world of training

By the year 2000, technology was increasingly being introduced to enhance the learning experience through active engagement, group participation, interaction and feedback, with the ability to connect to real-world contexts and access ongoing information.

With the advent of social media and collaboration tools, educators gained significant opportunities to connect learners and take education in new directions. Being able to simulate real-world situations enabled students to engage in ways that were not possible with previously available instructional methods.

Learning in the 21st century places new demands on learners to use technology to access, analyse and organise information. It places responsibility on learning providers to establish an environment that supports creativity, innovation, communication, collaboration, problem solving, decision making and engagement with the learner, to ensure learning occurs within the context of the real-world environment they are involved with.

Technology in training is driving change in terms of empowering and encouraging self-directed learning. For it to succeed, learning providers need to shift their emphasis to being facilitators and collaborators in the students' increasingly self-directed learning world.

This book provides guidance on how to establish, run and manage a commercial technical training organisation from a managerial perspective. It covers business disciplines, employee skills, risks and opportunities as it relates to supporting a training business within a broader product and service-oriented organisation.

For managers with prior knowledge of training provision, it provides a detailed insight into all aspects of running a successful business, be it a small to medium enterprise or large multinational organisation. For those new to training or progressing their managerial career, it provides knowledge, guidance and reference on the requirements one needs to establish a successful service-based training business.

1   THE TECHNICAL TRAINING ORGANISATION
Introduction to the key elements and activities

This chapter provides an overview of what a technical training organisation provides in terms of its scope, key activities, structure and rationale, and an introduction to the evolving discipline of customer success management and the part it plays in its overall success.

As a career, technical training provides a rich spectrum of opportunities to develop skills, knowledge and business acumen, which are briefly summarised at the end of the chapter in terms of key disciplines.

WHAT IS TECHNICAL TRAINING?

Technical training covers any aspect of an employee's job role where they are required to use and apply technical components in the execution of their job.

> Technical skills tend to be job specific, whereas so-called soft skills (such as management and negotiation) are independent of role and hence transferable.

The training can cover technology applications, products, sales and service implementation. The scope can be broad and cover the acquisition of knowledge, skills and competencies leading to overall individual or company performance improvement.

Technical training can be purchased directly from a vendor, authorised training partner, contractor or university/college, or it can be provided by an internal training group. Internal training, often known as in-house training, can be delivered by dedicated technical instructors or subject matter experts (SMEs) from within the company.

Vendors who have a service arm to their business will often establish a training group to focus on the provision of both customer and partner-related training, normally for a fee. When the training is diverse or requires a substantial investment in training delivery, they will use a combination of training partners and independent training contractors.

The benefit of investing in technical training is to ensure employees have the confidence and skills necessary to perform their work at a high level, resulting in improved employee morale, efficiency and gaining business benefit from the technology investment.

COMMERCIAL TRAINING

Customers who invest in technology often require support regarding implementation, obtaining expected returns on investment (ROI) and technical assistance. As a result, most technology manufacturers establish service departments comprising technical support, consulting and training.

On the training front, technology companies may engage third-party training companies or business partners, undertake it themselves or a combination of all three, dependent upon market opportunity and need. Whichever model they run with, it will involve some element of commercial activity. Table 1.1 highlights the pros and cons of this.

Table 1.1 Commercial training models

Commercial model	Description	Pros	Cons
Direct provision	Vendor provides training direct to customers.	Maximises revenue income and provides capability to sell broader customer solutions.	Profitability can come under pressure due to multi-geographical training demands. Can be viewed as non-core business and suffer from lack of corporate investment.
Training partner	Training is provided by the training partner on behalf of the vendor. These partners will either be distributors or value-add resellers.	Enables business partners to add value to their portfolio. Provides the vendor with greater coverage and minimises risk regarding inability to provide training in all countries the product is sold in. Reduces vendor need to invest in capital equipment and training resources.	Dependency on the training partners to provide appropriate level of coverage. Requires commercial models in place that may minimise profitability levels. Partner management structure needs to be implemented.

(Continued)

Table 1.1 (Continued)

Commercial model	Description	Pros	Cons
Independent training company	Training is provided by the training partner on behalf of the vendor. Will have business relationships with multiple vendors.	Customers often use independent training companies to manage their training needs and budgets. Often viewed as a trusted provider and hence can be an asset to a vendor. Many independents have international coverage capabilities.	Requires commercial models in place that may minimise profitability levels. Partner management structure needs to be implemented.
Contractor	Independent subject matter expert with instructor-related skill sets.	Flexible resource pool that can be accessed by vendor and other training partners.	Potential to lose customer control.
Multi-modality	Training may be available via electronic access (eLearning, video, web).	Provides customers with learning and cost flexibility. Can maximise profit levels on high volumes.	Cost of development can be prohibitive.
Combination	Vendor may apply one or more of the above regarding training provision to its customer base.	Provides vendor flexibility regarding training provision and investment decisions. Maximises training coverage.	Requires strong product management to ensure right modality is used for the appropriate market opportunity.

Vendors can achieve good commercial results and ensure customers are well provided for by assessing the prevailing market conditions. Through balancing customer need and potential versus access to training resources, a good commercial environment can be established and maintained.

TYPICAL TRAINING ORGANISATION STRUCTURE

Training organisation structures differ from one vendor to another, depending upon the size of the target market, the nature of what they want to offer, the investment profile and the functions that can be resourced within a shared services environment.

The organisation chart shown in Figure 1.1 is represented in terms of functional departments. Overall control comes under the remit of business management and is the responsibility of a training executive or senior manager, depending upon the size of the overall team and its financial structure for profit and loss (P&L), cost centre or breakeven.

Shared service functions, such as finance, accounting, legal, and systems and infrastructure, typically come under the respective corporate departments, with remits to allocate staff to support the training group on a daily basis. For the corporation, it represents significant savings in terms of minimising duplication of activities.

Marketing may also be under a shared services remit dependent upon the corporate position regarding alignment of messages, activities and allowable spend the corporation wants to allocate to general marketing activities.

Sales may reside under a professional services structure comprising consulting, technical support and training, dependent upon revenue targets and organisational need. The training sales team may be structured around direct and telesales activities.

Telesales focus their attention on transactional sales activities such as selling places on a public schedule or eLearning offerings below a certain value. The direct sales team undertakes customer account management and sells larger or more complex deals.

The training product management team liaises and works closely with corporate product management to ensure alignment of service-related offerings. Curriculum development with its instructional designers, content and lab developers works closely with product management to interpret their requests and develop training offerings.

Certification and publication teams also work closely with the curriculum team. Publications are responsible for ensuring training offerings – eLearning, instructor-led training (ILT) and virtual instructor-led training (VILT) – are available and distributed in accordance with requests from the administration and operations team following confirmed sales activities. Certification develops examinations on behalf of the curriculum development team and distributes examinations, including pass/fail results, to requesting students.

Training partner management has responsibility for engaging partners who sell and deliver training and for ensuring quality of delivery and sales targets are achieved.

Courses and offerings sold by the sales team are passed to the administration and operations team, who accept bookings and coordinate the distribution of joining instructions and scheduling of resources such as instructors and training rooms. On

Figure 1.1 Typical organisation chart

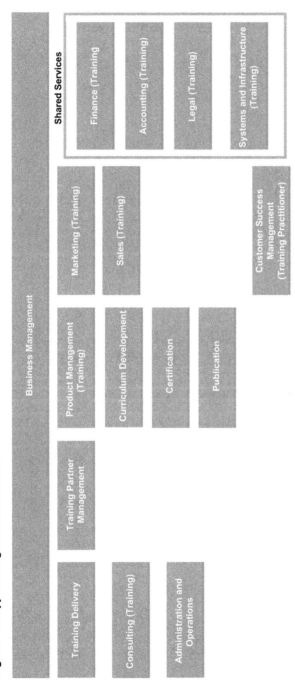

completion of an instructor-led course or student receipt of an eLearning or subscription offering, accounting are advised to initiate customer invoicing.

The training delivery team, working in conjunction with the administration and operations team, assists in the planning of course schedules and the delivery of training. The consulting team supports requests from customers requiring specialised training solutions specific to their needs.

To accommodate requests for training in geographies or markets where the training delivery team does not have a presence, the training partner management team enlists and manages authorised partners to sell and deliver on behalf of the training group.

Quality management, covering planning, assurance, control and improvement, comes under the remit of the training business management team. Each manager assesses how overall quality ensures the training service and offerings provided satisfy the intended function. All employees within the training group are held responsible for ensuring quality of service is maintained throughout their activities.

The organisation structure will vary from one company to another, but the functional elements will exist for all. For companies initiating a training department for the first time, many of the elements will reside with the training delivery team. For those who are servicing large training volumes, the elements may subdivide. One example of this is in the area of curriculum development where additional functional elements become departments in their own right, such as eLearning and lab development.

> The processes and organisational needs required to ensure all stages of the customer experience are effective need to be defined and in place before customers are engaged.

Customer success management

Customer success management is growing in popularity, specifically in the technical arena. Primarily, the role is based on understanding the needs of the customer and using this to develop a shared vision, establish joint accountability and prioritise their long-term success above all else.

Its key driver is customer retention and requires the provision of dedicated resources on the training side to help align provider and customer in a homogeneous manner. With continuous pressure from competitors, staying one step ahead is a key factor for continued success. For a technical training manager, customer success management alignment is as vital as that of sales account management.

From a training perspective, it is financially astute to assess which customers are crucial to overall company success and what type of coverage is required. This then allows a decision to be made on how many customer success training practitioners are allocated to support the company-dedicated customer success managers, and how best to ensure the full alignment of corporate and customer need.

TECHNICAL TRAINING MANAGEMENT AS A CAREER

Does being a technical training manager limit your career prospects? The simple answer is: no!

Executives of high performing organisations understand that commitment and vigorous pursuit of a clear and compelling vision stimulating higher performance standards is the catalyst behind a great company.

Achieving this comes from hiring managers who can organise staff and resources to be effective and efficient in the pursuit of pre-determined objectives. In that sense, whether you are running a technical department or a marketing department, the principles of management are the same.

Where technical training comes into its own is the diversity of the roles it encompasses:

- **strategic alignment:** aligning training provision with product and service needs to ensure overall corporate business objectives are achieved;
- **content development:** design and development of training offerings that enable customers to capitalise on their investment;
- **training delivery:** managing instructors and training resources to ensure customers have access to training when and where they need it;
- **technology management:** providing technical resources in support of system infrastructural needs;
- **administration services:** supporting registrations, bookings, invoicing, scheduling and coordination of resources;
- **partner management:** establishing partner networks to support coverage and expansion of geographic markets;
- **training product management:** the design, build, operation and maintenance of the training offering, including marketing need, position and pricing;
- **sales management:** selling and achieving desired revenue goals;
- **business analysis:** assessing market potential, coverage and price points for new and existing training offerings;
- **business development:** expanding the training organisation's reach into new and existing markets;
- **release management:** ensuring course and certification releases are clearly coordinated across both internal and external stakeholders.

In running the business, motivating the team is a key element. However, staying focused on the business itself is crucial. Synchronising training activities with the rest of the company is fundamental to its success and its ability to influence at the highest level. With that in mind, the role of a technical training manager provides a rich spectrum of skills, knowledge and business acumen to launch a move into higher executive management.

SUMMARY

Customers who invest in technology require training support in order to maximise their expected return on investment. As a result, most technology manufacturers establish training departments to educate and train customer employees to use and apply the technology in the execution of their job role.

Companies who provide training may engage third-party training organisations and business partners, or undertake it themselves to satisfy the market opportunity and need.

The organisational training structure will differ from one vendor to another, depending upon the size of the market, what they want to offer, investment availability and what business functions they need to provide or can be accessed within a shared services environment.

Business management and control is determined by the company's functional activity and financial reporting needs, such as P&L, cost centres or breakeven.

With the rapid and growing acceptance that customer success management is a crucial component of maintaining a strong and meaningful relationship, technical training must be a key consideration for inclusion.

As a career, training management provides a rich landscape in which to gain broad-based skills across multiple disciplines and contribute in an effective and productive manner to the overall success of a company.

2 STRATEGY AND BUSINESS EXECUTION
Developing strategies to produce working plans to execute and drive results

Successful commercial training organisations require a clear strategy and business execution plan in order to achieve, monitor and control the attainment of their goals and objectives.

This chapter looks at a typical approach to this, including the associated components and activities required to develop the strategy that can be used to develop an executable plan.

USING STRATEGY TO SENSE AND SEIZE OPPORTUNITY

Morris Chang (General Instruments, Texas Instruments and Chief Executive Office (CEO) of TSMC) once said: 'Without strategy, execution is aimless and without execution, strategy is aimless.'[1] This is another way of saying that strategy and business execution need to be in harmony in order to succeed.

Spending time strategising market opportunity based on knowledge, intuition, innovation and potential is fundamental to business success, and this is of equal relevance in the world of technical training.

Intuition or sensing training opportunities plays a key role in distinguishing a leader and the team from other organisations that simply provide solutions in line with generic offerings. Learning has changed and accelerated since the heady days of the burgeoning IT world of the 1980s.

Being able to understand and relate to these changes, be it learning technology, commercial demands on the time allocated to training or millennials who have grown up with the internet and smartphones in an always-on digital world, drives a new mode of business thinking.

Building a business plan of merit, confidence and expected results requires a strategy based on a structure that factors in strategic intent, market insight and innovation, leading to a business design that can be converted into a set of executable critical tasks.

---

1   http://entrepreneur.wiki/Morris_Chang#Inspiring_Quotes

CREATING STRATEGIC AND BUSINESS ALIGNMENT

Strategic and business alignment is achieved when strategic output in terms of business design is aligned with critical task execution. Various models abound on how to approach this, which in essence will be similar to the one shown and described in Figure 2.1. The model comprises two main sections: strategy and execution. Each section consists of four individual components and is supported by leadership and organisational values to drive the expected business results forward.[2]

Figure 2.1 Strategy to execution modelling

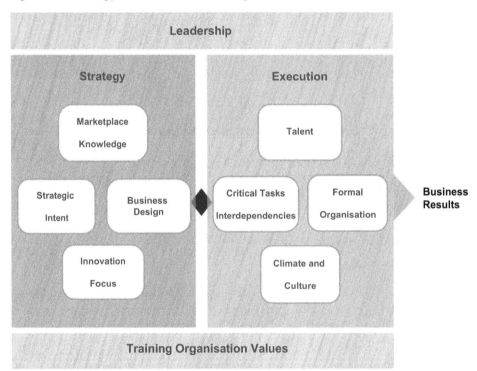

Leadership

'The greatest leader is not necessarily the one who does the greatest things. He is the one that gets the people to do the greatest things' – this quote from Ronald Reagan,[3] although stated 30+ years ago, still holds true today.

---

2   Computer Education Management Association (CEdMA) Europe Ltd thanks IBM for allowing reference and use of the IBM Business Leadership Model (BLM) throughout this chapter and recognises the content as © International Business Machines Corporation.

3   Ronald Reagan interview with Mike Wallace on the *60 Minutes* TV programme, 14 December 1975.

In order to achieve the desired business results from strategy and business execution alignment, a strong employee experience is critical. Certainly, from the leader's perspective, hiring to the needs of the strategy is vital.

Leaders need to work with employees to establish a climate of responsibility, accountability and active engagement. They need to ensure that employee feedback and commentary on their own and the entire training group's results are heard and acknowledged.

Figure 2.2 illustrates a strategy and execution closed loop environment where each individual attribute has an impact on the others. These need to be monitored and assessed in order to define the team's values and social interaction. On the subject of interaction, it is vital that the rest of the company outside the training team is included. One major danger is the training team operating in isolation, which can seriously undermine its corporate value.

Figure 2.2 Leadership and organisational values

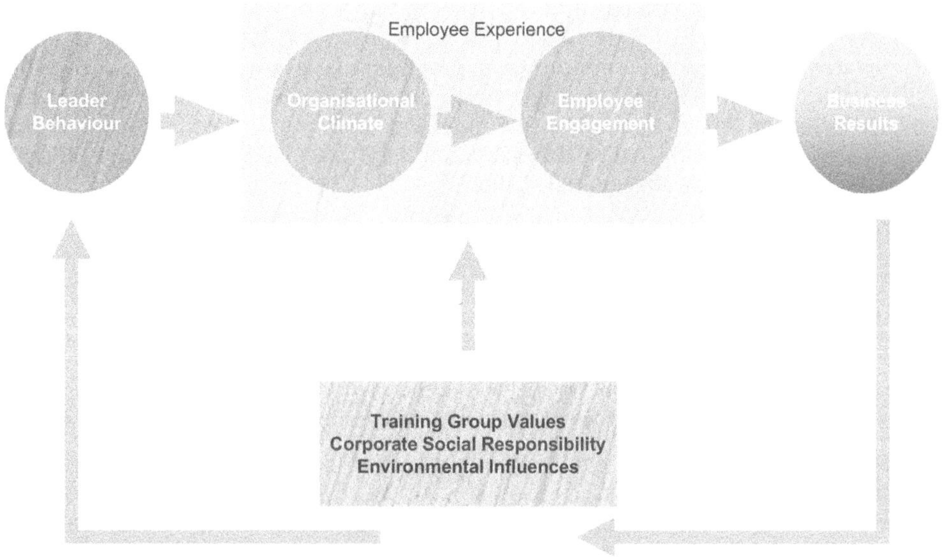

Employee Experience

Leader Behaviour

Organisational Climate

Employee Engagement

Business Results

Training Group Values
Corporate Social Responsibility
Environmental Influences

Training organisation values

Profitability, growth, quality and exceeding customer expectations, are not examples of values. These are examples of corporate strategies being sold to you as values.

Stan Slap[4]

---

4 www.goodreads.com/quotes/620501-profitability-growth-quality-exceeding-customer-expectations-these-are-not-examples

Organisational values guide an organisation's thinking and actions. When it comes to culture and values, actions speak louder than words. All organisations have values that assist in defining their actions for planned success. Establishing an agreed set of values can assist a training organisation to define its culture and beliefs, which helps in unifying its approach to dealing with various business-related issues. These values assist training groups and employees to decide what works and what doesn't.

Example value statements

- We strive to deliver the right training at the right time for our customers.
- All employees are treated equally irrespective of role or contribution.
- Selling at all costs is not a virtue; consulting to a mutually agreed benefit is.

Strategy

The four components of strategy are:

1. **Strategic Intent**, which sets the main focus for the organisation by setting the overall direction and goal for the training organisation, establishing priorities for the achievement of strategic advantage and factoring and combining training strategic intent with that of the overall company, is essential for solid market insight and business design generation.

2. **Marketplace knowledge**, which focuses on understanding the needs of the customer base (in terms of training, services and product), training partners, key competitors and their actions, market trends and current technology developments.

   It is a fact-gathering, analytical exercise, with the objective to specify in detail what is happening in both training and company marketplaces, how commercial success factors are shifting and their implications for the business.

3. **Innovation Focus**, which challenges the training group to actively explore and try new modes of working. This is achieved by reviewing and asking questions on the design and implementation of the strategy, how training can be designed and delivered (including idea generation) and creating pilot projects all aimed at shaping change for continued growth and success. *Innovation focus should not only be about new training offerings, but also include operational and business model innovations.*

4. **Business design**, which interprets the strategic intent in terms of how the training business will go to market by answering five key questions and incorporating the focused innovation and marketplace knowledge output:

   1. *Customer selection*: what industry segments (categorised according to the nature of the business sector they are involved with: finance, manufacturing, etc.) and size of customer should be selected?

2. *Value proposition*: what training offerings should be provided and why would customers purchase or engage with the offering?

3. *Value capture*: given the answers to the first two questions, how will money be made or strategic advantage be gained and measured?

4. *Partnerships*: what can be done internally and what activities will the business rely on through partner engagement?

5. *Sustainability*: how will profitability of offerings and investments be protected and grown?

The above five key go-to-market elements, along with the innovation and strategic intent recommendations, form the input into the execution stage, which is assessed and converted into key critical tasks and subsequent organisational needs.

Execution

This phase involves the assessment of the strategy and conversion of it into four tangible executables to form a practical and tactical interpretation of the training strategy.

1. **Critical tasks and interdependencies:** to execute the strategy, the critical tasks required to achieve the business design output need to be defined and any interdependencies highlighted and listed. These tasks need to be measurable and achievable.

2. **Talent:** assess and define the requisite employee characteristics, capabilities and competencies needed to execute the critical tasks, including whether employees and support partners are motivated and engaged.

3. **Formal organisation:** consider the explicit structures, metrics and rewards required to direct, control and motivate individuals and groups to perform the training group's critical tasks.

4. **Climate and culture:** in order for the critical tasks to be achievable, there needs to be a definition and plan of action regarding how people and the training organisation need to behave and operate.

CASE STUDY: STRATEGY TO EXECUTION MODEL

To assist in the understanding of how to apply the strategy to execution model, the following scenario will be used as a case study.

Scenario

An established global IT (software) company has been providing instructor-led training at centres in the main geographies of the Americas, Europe and Asia Pacific. With increased pressure to maximise its employee per head revenue in core product lines, the training group has been requested to reduce its training (service-based) headcount and expand its footprint and technical coverage via third parties while sustaining current monetary profit contribution levels.

Proposed solution

The proposed solution will comprise two stages. The first is definition of the strategy and the second is the conversion of the strategy components into an executable plan.

Define the strategy

Defining the strategy requires four separate activities to be undertaken: first, definition of the strategic intent; second, an assessment of the marketplace; third, consideration of any innovative approaches or activities; and, finally, the development of the business design based on the key points and implications from the three previous activities.

Step 1: Define the **strategic intent** in terms of bullet point-based statements:

- Reduce headcount across the following training-based disciplines: sales and marketing, operations, delivery and infrastructure.
- Establish training delivery partners in all geographies using market-leading providers with strong sales and marketing presence.
- Expand training coverage via a subscription-based model.
- Migrate from function and feature content provision to business outcome-based provision.
- Improve and grow monetary profit contributions year on year.

Step 2: Assess and define the **marketplace** in terms of bullet point-based statements:

- With the exception of Asia Pacific, all geographies have established third-party training delivery and sales teams in main target countries and cities of interest.
- Asia Pacific third-party training delivery coverage is inconsistent in terms of mainstream players. Universities do specialise in the company product at local country level.
- Product growth is strong in the Americas, moderate in Europe and slow in Asia Pacific.
- Two product competitors have successfully launched training subscription models.

Step 3: Assess any requirements around **innovation focus** to address the strategic intent points and implications, and factor in any engagement considerations regarding marketplace knowledge:

- Assess the existing company product-based subscription model and technical support portal. Consider relevance to training and suitability for adoption and modification.
- Develop role and task-based training offerings to align with the need to provide business outcome-based training.
- Adopt a distributed learning model to maximise training delivery headcount productivity.

- Investigate and initiate adoption of an integrated cloud-based solution to automate current labour-intensive operational and administrative procedures.

Step 4: Develop the **business design** based on the key points and implications from the strategic intent and marketplace knowledge activities:

1. *Customer selection:* which customer segments should be selected and which ones not?

   1.1 Focus to be directed on customer industry sectors currently targeted by the product sales teams.

   1.2 Responsibility for training delivery and sales in the Asia Pacific region to be covered by authorised training partners.

   1.3 Training delivery and sales in the Americas region to be divided on a 60/40 basis between the training team and authorised training partners.

   1.4 Training delivery and sales in the UK, Nordics and Netherlands to be covered by the training team. All other Europe, the Middle East and Africa (EMEA) countries to be covered by authorised training partners.

2. *Value proposition*: what training offerings should be provided and why would customers purchase or engage with the offering?

   2.1 All new courses developed and published based on role and task-based principles:

      - Function feature-based training no longer relevant to customer base. Customers are organised around job roles and require training to be relevant and specific to their needs.

   2.2 Existing courses modified to fit in with distributed learning methodology:

      - Customers requiring role-based training will benefit by being able to select training in line with actual need at a modular level, modality preference and on a timeline that maps to their deployment profile rather than a fixed duration course.

   2.3 Subscription model introduced:

      - Aligns the selling of training with the existing product subscription sales model. Customers prefer point of sales service (training) inclusion. The training subscription model provides customers with a more flexible financial solution.
      - Will include role-based and distributed learning solutions.

3. *Value capture*: given the answers to the first two questions, how will money be made, or strategic advantage be gained and measured?

   3.1 Realignment of the delivery and sales activities regarding the use of authorised training partners will provide:

      - Improved coverage in terms of:
         - closer alignment of training with product sales activities;
         - ability to deliver training in local language;

- measurement by number of product sales engagements and training volume.
- Revenue and profit contributions based on agreed percentages between the training team and authorised training partners.

3.2 Introduction of role-based training expands training relevance and opportunity:

- On the customer side of the business it provides:
  - broader opportunities to expand training market penetration;
  - the ability to supply training solutions and develop longer-term customer relationships;
  - measurement by increased training spend per customer and greater return on content developed, because it is modular.
- Improved opportunities for authorised training partners to engage customers with broader training solutions, because it is measured in terms of revenue and profit growth.

3.3 Introduction of distributed learning provides:

- customers with greater choice and flexibility regarding their ability to purchase training at a modular level and in accordance with their modality preference and desired timeline;
- training and product sales teams with the ability to sell to actual customer need;
- measurement in terms of number of engagements, revenue and profit growth.

3.4 Introduction of subscription model provides:

- training to be aligned with the existing product subscription sales model;
- customers with a flexible financial solution;
- both role-based training and distributed learning to be purchased as a subscription offering;
- a regular and reputable revenue stream;
- measurement in terms of the number of subscriptions, revenue and profit growth.

4. *Partnerships*: what can be done internally and what activities will the business rely on through partner engagement?

4.1 Training IT infrastructure will be transferred to corporate IT for them to run as a shared service.

4.2 Cloud-based infrastructure will require approval and support from corporate IT.

4.3 Enablement programmes will need to be redefined to accommodate the selling of role-based training, distributed learning and subscription models.

4.4 Sales commission and incentive plans will need to be reviewed and costed by finance.

4.5 Authorised training partner programmes will require additional enablement and revised contractual terms to reflect changes in delivery and sales models.

4.6 Executive support will be required to ensure that product sales in all geographies engage with authorised training partners to assist in the selling and inclusion of training.

4.7 Training-related marketing will be transferred to corporate marketing as a shared service provision.

5. *Sustainability*: how will the profitability of offerings and investments be protected and grown?

   5.1 Cloud-based infrastructure integrating administration bookings, registration, invoicing and content distribution with multi-language support:

   - assists in reducing operational and administration headcount and costs;
   - is scalable without associated headcount increase;
   - has costs based on actual consumption;
   - improves profitability;
   - ensures financial risk is low as costs are related to consumption and minimal capital expenditure required.

   5.2 Introduction of distributed learning, role-based training and subscription model:

   - supports reduction in instructor headcount and costs;
   - reduces instructor travel and expense costs;
   - minimises the need for instructor-led courses via the use of eLearning;
   - improves the potential for market and revenue growth via alignment with a product subscription model;
   - retains financial risk at medium to high, as it requires investment in new content development methods and skills – risk can be minimised by executive commitment to include training at point of sale and the introduction of strong governance.

   5.3 Authorised training partner programme expands market coverage and reach by:

   - improving revenue and profitability contributions;
   - keeping financial risk at low to medium because current authorised training partners have strong regional product sales relationships – new regional partners will need to be accepted and adopted by the local teams;
   - considering the reputational and quality risks of new training partners to ensure they share the same values and alignment with the strategy.

5.4 Marketing and IT infrastructure needs transferred to respective corporate groups. Service level agreements (to be established) will result in reduced costs due to headcount reallocation.

Develop an executable plan

The previous steps relate to the development of the strategy. The final step is the development of an executable plan. This stage entails interpreting and converting the business design via the four steps:

1. critical tasks and interdependencies;

2. talent;

3. formal organisation;

4. climate and culture.

For clarity purposes, only the critical tasks and interdependencies are shown below; the other three steps relating to this example can be found in the Appendix at the back of this book.

Step 1: Develop **critical tasks and interdependencies**.

Table 2.1 represents an extract of critical tasks by business functional area based on the strategy example developed above. In reality, there would be others based on normal training business requirements.

Table 2.1 Critical tasks

Key tasks

Financial critical tasks	Dependencies
Maximise route to market channels	
1.1 Engage and enable authorised training partners across the geographies	training partner management team and product sales team
1.2 Assess, recommend and implement sales commission and incentive plans	training management and finance
1.3 Develop and introduce revised authorised training partner contracts	training management and legal
Maximise margin contribution	
1.1 Implement cloud infrastructure	shared services infrastructure team
1.2 Implement subscription model	shared services infrastructure team
1.3 Implement training staff reorganisation across the geographies	training management and human resources (HR)

(Continued)

Table 2.1 (Continued)

Key tasks

Infrastructure critical tasks	Dependencies
Develop cloud-based infrastructure	
1.1 Assess and define requirements	shared services infrastructure team
1.2 Develop recommendations, costs and return on investment	shared services infrastructure team
1.3 Select solution and implement	shared services infrastructure team

Operational critical tasks	Dependencies
Metrics for success	
1.1 Define and implement metrics for distributed learning, role-based training, subscription model and authorised training partners	training management
1.2 Track and report metrics/incorporate with governance report	training management and finance
Implement functional matrix management model	
1.1 Define service level agreements between product sales and authorised training partners	legal
1.2 Deploy and monitor service level agreement performance and include in governance report	training sales team and partner management team

People critical tasks	Dependencies
Develop education services staff skills	
1.1 Distributed learning model	content development team
1.2 Role-based training	content development team
Develop sales skills of training sales team, product sales team and authorised training partners	
1.1 Positioning and selling education solutions	content development team
1.2 Opportunity management	training sales team and partner management team
Communication	
1.1 Monthly and quarterly updates on training metrics and performance	finance

Change management critical tasks	Dependencies
Training restructuring and new direction	
1.1 Reason for change	executive sign-off to implement the change
1.2 Enablement on new training offerings	content development team

(Continued)

Table 2.1 (Continued)

Key tasks

Authorised training partner critical tasks	Dependencies
Establish authorised partners in the geographies	
1.1 Assess training partner capabilities	training partner management team and product sales team
1.2 Select training partners in line with geography recommendations	training partner management team and product sales team
1.3 Develop legal contracts and financial terms and conditions	legal
1.4 Enlist training partners	training partner management team
1.5 Develop and run enablement training (sales, distributed learning and role-based training)	training partner management team
1.6 Engage and align training partners with product sales teams	training partner management team and product sales team

Training delivery critical tasks	Dependencies
Divide training delivery and sales by geography	
1.1 Training delivery and sales staffing numbers in the UK, Nordics and Netherlands finalised	training management
1.2 Training and sales staffing numbers in the Americas finalised at 60%	training management
1.3 Training and sales staff not required in the rest of EMEA and the Americas assessed for redeployment	training management
1.4 Training staff positions confirmed and finalised	training management
Enable training instructors to deliver distributed learning and role-based training	
1.1 Develop enablement training	content development team
1.2 Deploy enablement training	content development team

Content development critical tasks	Dependencies
Develop distributed learning	
1.1 Methodology	content development team
1.2 Modality formats	content development team
1.3 Content	content development team
Develop role-based curriculum (new courses only)	
1.1 Methodology	content development team
1.2 Assess technical roles and map relevant tasks	content development team
1.3 Content	content development team

SUMMARY

Commercial training organisations require clear strategy and business execution plans in order to achieve, monitor and control the achievement of their goals and objectives.

There are many models that can be used to achieve this, which all, in essence, comprise two main stages: strategy definition and development of the execution plan.

The first stage of strategy is based on a structure that factors in strategic intent, market insight and innovation, which are then interpreted and presented as a business design blueprint covering customer selection, value proposition, value capture, partnerships and sustainability.

The business design blueprint is then used to form the executable plan. This contains four tangible executables to form a practical and tactical interpretation of the training strategy: critical tasks and interdependencies, talent, formal organisation, climate and culture.

Having an executable plan enables an organisation to monitor and control its goals and objectives more efficiently. Any issues can be addressed by regularly reviewing the four tangible executables and implementing appropriate actions.

Changes to the overall strategy should only be considered if there are significant changes to the business design due to internal or external influences that cannot be addressed via the existing business execution plan.

3 TECHNICAL TRAINING PRODUCT MANAGEMENT
Planning and introducing the right offering at the right time and right price point

Technical training product management encompasses the process of designing, building, operating and maintaining the training offering. Many technology-based companies apply product management techniques to ensure they are creating a training service that motivates and adds value, with the end objective to ensure the customer wants to buy and continues to apply training for business benefit.

Product management also takes into account the current marketing need, position, price and lifecycle management to ensure continued fitness for purpose over time.

This chapter looks at roles and responsibilities of employees engaged in supporting the process, including details on the specific elements and activities associated in implementing a typical product management lifecycle.

ROLES AND RESPONSIBILITIES

A multi-disciplinary team normally performs product management, although this depends upon organisation size, departmental complexity and the number of products. Team members can include, for example, product developers and managers, training business development managers, training business unit owners, content developers and curriculum managers, certification specialists and training programme managers.

Normally, the training product manager or director serves as the leader of a cross functional team, in essence acting as a project leader by way of guiding, coordinating and supervising the work to deliver a training offering that launches with the technology product and remains aligned throughout its lifecycle.

Training product manager

Training product management defines the training offering. To achieve this, a product manager's responsibilities includes the following:

- interpreting the product-based, technology-strategic goals into tactical training tasks and deliverables to ensure consistency and alignment;
- defining and planning training offerings and curricula;
- establishing strategic training direction, based on customer needs and business goals;

- obtaining senior management buy-in for proposed training plans in support of technology releases;
- gaining internal and external client feedback on needs and market opportunities;
- evaluating risks and returns on investment versus not investing in training;
- proposing contingency plans;
- managing financial modelling and business analysis;
- branding and marketing;
- launching training products and enabling sales;
- managing the training product lifecycle;
- defining and implementing quality management throughout the training product lifecycle.

The training product manager engages the following employees in the execution of their role:

- **Technology/product developer:** a subject matter expert who works closely with the training content developer to provide insight on the product's features and the skills required to use or apply the technology.
- **Technology product manager:** responsible for technology product releases and ensuring that all service-based offerings are included for consideration and implementation within an overall offering prior to release.
- **Technology design manager:** provides advice on overall technology direction and works with the content curriculum manager to advise on product family direction.
- **Project manager:** works closely with the training product manager to ensure successful completion of the training offering lifecycle.
- **Training business development manager:** runs the training business at a geographic level and has valuable input into the process of new product launches.
- **Training business unit owner:** owns the commercial aspects of the business and is consulted regarding investment decisions.
- **Training content developer:** subject matter expert with responsibility to develop course objectives and course content. Both the technology product manager and training product manager sign off on course objectives. The project manager oversees overall progress.
- **Content curriculum manager:** responsible for managing and ensuring the development of relevant content and courses to support the broader technology family curriculum.
- **Certification specialist:** works closely with both the training content developer and the content curriculum manager to agree on the nature of testing (certification or accreditation) and relevancy to both customer and the company.
- **Marketing specialist**: responsible for developing the marketing programmes required to promote and drive both demand and lead generation activities.

- **Business analyst:** responsible for assessing market potential, coverage and price points for new and existing training offerings. In some training organisations this may come under the remit of the training programme manager.
- **Finance specialist:** works closely with the business analyst and training product manager to develop investment plans, pricing and the assessment of return on investment (ROI) potential.
- **Training programme manager:** responsible for managing all aspects of new and existing training offerings, including marketing requirements, sales enablement, lifecycle management and validating investment decision requests.

Training product managers are accountable to executive management for overall training direction, key decisions, training budget allocations and revenue/profits on individual training offerings. They play a lead role in ensuring a training offering aligns with technology service requirements, and evangelising training to internal and external stakeholders. They are also responsible for the lifecycle management of the training offerings. The training lifecycle comprises seven stages (see Figure 3.1).

1. concept;
2. feasibility;
3. design and planning;
4. development;
5. verification;
6. release;
7. maintenance.

Training product lifecycle management
A process used to manage the lifecycle of a training offering involving seven stages commencing with a concept phase and then: feasibility, design and planning, development, verification, release and maintenance. Explicit throughout the various stages of lifecycle management is the requirement to define and implement strong quality management. This entails quality control, quality planning, quality assurance and quality improvement.

The level of quality provided is also linked to value from the customer perspective and that of the sales team. Quality offerings help to provide confidence and boost motivation in sales teams to promote the training offering and provide confidence to customers that they are purchasing a quality product.

Initiating the concept phase of lifecycle management

All projects including training commence with a concept phase whereby the idea for the training is explored and expanded upon. The goal here is to assess the feasibility of the project.

The phase starts when either the training product management team, technology team, training business development manager or training business unit owner submits a request to the training product manager for a new training offering or modification.

Figure 3.1 Training product management lifecycle

Concept	Feasibility	Design and Planning	Development	Verification	Release	Maintenance
• Establish stakeholder meetings • Assess product training and market need • Create training requirements • Develop initial funding request	• Assess market opportunity • Define GTM and RTM • Assess infrastructure needs • Develop business case and make decision to proceed or cancel	• Plan and schedule project plan • Engage sales enablement and marketing	• Develop training content and supporting practical sessions • Develop train the trainer content • Develop certification exams if relevant • Create marketing and sales collateral	• Review training content and practical sessions and correct accordingly • Review sales and marketing content and correct accordingly • Where relevant undertake beta certification exam testing	• Enable instructors and training partners • Enable sales and training partner sales teams • Publish where relevant certification exams • Promote via marketing activities • Monitor student feedback and correct as required	• Monitor student feedback and correct as required • Assess and monitor relevant business metrics • Review product revisions and update content accordingly • End of life assessments based on training metrics and product relevance in the market

In a large organisation, the training product manager or programme management office defines prioritisation of requests. This is followed by a review of the requests, by stakeholders with an interest in training, to assess the business opportunity and viability of the request in the context of relevance to the training group's business needs and corporate strategy. Funding is allocated if the request gains approval. This is typically in the form of manpower, to undertake the feasibility phase.

Assessing business relevance via the feasibility phase

Before any investment decision can be undertaken, the training being proposed needs to be assessed in terms of its feasibility and relevance to the training business overall.

To assess business relevance, high-level training requirements are defined, including training objectives along with a proposed route to market (RTM) and go-to-market (GTM) strategy.

Once the RTM and GTM offerings are defined, ROI modelling is undertaken and balanced against the market opportunity. At this point, a business case is developed for stakeholders to review. If approved, funding to proceed to the design and planning phase is allocated to the request.

Undertaking the training offering design and planning phase

This is one of the most important phases, as it defines the structure and nature of the training offering. The high-level training requirements from the feasibility phase are used to design the overall specification of the offering, covering module content requirements and practical session needs. Other core documents are specified and completed, such as the marketing GTM requirements, training technical infrastructure descriptions, train the trainer requirements, sales and training partner enablement certification or accreditation requirements, and training operation updates.

Once these have been completed and aligned to a budget and ROI plan, they are combined into an overall planning schedule and checklist, which is then presented to the stakeholders for approval. Once approved, development of the offering starts.

Starting the development phase

This phase is where the training offering and business support functional requirements are developed with other teams, such as training instructors, working in parallel to test modules and practical sessions as they become available.

Certification exam development questions are written on a module-by-module basis. However, the final compilation and validation of the exam is not started until all the content is finalised. This is recorded in the planning document.

From the business support perspective, the project manager ensures all core planning documents and checklist activities are completed on time. Failure to complete tasks can be catastrophic. For example, if no sales enablement or technical infrastructure are in place, meeting a course launch date is seriously jeopardised.

The following set of conditions must be met before moving to the next phase of verification:

- Training offering content complete and ready for testing.
- All business support documentation and enablement programmes complete.
- Training infrastructure in place and functional.

Once the project manager has confirmed that all development items on the checklist are complete, the stakeholders are requested to approve the moving on to the verification phase.

Undertaking the verification phase

Verification, sometimes known as the testing phase, is where the developed training offering is validated and business support functions tested for their effectiveness prior to launch.

The training offering is validated for accuracy and the achievement of its objectives. A series of courses are delivered to a mix of internal employees, partners and selected customers to gain feedback. Any infrastructure changes are also tested.

Business and operational changes undergo functional and live testing to ensure operational readiness prior to deployment. Having completed quality assurance (QA) and operations readiness testing, including any change or corrective action requests, the project manager requests approval from the stakeholders to start the release phase.

Releasing training offerings

In this phase, the training delivery and the operations teams initiate and coordinate the deployment of the new or modified training offering. They work closely with marketing and sales to ensure traction and availability in the target market.

During this phase, training partners are enabled and, where appropriate, organisations are given access to any new support processes. Once deployed, the project manager and nominated training programme manager check that all aspects of the launch are complete and readily available.

Any corrections are addressed and the project manager passes control to the training programme manager, whose responsibility it is to deploy and drive the success of the new training offering.

Maintaining the lifecycle of a training offering

This is often known as the operation phase and is normally the longest of the phases, during which the training offering generates its ROI.

Sustaining the life of the new training offering requires the monitoring of sales results, customer satisfaction metrics and trends in the target market. These are then balanced against any changes to the technology that might affect its success and relevancy in the marketplace, potentially resulting in course content modifications to be implemented.

As a training offering moves towards its end of life, the training programme manager requests an orderly closing down of the product or service and instigates an agreed series of actions to ensure all relevant parties, partners and customers, are aware of its controlled removal from the market.

Product launch to training content release

With the development of any training offering when it is based around product launch dates, it is important that there is agreement between the training product management team, course development and the actual product, sales, channel partner and marketing teams on when the offering will be available. Table 3.1 represents typical training release times as reported by CEdMA member companies.

Note that some organisations will require training and enablement to occur before product release in order to be able to successfully position, sell, support and assist target customers.

Table 3.1 Product launch to training content release dates (PR = product release date)

Training event	Timeline
Partner awareness session	PR 90 days
Sales training	PR 60 days
Consulting service training	PR 30 days
Technical support services training	PR 30 days
Accreditation exams	Varies (~PR +30 days)
Certification exams	Varies (~PR +120 days)
Customer training	PR +90 days

GO-TO-MARKET STRATEGIES

Part of the product management role is to decide what marketing strategies should be used to launch a training offering to the market. Marketing in itself covers who to sell to, what to sell and how to offer it in terms of maximising training offering penetration.

From the perspective of this section, focus is on the 'how to offer', which falls into the category of GTM. GTM plays a significant part in the training product management lifecycle.

GTM strategy covers:

- how training connects with its customer base;
- how unique value is delivered to customers purchasing training;
- how brand promise is fulfilled.

Spending time on developing a training GTM strategy helps the business to succeed. The challenge is in understanding which aspects the strategy can assist with, including customer profile, industry sectors, promotional channels and training accessibility. The first is one that most product managers are aware of: reducing costs associated with failed training offering launches. The second is to ensure there is an effective customer experience and a plan with clear direction defined for all elements of the product management lifecycle.

The key objective of a training GTM strategy is to improve the required business outcomes and align with the needs of the customer. To be of value and provide a template for future use and development, the training GTM strategy should cover and define these six key points:

1. **Target market:** for a particular training offering, decide on what markets are to be targeted.
2. **Customers:** decide on which customers *and* which industry sectors to sell to.
3. **Channels:** where will customers buy the training offering and how will it be promoted?
4. **Training offering:** what is being sold and what is the unique value being offered to the targeted customer?
5. **Price:** what should be charged for the training offering?
6. **Positioning:** how does the training offering support the brand and its relevancy to the customer?

Let's take a more detailed look at the six key points.

Targeting markets

Not all training offerings are appropriate for every market. For example, positioning a five-day instructor-led course to traders on the stock market is not going to get much traction in an environment where time is money. However, if the offering is based around on-demand eLearning, then it has more interest and value.

Taking time to clarify in detail the ideal target market(s) is vital to maximise effectiveness and make judgement calls on where to invest development funds. Considerations include demographics, language, geography, strategic importance of the technology that training is proposed for, and the training drivers of need.

29

One business challenge that all training product managers are faced with is how to balance the training financial return against the need to provide a full technology product support service in the situation where the product may not have a large training target audience. It is important to balance the effects of not providing training against not getting product traction. By applying a value to both sides of the equation, it is possible to come to an amicable agreement – normally, the technology product team covering some or all of the training investment.

There are times in every market when it is not possible to attain profitability. It is therefore important to determine and locate the most profitable customers to benefit from the training offering.

When considering a target market, typical metrics to consider are the market size, growth trends, barriers to entry and the financial benefits. From a training perspective, considerations should also be given to:

- Identifying market segments with the biggest and most urgent training need.
- Identifying gaps in the market; for example, there may be comprehensive coverage of the technology at the competency level, but coverage may be lacking in showing companies how to gain business performance benefits.
- Identifying which markets are most easily reached; this helps in deciding whether a two tier (distributor/reseller) sales model and/or training partner model is required.
- Identifying which markets have the largest market size and least competition; this is crucial when considering the implication of grey market training. Large market volumes often attract competition from third-party non-authorised training partners.

Understanding customers

In order to make valid decisions on what to offer and how training should be positioned, it is important to understand how customers feel about the training in terms of how they value what is provided and what their training needs are.

This information can be obtained by running web surveys, focus groups, one-to-one interviews, or simply organising a visit with a product sales representative. For example, customers will appreciate that training addresses skills shortfalls, but other factors, such as how the technology is being applied and budgetary restrictions, can impact on the decision process and its timing. Being able to factor these considerations into the overall GTM process provides useful insight into positioning the training offering to satisfy the market and customer needs.

Channel selection

All organisations operate through channels in order to position and sell their training offerings to customers. Some channels are direct and others indirect. The level of involvement depends upon budgets, market complexity, size and geographic spread.

Direct channels include product sales, training sales, the web and trade shows. Indirect channels include distributors, resellers, value-add resellers, strategic alliances, authorised training partners and, in some instances, retail stores.

Whichever way the customer is being engaged, it is important that they have a consistent brand experience. Get this wrong and the market is confused with mixed messages and interpretations that are difficult to control, which may ultimately result in lost sales.

To be in a strong position to decide on which channels the training product manager should be targeting, the following assessment should be undertaken:

- Identify how to reach the target customers.
- Identify where the target customers normally buy.
- Identify where training offerings are to be promoted.
- Identify the right distribution model for the training offering.
- Identify how to develop the right distribution channels.
- Identify how the training offering fits with the target market and supporting channels.
- Identify how customers prefer to interact with the training group.
- Identify what level of interaction customers require from the channel.

Fitness for purpose is the key dynamic here. For example, selling a custom training solution requiring consultative selling techniques is not suitable for a high-volume product reseller or for selling via the web. A strategic alliance would not undertake the selling of public, scheduled instructor-led courses. For them, transactional selling is inappropriate.

Training offerings: value proposition

As with any product, it is important to define a training offering's unique value proposition. Understanding the offering's key features and benefits is the initial step, followed by understanding exactly how the training connects with the customer in terms of how it is used, the problems it solves and the benefits it provides.

Consider the following points when clarifying the nature of the training offering:

- Identify the specific customer needs that require solving.
- Decide if the training offering is feature-, function- or performance-based, or a combination.
- Identify which delivery modalities are required.
- Identify how the training is accessed.
- Identify how customers use the training offering.
- Identify the important attributes or benefits of the training offering.
- Identify how the training offering is differentiated in the marketplace. Is it disruptive?

Determine the all-important unique value proposition by considering it from the customer's position. Consider testing thoughts and ideas with trusted customers beforehand. Key considerations should be:

- What reaction are you looking for from your customers?
- What level of trust and respect do you want?
- What importance do they place on training as a worthwhile investment?
- What is the key takeaway from the customer perspective?

Pricing

A number of factors come into play when deciding on the pricing structure for a proposed training offering. The first consideration is the estimate of the costs to develop and produce it that need to be recovered over an agreed period. This varies from company to company, but is typically an 18- to 24-month period. The next consideration is the cost of delivery, followed by cost of sales, all of which need to contribute to an agreed return on investment over the lifecycle of the offering. In addition, the pricing model should also factor in:

- Additional value associated with the offering for which customers would pay more.
- Existing price points in the market.
- Pricing training relative to other similar technology company offerings.
- Using disruptive pricing to drive competitive advantage and grow market share.
- Channel considerations; all routes to market require some form of sales incentive – the incentive needs to be part of any profitability calculation.
- Discount policies for large volume transactions.
- Number of transactions.

As with any investment decision, it is important to consider the risks and undertake financial modelling to help mitigate them and provide ideas on what strategies might be required to overcome risk in the medium to long term. Pricing is discussed in more detail later in this chapter.

Positioning training offerings

Positioning is intended to create an impression about the training offering and brand in the customer's mind so they can relate to it specifically in a way that differentiates the offering and brand from the rest of the marketplace.

Before embarking on a unique training-related brand position, care must be given to assessing how it relates to the corporate one. With training not always seen as core business, it is important not to dilute the broader brand position message. It should be more about complementing it.

The objective is to create a unique impression in the customer's mind that associates the training with something specific and desirable that is distinct from that of competitors.

There are a number of steps to creating a position statement:

- Obtain and understand the current corporate brand position.
- Understand how technology competitors are positioning their training brand and aligning it with their corporate branding.
- Understand the uniqueness of the proposed positioning by comparing it with other technology competitors.
- Develop the unique value-based positioning statement.

These steps allow the creation of a positioning statement that will cover target customer, market definition, compelling benefit and evidence-based results that can be delivered.

For example, if the training group was part of a company providing web services, then this positioning statement might be relevant:

For web users of Company XYZ productivity tools, we provide access to flexible training services to develop skills and competencies. As part of our commitment to success we assess business performance improvement and follow up with post-training support.

Having established a positioning statement, create tag lines. For example:

BMW: The ultimate driving machine

Intel: Look Inside

For our example, it could be 'Performance Improvement: it's a commitment!'

OFFERINGS AND MODALITIES

Part of the training GTM strategy covers the training offering in terms of what is sold and the unique value it offers to the targeted customer. In making decisions regarding the offering, it is important to consider the delivery modality. The nature of the delivery depends upon market need, opportunity, cost of development and expected ROI.

As discussed, lifecycle management plays a key part in product management. This includes making decisions on whether the offering needs updating. This is a factor in deciding modality complexity due to increased cost of development.

At a high level, training offerings can be categorised as shown in Table 3.2.

Table 3.2 Training offering categories

Offering category	Description
Course	Covers an agreed number of topics over a sequential period of time. Typically, the duration is between three to five days, but can be longer or shorter.
Subscription	Provides access to a series of training offerings for an agreed period of time for a regular payment. The payment can be monthly or annual.
Seminar	Short duration session typically covering advanced topics presented by a subject matter expert. Can be used to exchange information and hold discussions.
Lab/practical	Normally included within a course offering, but can be provided as a separate offering to assist in the reinforcement of learning.
Certification/accreditation	Theoretical or practical test to validate that learning has taken place or skills have been acquired.

Training modality relates to a number of factors, which involve the preferred learning style, budget and logistical needs of customers, all of which can be factored into a solution that optimises the learning experience. If done well, it significantly reinforces brand awareness and loyalty. Table 3.3 summarises typical approaches that are currently prevalent in the market.

Table 3.3 Technical training modalities

Training modality	Description	Pricing
Instructor-led training	Instructor-led training presented in a classroom with each student being allocated a dedicated hands-on lab environment to undertake practical work. The advantages are: • Sharing ideas and questions with fellow classmates. • Experiencing hands-on labs with real-time support. • Learning in a fully equipped dynamic learning environment. • Benefiting from face-to-face interaction with a certified instructor. • Accessing electronic versions of course materials that can be optionally printed.	Pricing is based on a daily per-student basis.

(Continued)

Table 3.3 (Continued)

Training modality	Description	Pricing
Virtual instructor-led training (VILT)	Similar to ILT without the need to travel to a classroom. With virtual instructor-led classroom training, you get training from instructors using seamless over-the-web connectivity. The same content delivered in the traditional physical classroom is presented during virtual live classroom deliveries. Hands-on learning is provided via access to remote lab-based systems. The advantages are: • Ability to train from wherever you choose. • Access to a live instructor for the complete duration of the course. • Longer access to remote lab systems for hands-on activities that are not limited to traditional classrooms. • Access to electronic versions of course materials that can be optionally printed. • Full interaction with other remote students.	Priced like ILT on a daily per-student basis.
eLearning – self-paced	Interactive, web-based courses that complement the instructor-led classroom-based training, allowing users to improve or maintain their skills by building online learning into their schedules. Students have the flexibility to determine what, where and when to learn. They can repeat learning units as often as required and control the duration of learning sessions. The advantages are: • Students get the training they need without the cost of travel or time out of the office. • Interactive with reinforcement-based questions. • Supports on-demand training needs.	Depending upon the training supplier, content will either be free or priced on a per course download basis, typically charged at 25–30% of an ILT course.

(Continued)

Table 3.3 (Continued)

Training modality	Description	Pricing
Seminar	Depending upon the provider, a seminar is typically a short duration offering (4–8 hours) focused on a specific technical topic. Seminars are usually delivered to large or small audiences with minimal practical involvement. The advantages are: • Reduced content development time. The majority of content will be presentation-based with some supporting handouts. • Time to market is minimised. • Can be used to teach advanced and specialised topics. • Can be presented by subject matter experts rather than training instructors.	Can be free or command a premium price depending upon the nature and level of the topic being offered.
Learning hubs/ distributed learning	Learning hubs provide access to distributed learning, where students have access to multiple modalities providing maximum choice and versatility of usage. Learning hubs are based on learning platforms capable of providing access to a vendor's complete portfolio of training offerings. This can cover eLearning self-paced training, remote lab sessions, social collaboration, subject matter expert support and learning rooms where students can discuss and undertake training. The advantages are: • Instant access to latest training materials. • Students can plan a training programme to suit their specific learning needs. • Supports role-based learning and performance-support materials that are always available when and where required. • Maximises training budgets and provides all round, on-demand training. • Unlimited 24×7 availability of online learning materials.	Pricing is subscription based, which can support single-user or multi-user needs.

(Continued)

Table 3.3 (Continued)

Training modality	Description	Pricing
Lab session	Provides an environment to practice skills and build experience in a live, fully supported private environment. The lab environment is typically pre-configured with the data to carry out training exercises and can be freed up to allow students to practice their own exercises. The advantages are: • Direct access to a live, fully supported system. • Ability to access the lab environment on-demand. • Helps to reinforce learning from a practical perspective.	Pricing is based on a nominal, agreed number of hours on a renewable basis.

PACKAGING AND BUNDLING

Being able to package or bundle training is a powerful way that training product management and marketing can increase the value perceived by customers and increase sales productivity.

Packaging and bundling are terms often used interchangeably. In some circles, packaging is viewed as combining training service offerings with technology product sales, whereas bundling combines multiple training offerings. Either way, the benefits of packaging or bundling training, apart from increasing sales, also provides:

• The ability to position and sell advanced curriculum offerings that might normally have a lower volume uptake.

• Automation of the up-selling process.

• A more efficient way of using the marketing budget with more than one training offering being positioned.

• Opening up new customer prospects if training is combined with product sales or a strategic partner.

• Higher perceived value to both the sales channel and the end customer.

One of the big challenges that training has is how and when it is positioned within the product sales cycle. Often, it is left to the end when the customer has already mentally decided on the budget they are prepared to spend. One way of addressing this is to apply a little bit of psychology, by combining product and training as part of a bundled deal. This can result in influencing the buyer to think they need the combined offering or making them aware they need the training service later. It also adds value.

From a value perspective, it is important to understand what that means in the eyes of the customer. Typically, it relates to either lowering the overall price, increasing the benefits or a combination of the two.

In developing a training bundle or package, consideration needs to be given to the problem the customer may often experience and the potential solutions that can be offered to help solve the problem. Table 3.4 highlights some typical examples.

Table 3.4 Packaging and bundling examples

Bundle/ package	Description	Benefits – vendor	Customer problem and benefits
Combined curriculum offerings and product package	Product training, including basic, intermediate and advanced, packaged with the product sale. Overall the offering is 15–20% cheaper.	Assists in driving attendance of the more advanced courses. Typically, advanced courses only attain 30% attendance of students sitting the basic course. Increases the overall sales value and aligns product with services.	Customers need to develop advanced skills in order to maximise the benefit of the products. In many instances, training is not discussed at point of sale and no budget is allocated. Therefore, the training purchased is limited due to the unforeseen costs. Customer benefits: • Overall lower price point. • Encourages development of broader and deeper skills and competencies.
Multimedia bundle	Product training including ILT/VILT and eLearning bundled as a single offering. Typically, the eLearning is reduced by 50% when purchased as part of the bundle.	eLearning has high profitability, albeit with lower revenue contribution. Combining with ILT enhances the overall contribution to the company via a single point of sale.	Employee performance benefits will reduce after attending a course if reinforcement and access to reference material is not provided. This reduces the benefits of the initial customer investment. Providing access to the eLearning on-demand element can greatly improve retention of knowledge and further development of technical skills. Customer benefits: • Lower overall price point. • Supports post-training reinforcement. • Supports on-demand training needs.

(Continued)

Table 3.4 (Continued)

Bundle/ package	Description	Benefits – vendor	Customer problem and benefits
Certification and course bundle	Product training course bundled with certification voucher. Overall the offering is 15–20% cheaper.	Increases overall sales value and assists in addressing the differential between students attending courses and undertaking certification. Certification is a differentiator in the employment market and vendors who can show growth in this area have a greater sphere of influence.	Customers need to ensure employees have gained the right skills and are competent to deliver results. Certification is a known and proven mechanism for achieving this. Customer benefits: • Lower overall price point. • Assists in assessing overall ROI by way of proven examination of skills. • Validates student competency and can form part of an overall career development programme for the employees.

These three examples provide a view on what can be packaged and bundled to address customer problems and provide value to them and to the training provider. When implementing, there are a number of important considerations that should be factored into any decision before going to market, particularly:

• Do not offer a training package or bundle unless it is addressing a customer or market problem.

• Any additional training content or service included in a basic offering needs to be cost-effective to ensure it drives increased profit contribution while allowing a price to be charged that is attractive to the customer. Packaging and bundling training provides opportunities to increase its value in the eyes of the customer, especially when it is solving a problem, and provides a sales and marketing vehicle for increasing revenue and profitability.

ROUTE TO MARKET CONSIDERATIONS

In order to consider which routes to market to activate, a training group needs to consider the following:

• Understand the customer – main contact points, level and nature of engagement and buying behaviour.

• Understand the training offering value proposition from the sales channel perspective.

- Assess available sales channels and their fitness for purpose.
- Enable sales channels.
- Consider cost of sales, including operational management.

Understanding the customer

From the perspective of understanding the customer, it is important to understand where they buy, how they prefer to buy and why they buy. This needs to be tempered with relevant industry sector nuances. Doing this allows consideration to be given as to which sales channel would be most effective.

Sales are usually divided into direct and indirect channels. Direct typically includes product sales, professional service sales, training sales and inside sales. Indirect channels include resellers, value-add resellers, distributors, strategic alliances and authorised training partners.

Whoever is being sold to, it is important that the needs of the individual buyer are catered for from within the appropriate sales channel. Part of the equation for success is getting the value proposition right.

Training offering value proposition

In terms of the training offering value proposition, there are two recipients. The first is the customer in terms of the compelling reason to buy and its relationship to a value proposition. The second, which is relevant to RTM, is what the business value proposition to the sales channel is. This normally relates to how they make money and, if it is a channel partner, why they should sell the training being offered.

From the direct sales perspective, it is an easier proposition as training is seen as a natural extension to the product sale. Normally, once sales compensation and support from senior sales management is obtained, it tends to be reasonably straightforward to action.

In partner channels, it is more challenging as they normally want to know how they can make money from your training offering compared to other vendors' training offerings. To achieve this, one approach is to consider how the training offering fits within the solutions they sell, their ROI needs, brand relevance and market opportunity.

From the solution fit perspective, it is important to understand how the training offering complements what they sell. If the training assists in enhancing their service provision and establishing stronger, more trusted ties with their customers, the more compelling it is for sales to include training in the solution offering. If the training is easy to understand and matches with their current sales competencies, the solution fit is further reinforced.

From the ROI perspective, the partner sales channel wants to know what is in it for them. Margin contribution is critical to any channel partner. While they may be given 20–25% discount off the retail price, they still have to factor in staff training, operational changes and marketing costs. These can be compensated for by increasing discounts and offering access to marketing funds in return for achievement of forecasts.

Brand recognition for a channel partner is a definite plus as it validates their involvement and credibility with potential customers. It also implies a good potential market opportunity.

Finally on the topic of the value proposition, being able to show the nature of the training market opportunity provides partners with information allowing an analysis of potential revenue streams and validation of expected ROI.

Assessing sales channel fitness for purpose

Locating a sales channel is arguably straightforward; the challenge is being able to validate its fitness for purpose. From the direct channel perspective, there tends to be three key options: selling via product sales, services sales or dedicated training sales staff. Therefore, unless there are internal restrictions on the use of sales outside training, their fitness for purpose once initial sales enablement has been undertaken should be very effective.

On the topic of indirect partner channel sales, the advantage over a direct sales team is one of size and coverage. The challenges relate to their relevance.

One approach to filtering out who to engage is to understand what segments they specialise in. From a technology perspective, there are three broad categories: hardware, software and services.

As a training provider, if the supported product is software-based, then, obviously, it would not be relevant to engage hardware partners. However, if the partner is a value-added reseller or solution provider, they would be worth consideration. Of course, this is an over simplification and Table 3.5 provides other factors that need to be considered when deciding on sales channel fitness for purpose.

Sales channel enablement

Having assessed sales channel fitness for purpose, the fourth element to be considered regarding RTM is that of sales enablement. Having a good training offering and a market opportunity to match is of no benefit if the sales channel is not enabled.

In essence, this means providing sales with an insight into the market opportunity in terms of why the customer would want to buy, how they buy and the value it provides them, including motivating the sales channel to achieve the desired business results of increased sales figures. A typical approach to the provision of sales enablement is:

- Ensuring there is appropriate sales content available and mapped to the buying cycle covering prospecting, qualifying, presenting, objection handling and closure.
- Aligning sales content with the appropriate sales person; a sales representative requires presentations and cheat sheets (quick reference guides with key points regarding the specific training offering), whereas an inside sales person requires pre-written narrative and content to send to prospective customers.
- Providing sales with content that is readily available in multiple formats (PDF, email, hard copy and presentations for laptop or tablet).

Table 3.5 Training sales channel fitness for purpose

(The Revenue column in this table displays US$, €Euro and £Sterling as many commercial training providers report in multiple mainstream currencies; exchange rates at December 2018.)

Channel segment	Target market	Industry specialism	Geographic coverage	Competency levels	Revenue, millions (M)	Training fitness for purpose
Reseller	Small to medium business (SMB)	All	Southern England	Software sales	$1 €0.9 £0.8	Low due to no specialism in selling training
Value-add reseller	Enterprise	Finance	London	Software, consulting, training	$5 €4.4 £4	Medium to high, depending on the training group's own coverage of London
Application service provider	Enterprise, SMB	Healthcare, telecommunications	Northern England	Hardware, software, consulting, customer support, training	$15 €13.2 £11.8	High due to high revenues and specialism in selling training
Managed service provider	SMB	Fast moving consumer goods (FMCG)	UK	Customer service support and training	$20 €17.5 £15.7	Medium due to national coverage with limitations due to SMB market focus
System integrator	Enterprise, SMB	Government, education, finance	UK, Europe	Technology integration all major vendors, professional service and training provision	$100 €88 £78	High due to European and industry coverage
Distributor	Enterprise, SMB	All	UK	Sales, technical support	$50 €44 £39	Low due to no training sales coverage
Training provider	All	All	UK, Europe	Training	$75 €66 £59	High due to high revenues and specialism in selling training

42

- Providing sales enablement sessions that clearly define market opportunity, pricing and discount policies, incentives and how to engage training sales support.

Cost of sales

The final element regarding RTM considerations is cost of sales and operational management. On the cost of sales side, this typically relates to the cost of training products sold. Product management needs to assess which training offerings yield the best results for particular routes to market. Some training prospers better than others depending on target audience and sales channel segmentation.

Another sales cost that includes the actual cost of selling is often referred to as selling, general and administration (SG&A) and also needs to be considered when deciding which RTM to use. SG&A includes sales compensation, commissions, advertising and promotional materials.

In relation to RTM, it is critical to monitor progress in order to assess and understand what actions need to be taken to capitalise on sales growth or address any unexpected shortfalls. This includes the number of enquiries, sales conversions, discounts and sales cycle duration from each of the engaged sales channels.

This level of detail provides valuable information regarding which training offerings and RTM are effective and which ones require review and adjustment. This in turn assists in measuring the training ROI, not just at the offering level but at a specific market level, which helps to decide on where the business focus is applied.

ROI VERSUS ROE

In the commercial world of technical training, ROI relates to the financial return on the committed and operational expenditure associated with the development and delivery of a particular training offering. With return on expectation (ROE), it is more to do with what level of change, be it behavioural or developmental, occurred at individual or group employee level. In the longer term, ROE leads to ROI whereby employees are being more effective and productive in their roles.

From a commercial point of view, ROE can be used very effectively in the sales process. All courses have defined objectives, which can be viewed at a high level as expectations. In a consultative selling situation, sales and the customer agree on the required training outcome, which in itself is setting an expectation.

In taking this approach, it is important to be able to measure the expected outcome. This is done by way of certification or the setting of practical tests. For example, a customer may require all staff to be knowledgeable in the concepts of client–server security and be able to demonstrate their ability to implement it on a live system. From an expectation perspective, there are two components: the first is testing that knowledge has been gained, and the second is that the student can demonstrate they can implement the skills successfully. Both of these can be monitored and tested, which in turn provides a measurable ROE.

Depending on the sales relationship with the customer, this can be expanded to a measurable ROI by way of measuring improved time to implement and number of reduced support calls made over an agreed extended period.

From a training product management point of view, ROE provides a mechanism by which to validate what opportunities are out there in the market, as it reflects the actual need of the customer.

PRICING STRATEGY

As part of the training product lifecycle, training product managers with feedback from marketing set prices during the development stage. To do this, there needs to be a pricing strategy in place. Setting this is part of ensuring the training product or offering is a success and delivers to its ROI commitment.

Pricing strategy defines how the training group sets the price of its offerings based on costs, value, demand and competition, which in turn must align with corporate directives in force at the time. Table 3.6 summarises some well-known pricing strategies.

Table 3.6 Pricing strategies

Pricing strategy	Description	Comments
Cost-based pricing	The principle of cost-based pricing is simple as it equates to Cost + Required product offering profit. Cost-based pricing considers all fixed and variable costs, including SG&A. Once the total costs are known, the required profit margin is added to what becomes the market sales price.	• This is a fairly simple and quick pricing method as prior knowledge on costs can easily be extracted and referenced. • Its limitation is that it does not factor in market or competitive factors. • In addition, it is easier to defend from a vendor specific objective evidence (VSOE) perspective, with pricing being based on costs, and agreed profit percentages.
Value-based pricing	This requires a good understanding of customer needs and expectations in terms of what value they would place on the training offering versus what they would pay.	• Requires extensive research to assess market need and interest, including comparison of competitors' offerings of a similar nature. • Requires strong justification in relation to VSOE.

(Continued)

Table 3.6 (Continued)

Pricing strategy	Description	Comments
	Value pricing is used to increase profitability by aligning with more of the training product's value attributes.	• Can lead to continuous discounting especially when selling in competitive or challenging markets.
		• Requires significant advertising to communicate the value of training in order to motivate customers to pay more if not used to value pricing.
Demand-based pricing	This is based on the level of demand for a training offering and not specifically on the cost of development and materials.	• Demand-based pricing is geared to maintaining customer loyalty in high-volume markets.
	It requires an assessment and forecast of customer volumes in order to determine the price based on assessed demand. Once the demand is known, the price can be finalised by considering the costs at different sales levels and factoring in required profit levels.	• The success of this type of sales policy depends on the reliability of the demand assessments.
	Demand pricing is used to balance prices in high-volume competitive environments.	
Competition-based pricing	Competition-based pricing is based on assessing what other companies provide for a similar training offering.	This pricing policy can be used as a disruptive agent when training is involved in a highly competitive market.
	Following this, the pricing would be set higher, lower or the same, depending on what strategic advantage was required.	
Penetration pricing	This is similar in a way to competition-based pricing and is designed to gain market share by setting a low price to increase sales and market awareness.	• Once market share has been captured, the price may be increased.
		• Requires careful monitoring to ensure overall profitability is not impacted if the sales campaign extends beyond an expected end date.

(Continued)

Table 3.6 (Continued)

Pricing strategy	Description	Comments
Bundle pricing	The inclusion of several training products (ILT, eLearning, certification) in a bundled offering at a reduced price.	High-value offering that can be used to differentiate itself in the market.
Premium pricing	Typically used when the training offered is of an advanced nature and with low volume opportunities. The price is high when compared to other high-volume or mainstream training offerings.	Normally used when the training requires specialist subject matter experts and the content being provided is of a very high level.

TIME TO MARKET

Many factors affect decisions regarding timing, specifically in relation to training availability prior to alpha, beta and market readiness releases. Typically, in terms of the nature, depth and quality of content, this requires decisions on who, when and how it is developed, and complicated further by costs and availability of subject matter experts and content developers.

In some instances, content development work may need to be subcontracted out to either other internal groups or third-party developers. From the training product management perspective, this has to be balanced in relation to training ROI versus loss or slower product market growth and traction. Loss of market traction can significantly affect the longer-term training ROI and therefore requires a risk assessment to be undertaken with respect to the factors given in Table 3.7.

Table 3.7 Time to market ROI assessment factors

Key factors	Positive implications	Negative implications
Assess training market potential in relation to product sales.	Provides training volume opportunity overview.	May highlight restrictions regarding content price points and ability to recover required ROI if extra investment required to accommodate time to market challenges.
Increase training investment to access additional content development resource.	Minimises time to market.	Increases cost and ROI profile, which may require price point increase at release date or later in product lifecycle.

(Continued)

Table 3.7 (Continued)

Key factors	Positive implications	Negative implications
Apply rapid content development techniques to support phased introduction.	Training content available, which, if positioned correctly, can be targeted at early adopters. Phased content development and release minimises time to market implications.	May result in lower content quality look and feel, and only support a subset of actual product need.
Consider alternative modalities.	Early adopters gain access to material quicker and cost of entry for training providers is significantly reduced. Content can be released as subject matter-led workshop training with quick reference notes and/or YouTube 'how to implement' videos.	Requires careful market management and communication to ensure minimised brand damage and lack of support perception.

ACCREDITATION, CERTIFICATION OR ALTERNATIVE TESTING

From a training product management perspective, the business goal is about ensuring that the service or offering motivates and adds value to customers. This ensures customers want to buy and continue to apply the training for further business benefit.

To ensure fitness for purpose, proof points need to be established. In training, this comes in the form of testing. Testing itself comes in a variety of forms:

- **End of course survey:** a series of questions to establish the level of customer/ student satisfaction.
- **Qualification:** typically involves passing an examination that tests whether students can demonstrate their knowledge of a particular subject.
- **Accreditation:** often used interchangeably with certification and tests a student's competence level to perform specific tasks.
- **Certification:** a formal process validating that students have met a recognised standard. It usually involves attending a training course, gaining experience in the use of the technology and ratification by way of sitting an exam to test knowledge, skills and abilities required to perform a particular job or task.
- **Performance-based testing:** a formal process involving the testing and validation of knowledge, skills, competencies and the practical ability to implement them in a real-world situation to achieve desired business results.

For a product manager, the decision to develop and offer some form of testing is about four key factors:

1. Does the training undertaken by a student need to be validated in terms of their ability to prove in practice they have command of the technology?

2. Does it provide value to the student or business sponsor?

3. Does it drive market credibility?

4. Does it make economic sense in terms of ROI and minimising the total cost of ownership (TCO)?

With industry in general being short on skills, the business value of technical testing, particularly competency-based certification, and performance-based testing is high. The value of training staff and knowing that they can actually apply what they have learned for real business benefit makes testing an integral part of the overall training offering.

SUMMARY

Technical training product management involves the process of designing, building, operating and maintaining the training offering. The end objective of this is to create a training service that motivates and adds value, and ensures the customer wants to buy and continues to apply training for business benefit.

It involves multi-disciplinary teams being established comprising, for example, product developers and managers, training business development managers, training business unit owners, content developers and curriculum managers, certification specialists and training programme managers.

The training product manager takes responsibility for the lifecycle management of the training offering and ensures that it launches with the technology product and remains aligned throughout its lifecycle.

When launching a training offering, decisions will be made regarding how it will go-to-market (GTM). GTM plays a significant part in the training product management lifecycle, including what is sold, when it is sold, packaging, how training connects with its customer base, how value is delivered and the brand promise fulfilled. Pricing is also factored in, based on costs, value, demand, competition and required return on investment (ROI) needs.

The route to market (RTM) is also defined in terms of understanding customer behaviour, engagement and which sales channels to access.

The final stage of training product management ensures that the service or offering motivates and adds value so that customers want to buy and continue to apply the training for further business benefit, which is achieved via the validation process through testing and certification.

4 BUSINESS MODEL
Key components required to convert strategy to actual execution

Having established a clear strategy and business design, the next stage entails converting the output into tangible and measurable results.

This chapter looks at the steps required to establish the critical tasks and business interdependencies across the training and corporate organisation. This will include financial planning and management, business control and metrics, building or rebuilding an organisation, the establishment of a business climate and employee culture, and delivering the business value proposition.

ESTABLISHING CRITICAL TASKS

Critical tasks and interdependencies are the required activities to convert the business design strategy output into tangible and measurable results. They are primarily the key success factors to deliver the value proposition and other related business design activities such as:

- **Customer selection:** the customer segments selected for business focus.
- **Value proposition:** the training offerings to be provided, with justifications as to why customers would purchase or engage with the offering.
- **Value capture:** how revenue, profit or strategic advantage can be gained and measured.
- **Partnerships:** the activities and relationships required to drive the business forward.
- **Sustainability:** how profitability of offerings and investments will be protected and grown.

Table 4.1 represents an extract from the example in Chapter 2. It references tasks and dependencies, but not costs, measurable objectives or timelines, which are also fundamental requirements.

To ensure that critical tasks are achieved, it is important to establish a critical task list, factoring in all required elements to ensure success. The process in Figure 4.1 provides a simple approach to achieving this. However, to assist in more effective and interactive management, more sophisticated project management tools can be used when the tasks are many and complex in nature.

Table 4.1 Critical tasks example

Key tasks	
Financial critical tasks	**Dependencies**
Maximise RTM channels	
1.1 Engage and enable authorised training partners across the geographies	training partner management team and product sales
1.2 Assess, recommend and implement sales commission and incentive plans	training management and finance
1.3 Develop and introduce revised authorised training partner contracts	training management and legal
Maximise margin contribution	
1.1 Implement cloud infrastructure	shared services infrastructure team
1.2 Implement subscription model	shared services infrastructure team
1.3 Implement training staff reorganisation across the geographies	training management and HR

Figure 4.1 Establishing critical tasks

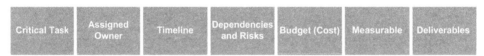

A critical task can comprise several sub-elements that may be dependent or independent of each other or rely on other parts of the organisation. These should be listed and defined with associated risks.

All activities should be assigned an owner with responsibilities to track progress via agreed timelines, budgetary expenditure and deliverables.

In terms of measurable goals, the responsibility may be spread across many groups. For example, a sales goal may be distributed across product sales, training sales and partner teams, whereas the development of a cloud-based infrastructure could be a shared services infrastructure team responsibility.

Sponsors and owners should both regularly monitor and review the progress of critical tasks in terms of resources, budgets and achievement of goals. Any deviation should be addressed and actioned accordingly.

UNDERSTANDING BUSINESS MODEL INTERDEPENDENCIES

Training success will depend on a variety of factors covering the robustness of the business model and interdependencies with other departments and business partners.

For instance, Figure 4.2 shows two linked but separate systems. The one labelled 'Training Department' represents a simplified business model reflecting the main elements of the business execution plan with its associated costs and revenue contribution. Similarly, the second system, labelled 'Corporate and Training Partners', also has associated costs and revenue contribution from a combination of partner activity and direct sales, plus shared service costs by way of finance, accounting and corporate support.

Figure 4.2 Business model interdependencies

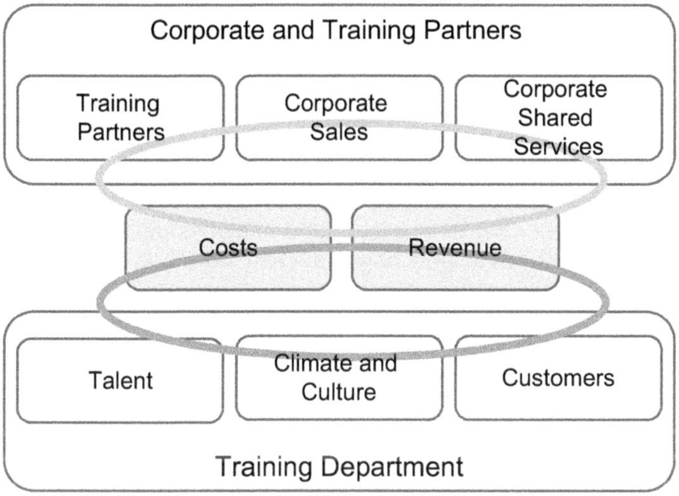

If a training department depends on corporate shared service functions and other sales team activities, effective coordination is key. Any misinterpretation or lack of support can have a significant impact on operational effectiveness, costs and revenues. The impact of corporate misalignment can result in financial decisions having to be made to address any shortfall at the training level.

Similarly, within the training-specific elements of the business model, any issues surrounding the competencies of the staff or changes in the climate of the team can have adverse effects on the results.

In effect, the two related systems both need to work in harmony. At one level, there is the internal interaction of the training team, while at the other level there are the corporate and partner interactions. Open communication, engagement and, above all, clarity of purpose is vital in order to have a business model that can deliver expected results based on expected levels of interactivity irrespective of where they occur.

FINANCIAL PLANNING AND MANAGEMENT

Financial planning is a key part of the strategy and business design process. The financial plan allocates costs, revenues and profit contribution according to the activities, resources, equipment and investments required to achieve the goals and objectives of the training business plan aligned to its expected time frames (typically 12 months, but can be part of a longer-term plan of two to five years).

It is a comprehensive exercise, involving the following activities:

- Assessment of the business environment.
- Confirmation of strategic intent and business objectives.
- Identification of the required level, amount and type of resources (employees, equipment, materials).
- Calculation of costs, revenue, profit and expected ROI.
- Identification of risks and issues associated with the agreed budgets.

Financial planning is critical to training group success as it provides the business plan with rigour by validating that the objectives set are achievable from a financial point of view.

Financial management involves the control of assets and liabilities, and monitoring expenses, revenues, accounts receivable and payable, cash flow and profitability. Working in conjunction with the training management team, it also provides ongoing assessment, evaluation and guidance to ensure focus is maintained for both short- and long-term gain.

Finance is a pivotal function and constantly undertakes risk management, review and evaluation. With its remit to ensure corporate fiscal stability and growth, the finance team may readjust short-term goals in order to achieve the company's long-term goals more efficiently. This could result in restructuring, for example. It is imperative that training management establishes strong working relationships with finance, and puts in place strong governance and metrics.

More detailed information on finances can be found in Chapter 15.

BUSINESS CONTROL AND METRICS

Business control, involving regular reviews, financial checks, accounting accuracy and adherence to agreed procedures and policies, is effective when a governance process is established. It provides an insight into the processes, systems and controls that are used to protect and develop the training assets.

The World Bank describes governance as 'promoting fairness, transparency and accountability' (World Bank 2017) and the OECD describes it as 'a system by which business organisations are directed and controlled' (OECD 2017).

To establish a training group governance policy, the management team needs to be clear on the current state of the business, where it intends to go and what is required to get there. In many instances, the work done in developing the strategy and business execution plan also assists in establishing the foundation for achieving this.

Metrics provide insights into how to improve a training business and they focus on what is important. The number of metrics can be many and varied, from mandatory and financial through to operational. The key element is simplicity, for if they are too many and complex in nature, they will be ineffective.

Metrics are effective when they are aligned to the business design requirements of the training group. Typically, they include finance, marketing, sales, training delivery, content development, customer satisfaction and financial needs.

The metrics should be monitoring and supporting key critical task activities, allowing the training group to assess whether there are issues or opportunities to be addressed and when goals have been achieved.

For more detailed explanations and examples, see Chapter 14.

BUILDING THE ORGANISATION

The training group's organisational structure should be based on how it supports strategy and business design needs. It is not a one-time activity, and should be reviewed in accordance with changes taking place in terms of growth and business need.

When building an organisation, three considerations need to be factored in:

- The functions it performs in terms of its core activities; for example, training delivery, content development, training partner management, sales and training operations.
- Organisational position in terms of reporting lines and interactivity with other functions.
- Functional authority in terms of its ability to make decisions and perform activities without seeking guidance from others within the structure.

From a functional structure perspective, there are four basic types of structure to be considered, depending upon the nature and complexity of the training group being built or evolved. The four types are:

- **Simple:** effective when a company is embarking on the introduction of a training group comprising a training manager, instructors, content developers and administration. Typically, this comprises a maximum of 20 employees.
- **Functional:** based on functional activities such as marketing, sales, operations, training delivery, content development and product management. Each function or department has a designated manager with the authority to coordinate activities and deliver defined results. Employees within the departments have specific

specialist skills. This is suitable for large training groups in medium to large enterprises.

- **Multi-divisional:** particularly relevant within large multinational companies where geographies or product lines are responsible for providing training. Each division is responsible for achieving its business results and reporting to a centralised office for strategic purposes only. This is suitable for corporates with decentralised structures and business models.

- **Matrix:** functional and multi-divisional organisational structures exist within a vertical reporting line, whereas matrix-based organisations interact on a horizontal basis. This type of structure is more suitable for project-oriented, service-based companies.

The key consideration is fitness for purpose and suitability to achieve the business design criteria.

ESTABLISHING A BUSINESS CLIMATE AND EMPLOYEE CULTURE

Establishing a business climate and culture takes time. For a newly formed training group, the employees may be influenced by an existing corporate culture. If the culture has already been defined in terms of its values, beliefs and behaviours, the employees will already know what the organisation's personality is and accept or accommodate it.

For example, the culture may be one of positive support where employees behave as an extended family, mentoring, nurturing and participating in active support. Another organisation may have a market-oriented culture where its employees are results-oriented and focus on the achievements of their roles and the teams they are members of.

Establishing a strong and recognisable culture is important as it contributes to business success, especially if it is built on shared values, attitudes, standards and beliefs that reflect the overall goals of the training group. To be effective, it has to be based around the group's values and vision, which feeds into the organisational design in terms of processes, structure and required hierarchy. This allows for the crafting of expected behaviours and the way employees should approach their work and interaction with others, enabling the culture to be established and nurtured.

Organisational climate reflects the mood or current atmosphere within a business. It is prone to short-term fluctuations and is determined by many factors, which include leadership, structure, rewards and recognition.

Developing a high-performing training group climate can be created by focusing and maintaining attention on a strong employee engagement model, and is achieved by ensuring communication clarity, and where commitment, responsibility, development and enforcement of standards, recognition and teamwork is established and defined.

Establishing regular feedback based on a measurable engagement model assists in influencing the work environment and steering employees towards the achievement of training group success.

DELIVERING THE BUSINESS VALUE PROPOSITION

When developing a strategy, the key objective is to develop and produce a business design, which is converted into critical executable tasks as previously described at the beginning of this chapter. One of those tasks, namely the value proposition provides the linkage between the customer and the training group in terms of what offerings are provided and why. The delivery of the proposition is defined and measured in terms of value capture and sustainability.

At the executable level, governance and metrics management provide active feedback on how the value proposition is being achieved. The challenge is ensuring the right measurements are in place and being cross-referenced to the original business design elements.

Any changes affecting the achievement of the value proposition can be addressed by assessing either the business design, which is strategy-focused, or the critical tasks, which are execution-based. This provides a powerful and effective active-based feedback control mechanism, providing the ability to adjust and address issues as they arise.

REBUILDING AN ORGANISATION

When building a new organisation, a training manager has the benefit of selecting staff according to the business need and establishing a joint working culture for combined success.

When a new manager is hired or required to rebuild an organisation, a couple of key challenges arise. The first is recognising who is performing well versus those who are not. The second, which is linked, is establishing trust.

Building trust is one of the most important leadership competencies required and needs to be consistently maintained. Without it, individual and group development will be seriously hindered and flawed.

One of the many management techniques that can be adopted to assist in group development, and ultimately trust, is that of forming, storming, norming and performing developed by Bruce Tuckman (Tuckman 1965).

The forming stage places a high dependence on the manager to provide guidance and direction. While employees will have degrees of anxiety and uncertainty, the manager will obtain a high-level view of how the group currently operates and provide an outline of how the team will be organised and its key goals.

Storming, the second stage of group development, is where a new training manager needs to establish authority and respect when employee conflict and competition are very prevalent. When employees begin to understand what is expected of them at training group level, they will start to challenge and vie for position, defining their roles and how required tasks will be implemented. The manager must provide clarification regarding the responsibilities, structure, measurement criteria and recognition systems for the group and the individuals. It is at this stage that the training manager must provide strong leadership, as observed through daily positive actions, communications and overall behaviour regarding decisions to be made on staffing levels, roles and responsibilities.

The third stage, norming, is where the training manager facilitates and obtains agreement and consensus among the group at large. This is typically achieved through the establishment of well-defined roles and responsibilities and encouraging group cooperation for the common good. This drives cohesion and focus on the achievement of collective goals.

The final stage, performing, is based on the group understanding why and what it is doing, including operating with high degrees of autonomy. The teams within the group strive towards overachievement and making valid business decisions. The training manager maintains direction by delegating tasks and projects and providing strong positive communication and problem resolution.

SUMMARY

Establishing critical tasks and business interdependencies across the training and corporate organisation are key and important activities. They involve financial planning and management, business control and metrics, business climate and culture development, organisational structure, and delivering the business value proposition.

Financial planning provides the business plan with rigour by validating that objectives set are achievable and, on the management side, providing control and monitoring of expenses, revenues, cash flow and profitability.

Business control, in conjunction with a governance process, provides insight into the processes, systems and controls that are used to protect and develop the training assets.

Organisational requirements are typically based around three considerations. The first is the function it performs regarding core activities; the second is its organisational position in terms of reporting line and interactivity with other functions; and, thirdly, the functional authority in terms of its ability to make decisions and perform activities without seeking guidance from others within the structure. Should an existing organisation require rebuilding, establishing trust with existing employees is key, as is understanding which staff are performing well versus those which are not.

Business climate and employee culture also needs to be considered and directed towards the development of a high-performing training group. In conjunction with the previous points, this helps to deliver the business value proposition.

5 BUSINESS DEVELOPMENT AND MARKETING MANAGEMENT
Building a training business and managing its success

Establishing, growing and maintaining a training business as it moves forward requires strong skills in business development and awareness of marketing management.

This chapter looks at the roles and responsibilities of a business development manager (BDM) in terms of the activities required to develop and grow the business in line with the agreed strategy.

Sales and marketing components of business development are also covered. The sales element covers discount policies, vendor specific objective evidence (VSOE), attach rates, and competitive and tactical strategies. The marketing element covers demand and lead generation, promotional materials and the implementation of customer, advisory and reference programmes.

As new technologies enter the training sphere, they have the potential to influence the way in which organisations gain a competitive edge through disruptive business growth. This is briefly discussed at the end of this chapter.

ROLES AND RESPONSIBILITIES

Sales and business development are often considered to be one and the same in terms of selling an offering to a customer. The reality is that they are different: sales provide the connection between an organisation and its customers regarding the positioning, presenting and selling of training, whereas business development refers to activities based on expanding the training organisation's reach into new and existing markets – for example, forming partnerships with other businesses to sell or include offerings that complement each other or provide greater market reach and sales coverage.

The BDM role is a combination of quality management, strategic analysis, marketing management and sales. The objective is to identify new business opportunities, expand market share and develop partnerships to generate new and increased revenue.

Building a training business requires the BDM to actively engage specialists to assist in establishing, growing and maintaining the business as it moves forward. The BDM also needs to have strong skills and awareness of market management. This involves expanding the customer base, maintaining influence and awareness, improving customer opinions of the training offerings, and raising the company's overall perceived value in the eyes of the customer. Marketing management can sometimes be overlooked or lack investment when comparing the training contribution to overall company product or service offerings.

BDMs need to justify and show the value of marketing management or risk the challenge of failure and ineffectiveness.

To win in the training business, the training offering, along with the sales and marketing effort, needs to be relevant and effective. Without engaging the market, it simply will not happen!

BUILDING SUCCESSFUL VALUE PROPOSITIONS

Value propositions are used by companies to summarise to potential customers why they should purchase a product or service such as training. They should be clear and concise in terms of explaining how training would address a customer's issue of concern, the benefit it provides and why it is a better solution than other competitors' solutions.

If a customer's training needs cannot be explained quickly or succinctly, then it is not a value proposition. Without a need, there is no incentive for customers to engage or purchase. The key to building successful value propositions is to:

- relate to the needs of the customer;
- outline how the training offering stands out from others;
- provide evidence that the deliverable will meet the customer's need.

The two example value propositions shown below highlight the need to develop a solution to address the specific opportunity. The first example is based on a training group's generic view, and the second based on a specific customer need.

- **Training group view:** Maximise customer skills and their return on investment in our technologies by providing high-quality and relevant technical training aligned to the achievement of their required business outcomes, while differentiating the learning experience through task-based rather than role-based training provision.

- **Specific customer need:** To protect your corporate environment against cyber-attacks, by investing in our cyber-security technology, we propose to align the required training based on assessing employee risks, vulnerabilities and exposure to the security challenges facing your organisation. With our security implementation teams working together, we will be in a strong position to develop employee competencies and confidence via a combined and aligned training solution.

Both are value proposition statements. The first is stating at a high level the rationale and value the training group brings internally and externally when undertaking an initial sales pitch. The second is more specific to the actual customer need and minimises the detail required later within a sales proposal.

DISCOUNT POLICY IMPLEMENTATION

Within any organisation there will be different and varying views on discount policy implementation. For example, finance will argue that while the opportunity for winning a deal is maximised, the margin contribution is minimised. However, the head of sales will fight for discounts to win against competitive forces.

At the end of the day, the training business unit owner will need to sign off on the discount policy a BDM is proposing, while simultaneously recognising that the role of the BDM is to ensure the right tools are in place to gain and maintain market traction. Discounts are part of the marketing tool set and can be very effective if used and applied correctly. To achieve correct application of a proposed discount policy, it needs to be defined, monitored and administered. Table 5.1 highlights the objectives, benefits, shortfalls and considerations of applying discounts in the world of training.

Table 5.1 Discount policies (factors for consideration)

Discount objective	Benefits	Shortfalls	Administration and monitoring
Gaining market traction	Initiates early market adoption for new training offerings. Expands market penetration when operating in a competitive environment.	Can set a precedent regarding expected price point in the long term. Depending on the depth of discount, may damage ROI expectations. Need to set right level of expectation with repeat customers.	Training sales operations, if in existence, or booking administration team. Need to monitor progress against predefined bookings and timelines.
Achieving month- or quarter-end target attainment	Can boost end of month or quarter sales results. Increases fill rate and the potential to increase bottom-line profitability. Minimises course cancellations that can damage brand reputation.	Customers may wait until month or quarter end before booking. Potential VSOE implications.	Training sales operations, if in existence, or booking administration team. Finance team, regarding profitability implications.

(Continued)

Table 5.1 (Continued)

Discount objective	Benefits	Shortfalls	Administration and monitoring
Improving sales value by bundling training	Improves order level value. Improves customer commitment beyond the short term.	Potential VSOE implications. Can impact on ROI and profitability expectations if not managed and tracked correctly.	Training sales operations, if in existence, or booking administration team. Finance team regarding profitability implications.
Training sold with products	Encourages training to be sold at point of sale. Supports solution selling.	Can impact revenue recognition and product sales compensation payments via VSOE rules. Can result in training not being consumed due to the sale going via the customer's procurement team.	Training sales operations and product sales, to ensure correct allocation of the booking and revenue. Finance team, regarding profitability and revenue allocation implications.

VENDOR-SPECIFIC OBJECTIVE EVIDENCE (VSOE)[1]

Generally Accepted Accounting Principles, also called GAAP or US GAAP, are formal principles adopted by the United States Securities and Exchange Commission (US SEC).

As part of these accounting practices, VSOE is a method of revenue recognition. VSOE is intended for use by US-based companies to maintain GAAP compliance with the American Institute of Certified Public Accountants (AICPA). Any US subsidiary operating outside the USA must support and report VSOE. UK and European companies do not have to follow VSOE.

VSOE enables companies to recognise revenue on specific items included within a multi-item sale, based on evidence (specific to the company) that the product has been delivered.

The purpose of GAAP is to ensure that financial reports reflect earnings in the period they were delivered. For example, a company selling a solution comprising software, installation and a one-year training contract can only record the overall sale on a deferred basis, with earnings being recognised over the term of the training contract. However, based on VSOE, allocation occurs by splitting the revenue among

1 Content provided by Wikipedia under the Creative Commons Attribution-ShareAlike License.

the products and related elements, which is the price established by the vendor for the separate sale of each element, allowing them to recognise the individual revenue components at their respective delivery stage. This allows companies that sell items comprising software licences, training contracts and hardware items to recognise the revenue of the hardware items on delivery, with the software licence and training contract being recognised at the time of their individual fulfilment.

VSOE revenue recognition is commonly used by companies that sell software products and services in multiple-element bundles. VSOE focuses on the fair market value of an item sold individually, as opposed to the assigned sales value of the item sold as part of a multiple-element bundle.

From a training perspective, it is common practice to maintain the overall average price charged to customers, irrespective of how the product is bought (bundled, discounted), to within 15 per cent of list price, to satisfy and justify VSOE fair pricing assessments. Note that VSOE interpretation varies by company, so it is important to discuss this aspect with the finance department to get a definitive answer.[2]

CARVE OUTS, ATTACH AND INCLUSION RATE STRATEGIES

Maximising training revenue by leveraging product sales teams can be challenging and also rewarding. It can be challenging when looking to encourage them to include training within the sales process. It is rewarding when they apply one of three strategies, namely Carve outs, Attach or Inclusion to include training within their customer engagement and resultant sale.

Carve outs

If a sales person sells an IT software solution to a customer at an all-inclusive price, it is up to the training team to request a percentage of the deal to be allocated to the department; this is known as carve out. Initially, this seems a good opportunity for the training department to ensure revenue flow; however, the reality in many instances is that the accounting department cannot recognise the revenue without applying VSOE principles and obtaining agreement from the product sales teams that the product revenue is lower than the full amount charged.

Carve outs are not popular or welcomed in many organisations but often requested by sales representatives who are eager to close deals without building the cost of training into the overall sales price. It can be viewed as a form of discount that is beneficial to the customer but detrimental to the overall true value being sold by the vendor.

Problems can arise with this type of sales approach in respect of VSOE implications, booking and revenue recognition, and sales and delivery compensation.

From a training perspective, carve outs offer a way of ensuring training is included seamlessly within most sales transactions. The downside is overall company revenue

---

2   Content provided by Everipedia under the Creative Commons Attribution-ShareAlike License.

is reduced and, unless the business unit training manager is particularly savvy, no revenue is recorded as training and delivery costs have to be absorbed. The golden rule, therefore, is to gain corporate agreement on any carve out strategy regarding booking and revenue allocation.

Attach rate

Training attach rate strategies, whereby sales teams automatically include training in the sales discussion and as a fully priced offering, should be the norm in any product- and service-based business. In many companies, product support or maintenance is attached, but for some reason this is not always the case with technical training.

The challenge is often around positioning the value, not just to the customer but to the organisation at large. Many surveys over the years have shown that customers are more inclined to purchase training if positioned at the initial point of sale. For a customer to invest and allocate a budget for buying a product only to find after the sale has been concluded that they then need to invest in training is ludicrous. The result is loss of trust and a customer now looking to locate the training at the cheapest cost possible.

Time spent by the BDM and training business owner with sales, marketing and product management leaders is crucial, especially regarding new product releases. Customers purchase business outcomes, not functions and features. As with all business outcomes, there are three components: technology, process and people. All these are important and entwined, so training should be part of the overall solution being sold.

Whether BDMs can sell an integral solution or a combined package, attach rate strategies are important tools in their arsenal. Attach rates are typically defined as a percentage of product sales or deals. For example:

- training revenue as a percentage of product (that is, £50,000 training with £1,500,000 product sales would be a 3.3% attach rate);
- assessing the number of training deals to overall product deals (that is, 500 training deals versus 5,000 product deals can be classified as either an attach rate or inclusion rate of 10%).

Inclusion rate

Attach rates tend to be revenue-based which is a measure of training revenue sold versus product revenue sold, whereas the inclusion rate is a measure of the number of deals that have been included with a sale.

Within the software industry, a 2 per cent attach rate is deemed typical, if not disappointing revenue-wise. However, if an inclusion rate of 10 per cent was achieved, this would be much healthier. Revenue attach can be misleading as large amounts of revenue may have come in from a small number of deals, whereas inclusion highlights the percentage of customers including training within a broader vendor solution.

Adopting inclusion over attach is a matter of choice; certainly, the ability to influence customers in the short and longer term is more effective with the inclusion strategy. Whichever one is favoured, Table 5.2 summarises some of the strategies that could be adopted.

Table 5.2 Attach and inclusion strategies

Attach and inclusion strategy	Benefits	Shortfalls	Notes
Attach: new product launch	• Initiates early market adoption with aligned company offerings support. • Improves customer spend contribution.	• Requires sales training to ensure right level of expectation is set with customers. • Potential VSOE implications if training is discounted.	• Training sales operations and delivery teams need to be aware and aligned with what has been sold and positioned.
Attach: geographic and region based	• Can be used to trial customer acceptance of a broader sales model. • Can be aligned with a phased introduction of new product releases.	• Countries may respond differently to training being attached at point of sale. • Potential VSOE implications if training is discounted.	• Training sales operations and delivery teams need to be aware and aligned with what has been sold and positioned.
Attach: overall revenue growth	• Can set attach rate growth targets to encourage sales adoption in both the short and long term. • Increases overall spend per opportunity.	• Potential VSOE implications. • Requires sales training to ensure right level of expectation is set with customers.	• Training sales operations and delivery teams need to be aware and aligned with what has been sold and positioned.
Inclusion: move towards business outcome or solution-based selling	• Encourages training to be sold at point of sale. • Supports solution selling. • Potentially improves customer loyalty and confidence. • Supports account management across the vendor portfolio.	• Requires sales training to ensure right level of expectation is set with customers. • May slow down the product sales activity if included across all deal types.	• Training sales operations and delivery teams need to be aware and aligned with what has been sold and positioned.

(Continued)

Table 5.2 (Continued)

Attach and inclusion strategy	Benefits	Shortfalls	Notes
Inclusion: large account management	• Focused selling on key accounts. • Provides an expected solution level of account management. • High-value customer and vendor engagement.	• Requires sales training to ensure right level of expectation is set with customers. • Good account management planning required to ensure training is positioned at the appropriate time and deal.	• Training teams need to be fully aligned with the account management team to ensure continuity of engagement.

COMPETITIVE AND TACTICAL STRATEGIES

BDMs need to be fully aware of the competitive forces affecting the success of the training business as well as the tactical actions required to implement and ensure any challenges or growth opportunities are exploited accordingly.

Competitive strategies can take many forms, as shown in Table 5.3. Also shown in the table are corresponding tactical strategies and key activities that BDMs can implement to stay ahead.

Table 5.3 Competitive and tactical strategies

Competitive strategies	Tactical strategy	Key activities	Notes
Market awareness: monitoring market conditions regarding buying patterns and price sensitivities	• Monitor market conditions as they affect the customer and business climate. • Develop promotional activities that address changing conditions and opportunities.	• Assess won and lost opportunities. • Monitor local and national business climate. • Focus training on specific key pain points. • Consider alternative training modalities to reduce the cost of training to the customer and the time required for them to attend the course.	Marketplace awareness and knowledge is key to understanding the needs of the customer base regarding training offerings, training partners, key competitors and their actions, market trends and current technology developments. This is a fact-gathering analytical exercise with the objective to specify in detail what is happening in the business training

(Continued)

Table 5.3 (Continued)

Competitive strategies	Tactical strategy	Key activities	Notes
			environment, and how commercial success factors are shifting and impacting the business.
Competitor offerings: monitoring their offerings, mode of engagement, go-to-market activities, value and key differentiators	• Assess competitor offerings and what differentiates them. • Monitor and compare competitor success rates regarding customer acquisition and retention.	• Assess go-to-market tactics and success rates. • Understand their value-add actions. • Assess how they differentiate themselves and compare with own current activities, and what lessons and actions can be undertaken to improve.	Good lessons can be learned from assessing competitors. Vendor-specific training tends not to overlap. Hence, monitoring competitors' growth or challenges provides a rich ground for assimilating industry best practice.
Grey market (independent unauthorised offerings): monitoring their offerings, mode of engagement, go-to-market activities, value and key differentiators	• Develop key marketing messages that reinforce the value of vendor-specific training. • Offer integrated solutions with training included.	• Enable product sales to offer an integrated solution, with training included to minimise grey market opportunities. • Targeted marketing highlighting the cons of using grey market versus the pros of vendor-specific.	Grey market tends to undercut on price and quality. However, they can be more flexible in terms of training offering provision.
Partner development and market penetration: monitoring and controlling growth, addressing market and quality challenges	• Assess product growth via partner network. • Establish training partner network to provide geographic and business growth coverage.	• Develop a training partner programme. • Align market opportunity to a partner coverage model.	Partners offer market expansion potential in regions in which it may not be cost-effective to establish a permanent presence.

DEMAND AND LEAD GENERATION

As explained earlier in this chapter, business development covers many aspects, from the right market offerings and discount policies to competitive strategies. All are important and very much entwined.

Another key area is that of demand and lead generation. However, an issue that often arises is understanding the difference between lead generation and demand generation, which are quite often used interchangeably, but are very different.

When allocating budgets to these types of marketing activities, it is important to know which one does what and how their value is measured:

- **Demand generation** is focused on shaping the target audience perspective on what they should consider buying and, hence, is measured in terms of bookings or revenue generated.
- **Lead generation** is focused on capturing customer information, which can then be used to drive demand via well-crafted messages and campaigns; typically measured in terms of the percentage of leads that led to revenue generation opportunities.

It is certainly not possible to have one without the other. From a vendor training perspective, lead generation can be eased by referencing and using product-based customer information and accessing customers who have support contracts, which can then be targeted with relevant demand generation campaigns.

Demand generation

For demand generation to be effective, the requirement is to have a clear view of the characteristics of the target customer and their buying process and to build a content framework by which to launch targeted messages.

The most crucial of these is knowing the customer characteristics. Without this, it will not be possible to decide:

- on what marketing message content is to be created;
- what tone, style and delivery vehicle is required;
- what training topics and targets to focus on to develop and grow the business;
- who within the target audience needs to be focused on and why.

To understand the training buyer characteristics, the BDM should organise a series of meetings between marketing, training sales and the delivery teams. This is important as all groups can share their unique insights on the customer rather than generating a biased and skewed one, which can result in an incorrect and invalid view. From these discussions, the buying groups can be structured around job function (such as training management, buyer, end user, system designer) rather than job title (such as vice president, director).

The next stage is the customer buying process and understanding and identifying the specific decisions or steps the training buyer goes through. Typically, this stage is asking what motivates them to start looking for a training solution. Often, this can be answered by assessing how the BDM's own company positions the product and what importance they place on the business outcome. From this data point, it becomes possible to determine and analyse further how the buyer progresses through to making a purchase.

Demand generation normally fails when not enough objective research has been undertaken. By working closely with product sales, the value of training can be positioned and investigated via the use of customer focus groups.

The next stage is to develop a content framework. The framework uses the output from the previous stages to assist in developing the message to be used to drive demand based on valid justifications. The content framework is based on building a matrix using the buyer characteristics and the collected buying process information, and asks the following questions:

- What are training buyers asking?
- What response should be provided?
- Which communication vehicle should be used to reply?
- What customer behaviour is expected from the responses?

A typical content framework could look like Table 5.4.

Based on the agreed framework and required customer behaviours, business development and marketing can construct a series of targeted demand generation campaigns. These types of activity take between two to three months when working across a large corporation or one to two months for a medium-sized company.

Lead generation

Lead generation is a marketing activity used to generate interest in training. The leads themselves are then passed to sales for the purpose of developing a sales pipeline. Obtaining the leads can be undertaken using various methods and approaches.

Advertising and emailing customers, which used to be the norm, is no longer an efficient way to establish and maintain an ongoing meaningful relationship. With the increasing use and interest in social media networks (LinkedIn, Instagram, Facebook, etc.) and subscription-based communication channels such as YouTube, and in some instances the training organisation's own website, a stronger and more relevant relationship can now be developed and matured.

When training buyers undertake their own research for information on courses and training products without engaging in conversation with a sales person, there is a requirement to establish a strong and relevant digital presence. Attracting attention and, more importantly, maintaining it, especially with respect to training, requires the provider to become a trusted advisor by publishing and creating valuable content assets and thought leadership.

Table 5.4 Demand generation content framework

	Buying process stages				
Buying characteristics (example based on a business sponsor)	**Addressing need**	**Data collection**	**Training relevancy**	**Budget and ROI**	**Training solution aligned to required business outcome**
Typical questions	How do you ensure the deployment delivers expected results?	What evidence do you have regarding training capabilities?	How do you know the training provider can deliver training that reflects the needs of the business and employee profile?	How do you maximise available budget and show a return on investment?	How do you align the training solution to the overall deployment and monitor that it delivers the required business outcome?
Training response	Consultation based on required business outcomes related to employee impact.	Outline training capabilities and coverage.	White paper and case studies.	Training needs assessment aligned to budget maximisation and delivering required ROI.	White paper highlighting how to achieve desired business outcomes via employee specific training.
Delivery media	White paper or case study.	Summary paper highlighting offerings supported by customer references.	Industry-specific case studies; certification results related to employee competency improvements; customer presentation.	Invitation to request an appointment to undertake a high-level assessment and presentation.	White paper and presentation.
Required behaviours	Requests meeting or presentation.	Requests further evidence.	Requests training needs assessment.	Requests meeting.	Requests meeting.

Other marketing techniques still apply, but it is important to prioritise these in relation to marketplace need and current lead marketing trends being deployed. Lead generation can be deemed to be inbound or outbound. Both are relevant and need to be considered as part of a broader training marketing strategy. Tables 5.5 and 5.6 highlight the differences between the two.

Table 5.5 Inbound lead generation matrix

Distribution method	Description	Key objective	Notes
Website	Main window highlighting what training you offer, why, benefits and how to engage.	Motivate potential training buyers to request more information.	Ensure message is clear and concise.
Blog	Populated regularly to maintain interest and position as a gateway to conversation and engagement.	Create buyer trust by maintaining interest and curiosity; encourage customer to subscribe.	Ensure it is search engine optimisation (SEO)-enabled as blogs are often found by random search.
Social media	Provide potential buyers with an environment to research and learn about your training from other influencers and peers.	Lead generation.	To maintain customer contact and engagement, it is important to understand which social sites they are active with, for example: Facebook, Twitter and LinkedIn.

Inbound marketing is about helping customers to find and be aware of the training group before they are seeking to buy training. Then progress them towards being a valid lead and ultimately becoming a training revenue stream.

The important point to remember in relation to the use of the internet is to focus on quality not quantity, and, particularly, useful reference-based material which helps SEO tools to be more effective.

From the broader training marketing strategy point of view, inbound lead generation activates broad interest, whereas outbound lead generation allows the acceleration of inbound efforts and targets specific opportunities.

Using outbound channels enables the introduction of key messages and content to potential prospects. To be effective, outbound lead generation is normally highly targeted, with a call-to-action that is obvious. This effectively means that well-focused outbound marketing can encourage potential buyers to move closer to being ready to buy training offerings.

Table 5.6 Outbound lead generation matrix

Distribution method	Description	Key objective	Notes
Email	Promotes new training offerings and enables the maintenance of regular communication.	Puts training content in front of prospects who may not be looking for information.	Small volume segment-based emails are more engaging than large un-targeted ones. Relevance is key regarding what the training audience requires.
Display advertising	Highly targeted online placements, which can be further enhanced via cookie re-targeting advertisements.	Focused marketing messages to address broader audience demographics and behaviours.	Requires an understanding of where the potential buyers spend their time and helps to build brand awareness.
Pay per click (PPC) advertising	PPC on search engines allows adverts to show up as sponsored results on the top and side of relevant search terms.	Promote training based on keyword phrase searches.	Pay for each click on advertisements that are displayed on search engines such as Google, Yahoo and so on.
Content syndication	A content sharing strategy used to promote white papers, articles, news releases and so on on third-party sites. Leads are passed on via email.	Deliver high-value content to training prospects through content syndication on other websites for greater reach and engagement.	Training buyers will not always end up at the website, so it is important that a presence is established where they may show up.
Direct mail	Effective for targeted communications in situations where email would fail (CEO, CIO).	Highly targeted, creative and high-value message to engage senior decision makers.	Executives do not usually browse the web for information. It is difficult to access them via email, but they may respond more favourably to a direct, personalised communication.

(Continued)

Table 5.6 (Continued)

Distribution method	Description	Key objective	Notes
Events	Events provide the chance to define the training brand, clarify the solutions provided and establish personal connections with participants.	To deliver speeches and content that conveys what the training group's thought leadership is and raises perception with potential buyers.	Compared to other marketing activities, events are more likely to quickly turn a prospect into a strong lead.
Inside sales representatives	Inside sales representatives focus on reviewing, contacting and qualifying marketing-generated leads and delivering them to training sales account executives.	To ensure that every single lead marketing passes on is as qualified as possible. Assists in making a positive impression, creating future demand and becoming a trusted advisor.	This is critical in the lead generation process to ensure leads are not treated as blank faces to be simply questioned, qualified and harvested.

Irrespective of the depth, level and nature of lead generation adopted and implemented, it is vital metrics for success are clearly defined, measured and analysed. Without this the training budget will be scrutinised and reduced, which in turn minimises the ability to justify investment in the short and longer term. Common lead generation metrics that companies use include those shown in Table 5.7.

Table 5.7 Common lead generation metrics

Lead generation metric	Description
Marketing effectiveness in terms of its contribution to the overall sales pipeline	Measurement of potential training revenue contributing to the sales pipeline process as a consequence of marketing lead generation activities.
Marketing effectiveness in terms of generated revenue	Measurement of training revenue generated in relation to deals obtained as a consequence of marketing lead generation activities.
Number of valid qualified leads	Number of valid leads generated by marketing, as confirmed by the training sales team. Often reported as a percentage of the total number of leads provided.
Cost per lead	Total campaign costs/quantity of leads.

MARKETING AND THE INTERNET

As noted in the previous section on demand and lead generation, the use of digital techniques is of course standard practice. The important point with any form of marketing, and, in particular, the internet, is the need to focus on quality not quantity. The main objective is to attract, acquire and engage a clearly defined and understood target audience. Understanding the various options, their benefits and their shortfalls, is vital to ensure marketing investment is not wasted.

SEO

SEO is an important component in the use of digital marketing. Without it, content may well go unseen. Its main function is to expand visibility in generic search engine results, improve rankings and drive customer traffic.

There are many elements to SEO, from words on a page to the way other sites link to a specific website. SEO can simply be a matter of making sure the website is structured in a manner that search engines understand.

With the majority of internet traffic being serviced by the commercial search engines of Google, Bing and Yahoo, if the big three can't locate the training content then in the majority of instances it will go unnoticed. The use of social media sites can generate training website visits, but search engines are the primary means by which target audiences will navigate the web.

Push and pull digital marketing

Digital marketing can be very effective in promoting training as long as the principle of using 'push' (email) and 'pull' (pay per click, website presence, etc.) technologies to execute a marketing programme is understood. Its success is based on considering the following requirements:

- it must be targeted;
- it needs to be trackable;
- it has to be measurable;
- it involves the development of a relationship with the interested customer requiring training.

Table 5.8 summarises the main digital marketing methods currently in use, along with their chief requirements and the potential benefits to be gained.

Table 5.8 Digital marketing methods

Digital marketing methods	Push or pull	Requirements	Benefits
Website	Pull	• Maintaining interest requires quality content. • Requires regular updates. • Must support mobile and tablets.	• Great content for SEO. • Can attract links from other sites. • Can support pop-ups, banners and add-ons for other websites.
Email	Push	• Needs to be creative. • Highly targeted.	• Targeted customer engagement and awareness. • Can be used for sending direct mailers and newsletters.
Pay per click	Pull	• Budget allocation with known objectives. • Understanding of what benefits will be gained by positioning adverts based on keyword searches.	• Promotes training based on keyword phrase searches.
Social media	Push and pull	• Decide on what will be shared and why. • Think like a publisher: be prepared to publish videos, PDFs, ebooks. • Expand the social routes: YouTube, LinkedIn, Facebook, Twitter, blogs. • Operate in real time and respond daily to questions or trends. • Educate, don't sell; focus on informing and solving customer problems. • Don't stagnate with fixed modalities, review new and additional multimedia channels to satisfy consumer profiles.	• Ability to promote compelling headlines. • Ability to encourage consumer activity with those interested in training. • Enables online 24×7 visibility. • Provides an insight into what is important for training consumers. • Training is multi-modal and therefore you can target baby boomers with text, generation Y with video, and so on. • The training audience will communicate directly, providing a rich exposure to their needs and potential opportunities to support.

(Continued)

Table 5.8 (Continued)

Digital marketing methods	Push or pull	Requirements	Benefits
Social media	Push and pull	• Listen to the training audience. • Make the experience interesting, but don't market. • Listen to feedback and engage via messaging systems. • Target the right community.	• Building a wow factor in terms of content maintains and promotes a broader audience. • Following niche supporters provides an ability for content to be forwarded and helps to expand audience reach and profile.
Editorial	Pull	• Consistency in style and approach. • Make the topic informative and topical, but don't market. • Target the right community.	• Ability to place topical training articles in online news, industry magazines and portals.
Affiliate or content syndication	Pull	• Educate, don't sell; focus on informing and solving customer problems. • Ensure alignment of message with that of the affiliate. • Target the right community.	• Can provide high-value content to training prospects through other training or partner websites for greater coverage and engagement.
Promotions	Pull	• Budget allocation with known objectives. • Understand the importance of timing and alignment with other marketing activities.	• Digital version of a marketing and sales promotion.

PROMOTIONAL MATERIALS

Promotional material provided to potential customers should be a quick summary and reinforcement of what they actually require.

Leaving them with a company mug helps to keep the name alive, as does a USB stick. From a product perspective, it is about creating brand awareness and brand loyalty. From a training department perspective, the promotional value is low. Reinforcing the company name does not provide any meaningful engagement, whereas fact sheets, course outlines and catalogues provide data that can be used and referenced and form a component part of demand generation. When considering the use of promotional products, the following guidelines apply:

- Promotional materials should be part of an overall promotion plan.

- Leverage corporate marketing and media activities where possible.

- Select an effective promotional product in terms of the overall contribution it will make to brand awareness, and what key objectives it is looking to achieve.

- Use a relevant promotional product that tempts the potential customer and provides some form of intrigue, not just for them, but others around them. T-shirts are good for this when used with quirky messages.

- Understand the what, the why and the cost/return; this is crucial, including its contribution to the overall marketing plan.

Time spent on defining the promotion plan, with the ability to include ad hoc promotional activities, is key. As is the need to explain in detail the required costs and expected revenue returns, especially if funding is required from corporate, as opposed to local, training department funding.

Apart from mugs, T-shirts and USB memory sticks, typical training promotional examples include fact sheets and catalogues.

Fact sheets

These are typically one to two sheets of information highlighting key training points with supporting data. The layout is often stylised and contains training course or offering information, technical data, answers to common questions and contact information.

Catalogues

Sometimes referred to as a training brochure, a catalogue is arguably the most important promotional aid available, highlighting the range of technical training courses and offerings provided.

For many influencers or purchasers of training, this document provides a professional insight into how the training is delivered, what course offerings and services are provided, purchasing options, recommendations for developing employee skills and competencies, and, very importantly, the training group's values.

Most training providers send an electronic copy to their customer base and print a smaller batch for use by sales personnel and for supporting targeted promotional activity. Table 5.9 summarises the key steps that should be followed in order to develop and produce a training catalogue.

Table 5.9 Course catalogue key summary steps

Key contents	Objective	Resources	Benefits	Notes
Develop outline contents	Define catalogue outline and structure.	Marketing, business development and training product management.	Aligns marketing messages with training product direction and business need.	Time spent here ensures the training group is holistically aligned.
Catalogue type	Decide on whether the catalogue is: • online and searchable or menu/dropdown-based; • print based; • online and print.	Marketing, business development and training product management.	Allows decisions to be made regarding: • costs and volume coverage; • online versus print.	Online is more flexible in terms of ability to alter and change versus print. Online development can be reduced by producing a PDF copy that mimics the print version.
Catalogue duration	Determine catalogue duration (shelf life).	Marketing, business development and training product management.	Defines the lifecycle of the catalogue. Enables budget management decisions based on catalogue type and frequency of content change.	Typically 12 months, although can be quarterly based. Many organisations extend shelf life by not including schedules.
Course offerings	Decide what courses will be offered during the lifecycle of the catalogue.	Training delivery, business development and training product management.	Provides single point of reference to list and structure the course offerings.	Provides broad overview of the courses, learning objectives, prerequisites, duration, topics and practical sessions.

(Continued)

Table 5.9 (Continued)

Key contents	Objective	Resources	Benefits	Notes
Training services	Decide what training services will be offered during the lifecycle of the catalogue.	Training delivery, business development and training product management.	Ability to enhance and differentiate the training experience and engagement with customers.	Provides an insight into the additional training services that can be purchased, such as consulting, custom training, training needs assessment and training managed service provision.
Curriculum road maps	Show recommended training paths leading to skills advancement.	Training delivery, business development and training product management.	Structures the learning experience for customers who want to move from knowledge attainment, through skills to competency.	For customers looking to develop employee skills and competencies, the curriculum road map provides a means by which employee development can be aligned with career progression and job requirements.
Training modalities	Decide which courses will be delivered by what modality.	Training delivery, business development and training product management.	Provides customers with choices regarding preferred learning styles.	Provides choices around employee learning styles, availability and budgetary needs.
Accreditation and certification	Outline what level of skills and competencies will be tested.	Business development and training product management.	Customers can attain recognised industry-based qualifications, which enhance their career prospects and capabilities to perform in their job roles.	Many customers require employees to be able to prove they have attained specific levels of competency. Certification achieves this requirement and is proven to assist with overall employee productivity improvements.

(Continued)

Table 5.9 (Continued)

Key contents	Objective	Resources	Benefits	Notes
Case studies	Provide actual case studies showing how customers have benefited from training.	Marketing, business development and training product management.	Provides reinforcement regarding the benefits of training.	Case studies provide tangible evidence that investment in training works.
Schedules	List all available courses that can be delivered by date and location.	Business development and training delivery.	Provides customers with a visual view of when, how and where they can attend training.	–
Booking instructions	Provides a mechanism that allows customers to book and enrol on courses, or request training services.	Training delivery.	A vehicle for accepting bookings and obtaining a view on the sales forecast. Also provides an insight into whether additional courses should be scheduled or cancelled if low enrolments.	From a training delivery standpoint, provides an insight into how the business is performing on a course by course basis. Decisions regarding the running of additional courses or promotion of slow enrolment courses can be made on a weekly basis.
Terms and conditions	Outline the terms and conditions that apply when customers book courses or training services.	Legal and business delivery.	Protects the training provider and the customer through understanding each other's responsibilities in the training transaction.	Is a legal requirement.

(Continued)

Table 5.9 (Continued)

Key contents	Objective	Resources	Benefits	Notes
Contact details	How to contact key staff regarding queries, booking courses or services.	Marketing, business development and training product management.	Ease of communication with a dedicated point of contact.	–
Useful links	Provide additional external reference points to reinforce the value of training.	Training product management.	Provides access to additional information without overloading the training catalogue.	Links can be inserted on the training website, company website or other points of reference (such as social media).
Contents	Contents page for ease of customer reference.	Publication and editing.	Provides a reference point for ease of locating information.	–
Editing	The process to be followed to ensure the content produced is accurate and ready for publishing.	Publication and editing.	Minimises errors before publication and maximises the training group's professionalism.	–
Publication	Define the quantity of catalogues to be produced, when, and the lifecycle management and maintenance.	Publication, business development and training product management.	Provides volume access to broad audience base via print and digital means.	–

(Continued)

Course outlines

Course outlines are an important part of the promotion process (see a sample in Figure 5.1), allowing influencers, buyers and training managers to gain an insight into how the learning process will occur and its relevance to their specific needs.

Figure 5.1 Sample course outline

Project Portfolio Management Fundamentals[3]		
Manage projects from initial demand to project closure		
Duration: 2 Days	Modality: ILT/VILT	Cost: £1,200
Project management is the application of methods, tools and techniques to achieve new capabilities, meet demands, respond to changes and realise new opportunities. In this 2 day course, attendees are introduced to the Project Portfolio Management suite (PPS) and learn how to efficiently manage the project lifecycle.		
A combination of lecture content and lab work helps attendees to achieve the following:		
• Get introduced to the suite of PPS tools and understand the specific role each application plays in Project Portfolio Management		
• Understand the solution architecture and deployment options with respect to the organisational structure and goals		
• Master the project management toolbox including Workbench, Templates, Scheduling Engine, Import and Export, Status Reports		
• Learn the secrets of efficiently working with the Planning Console and My Gantt		
• Dive into advanced project scheduling and learn to track risks, issues, goals, milestones and baselines		
• Become proficient with Portfolio Financial Planning and project and demand financial estimation and budget vs actuals tracking		
• Implement Resource management to allow for a structured request-fulfil process and accounting of project resources		
• Use the Demand application to prioritise business ideas and generate and manage strategic demands		
• Monitor Portfolio, Programme and Project health on Workbenches and via role-based dashboards		

(Continued)

---

[3] Computer Education Management Association (CEdMA) Europe Ltd would like to thank ServiceNow for allowing the use of the Project Portfolio Management Fundamentals course outline.

Who Should Attend:
This course is designed for Project, Programme and Portfolio Managers, members of the Project Management Office (PMO), project teams, project subject matter experts, and all stakeholders who will be actively interfacing with the Project Suite of applications (PPS).
Prerequisites: None
Certification: This course does not offer certification.

In some instances, this can lead to requests for customisation of content, which opens up broader customer opportunities. It is potentially one of the most important promotional assets to assist in closing out the final stage of lead generation or influencing a final purchase. Table 5.10 summarises the essential elements that should be considered for inclusion when producing a course outline.

Table 5.10 Course outline key elements

Key elements	Objective	Notes
Course title and reference number	To provide a generic course title representing at a high level what the course covers.	The reference number provides a unique identifier for booking, revenue reporting and invoicing recognition purposes.
Course overview	To highlight the purpose of the course and who should attend.	The overview should be concise, accurate and enable potential purchasers of the training to obtain a quick snapshot of its relevancy to them.
Course prerequisites	To define what prior knowledge and skills are required in order to enrol on a course.	In order for the course to be effective, it is important that any prerequisites for attendance are adhered to by the attending student.
Course objectives	To describe the knowledge, skills and competencies that should be acquired by students by the end of the course.	The training objectives should be precise statements such as 'The student should be able to ...'.

(Continued)

Table 5.10 (Continued)

Key elements	Objective	Notes
Duration	To confirm the length of the course.	Course duration can vary, and it is important to define prior to a customer placing an order.
Delivery method	Describes the learning modalities used to deliver the course.	The learning modalities offered vary, depending on their suitability for the target market opportunity. Typically, they comprise instructor-led training, virtual instructor-led training, video-based, self-paced or a combination of all of these.
Course outline	To outline what topics will be covered in the course.	Course outlines provide a brief summary of the main topics that will be covered on the course. This can result, in some instances, in requests for customisation.
Certification and evaluation	To provide guidance on how students can or will be assessed and evaluated during attendance of a course, or what certification exams are available afterwards.	Some countries and organisations do not allow evaluations or certification to be conducted. Care should therefore be taken when promoting in a multinational market.
Copyright protection	Protects against non-authorised training providers using existing course content.	Protects the training provider from loss of revenue, and the customer from receiving inferior non-authorised training.

Course schedules

Customers often search online for course offerings they are interested in. The next stage in the sales process is to close the sale with a definite booking date. This is where the course schedule comes into its own. Typically, it lists the courses on offer, available dates, locations and price in local currency.

Course schedules assist in generating demand and progressing revenue. However, care needs to be taken not to damage brand reputation and customer confidence if the schedules offered cannot be delivered or have to be cancelled. It is important to put in place a course schedule that reflects the actual demand in the marketplace. See the example given in Figure 5.2.

Figure 5.2 Typical course schedule

	Course ID	Duration (Days)	Spoken Language	Price	July	August	September	October	November	December
Technical training schedule for the UK										
Control Compliance	CC1.1	3		£2,100						
Virtual Academy			English		5		7		12	
Classroom – London			English			11		17		14
Classroom – Bristol			English				15		21	
Data Centre Security	DCS2.1	5		£3,500						
Virtual Academy			English		15			19		
Classroom – London			English			23			14	
Classroom – Bristol			English				24			19
Data Loss Prevention	DLP1.1	4		£2,800						
Virtual Academy			English		12	18	9	11	17	
Classroom – London			English			24		3		7
Classroom – Bristol			English		3		23		11	

MARKETING, PUBLIC RELATIONS AND PROMOTIONAL EVENTS

Marketing is a broad discipline covering direct marketing, advertising and promotional activities to drive and encourage interest in purchasing training. Public relations (PR), on the other hand, is focused on managing a training group's reputation by generating positive media coverage.

Marketing

Marketing covers a wide range of activities to ensure that the needs of the training customer continue to be met and to encourage positive interaction. Marketing in general tends to be fairly standard in its approach; where it differs in execution is around the nature of the offering. For example, marketing instructor-led training versus eLearning will be very different because the buying characteristics, needs and availability are not the same. In fact, positioning one against the other is not a good approach. In training, it is all about providing value decision-based choices. It is encouraging the customer to view training as a requirement that can be consumed to satisfy a variety of variables and needs; for example, learning preferences and maximising use of their available budget. What is important is knowing the customer and aligning them with what can be offered, rather than setting the wrong expectations.

As previously covered in this chapter, demand and lead generation play a role within the marketing function and part of these activities can lead to an understanding of broader opportunities or risks. These can be further explored in terms of investigating new training products or services, price points and what the competition is providing. Depending upon the structure of their training marketing department, some vendors place this activity under corporate product management (see Chapter 3) or as part of the training group, sometimes under the curriculum development umbrella.

PR

Public relations covers ongoing activities to ensure training has a strong public image. In reality, this resides at the corporate level, which requires training management to be well versed in broader company messages in order to assess how best to entwine the training offerings into the broader PR activity.

PR is often conducted through the media by way of press releases via trade magazines and sponsored events.

Promotional events

Promotional events can comprise invites to attend a 1–2-hour introductory training session, dialling in to a virtual seminar, or part of a broader company-wide promotional activity. They can be used to launch a new training curriculum or offering in order to generate interest and awareness in the market in support of a product that is due for release.

For an event to be successful, it is important to understand what the goals are, how success is measured and what the target market is. For example, in supporting a new product release, the training department might want to raise awareness among customers who are early adopters of the technology about the level and nature of the training and how it would assist them to capitalise on the new technology. The goals are usually around raising awareness to drive attendance and bookings on the new training curriculum. Success could be measured in terms of the number of advanced bookings made within the target market of early adopters.

Promotional events can be costly to organise, and it is important to assess the financial returns and risks before undertaking them.

CUSTOMER AND TRAINING PARTNER ADVISORY MEETINGS

In order for the training business development and marketing teams to expand the group's reach into new and existing markets, it is an advantage to obtain the views of current customers and training partners. One way of achieving this is to establish customer and partner advisory meetings.

Customer advisory meetings

Customer advisory meetings (CAM) can be productive for both parties. For customers, it provides an opportunity to share ideas among themselves and to advise the training team on their needs, concerns and observations. For the training team, it provides legitimacy in probing for market intelligence and positioning new offerings with a view to obtaining a candid response in a safe environment.

In order for the CAM to succeed, and be seen as a good use of valuable time, the meetings need to encourage active participation both during and in between the sessions. It is important to maintain momentum between meetings if customer involvement is not going to ebb and flow in terms of interest and activity.

To initiate and maintain a CAM, the recommendations shown in Table 5.11 should be considered. By implementing these actions, there is a better chance of ensuring ongoing participation and active engagement. This in turn validates the investment and should provide good ongoing value and insight into what customers require and need in a trusted commercial partnership.

Training partner advisory meetings

Training partners face many challenges: constant changes in technology and delivery models, dealing with business model transitions and maintaining profit margin contributions. By establishing a training partner advisory council (TPAC), the training business development and marketing teams can both obtain an insight into how best to represent and address the broader interests of this community.

The process and approach are similar to that of the customer advisory meetings. The key consideration in setting up a TPAC is to ensure that it represents all partners around the geographic area of operation and covers a cross section of partner types from small through to multinational organisations.

Table 5.11 Customer advisory meeting recommendations

Recommendation	Rationale		Key actions	
Provide thought leadership	By providing an authoritative and influential view, including being an agent of change in the field of technical training and learning, customer advisory members will be motivated to participate.	Introduce topical articles with alignment to a common industry theme with input from several members. Consider running a series of webinars with support from the CAM members.	Look to publish the articles in industry publications. Invite key customers.	Consider using as part of an ongoing demand generation programme. Consider using case studies and or research studies.
Gain industry insight	Obtain a view on how the CAM members are looking at training, its values or issues so that informed decisions can be made.	Undertake CAM member interviews. Explore CAM member topics of interest.	Use the information to formulate opinions that can be actively discussed. Publish selected topics on social media, such as LinkedIn, to obtain a broader audience measure of interest.	Consider publishing the findings to your customer base via the training website. Use findings to aid input into demand and lead generation campaigns. Share findings with CAM members.

(Continued)

Table 5.11 (Continued)

Recommendation	Rationale		Key actions	
Establish subcommittees	Use subcommittees to focus on training topics of interest. These can then be explored with a view to being adopted for the common good.	Capture topics that are worthy of deeper investigation from within the CAM.	Establish a subcommittee to define the scope and what support is required from the training group.	Share findings with board members. Where relevant, consider adoption by the training team.
Share research findings	Research undertaken by the training team will benefit in some instances by obtaining independent feedback from the CAM members.	Present research findings and the rationale for undertaking it.	Factor CAM member feedback into final research findings.	Share final research and associated recommendations with CAM members.
Engage support for joint marketing	CAM members can provide marketing support to reinforce the value of training from the customer perspective.	Discuss CAM member training success stories and investigate if these can be used as either case studies or be presented at trade shows.	Develop the case studies and publish. Develop the presentations and invite CAM members as keynote speakers.	
Maintain CAM communications	Develop an agreed style of communication to ensure ongoing and meaningful engagement with the CAM members.	Consider establishing quarterly CAMs and monthly newsletter updates.	Use a newsletter to update members on training and company developments. Provide quarterly minutes following the quarterly CAM.	

CUSTOMER REFERENCE PROGRAMMES

Customer reference programmes help to enhance sales and marketing activities and support active demand generation. Customer testimonials influence and encourage buyers to proceed further in their decision making by explaining how a real solution solved their training need. Tangible and demonstrable results are a sales person's dream for training!

Customer reference programmes should be centrally managed to ensure sales and marketing know where to go in order to maximise their effectiveness. With training often being side-lined in larger organisations, a library of training case studies that can be referenced helps to validate and legitimise the importance and contribution of having training included in a broader product sales offering.

One final note is do not over demand requests on any one customer as it can quickly undo long earned relationships.

Table 5.12 highlights some best practices that should be considered when introducing a training-related customer reference programme.

Table 5.12 Customer reference programme best practice summary

Best practice	Approach
Establish the structure	• Locate an environment to store and search customer references. • Nominate personnel to fulfil incoming customer requests. • Establish tracking and reporting requirements.

Identify key stakeholders	• Locate executive sponsors and major influencers outside the training group:
	  ▪ sales and marketing;
	  ▪ product management;
	  ▪ public relations and analyst relations;
	  ▪ professional services;
	  ▪ customer advisory boards.

Define the format of the customer reference	• Decide on the format and approach, based on assessing target audience and need:
	  ▪ case study;
	  ▪ ROI study;
	  ▪ success story;
	  ▪ audio or video recording;
	  ▪ press release.

(Continued)

Table 5.12 (Continued)

Best practice	Approach
Customer and employee incentives	• Consider setting up an incentive programme to encourage customers to provide references and for employees to recommend specific customer references.
Establish metrics to measure success and effectiveness	• Define the programme's objectives: ▪ increase training sales revenue; ▪ increase publicity and awareness; ▪ number of requests received; ▪ number of requests converted into sales.
Create the customer reference training programme	• Develop the launch, marketing and management materials: ▪ promotional brochure; ▪ frequently asked questions (FAQs); ▪ internal promotion and announcements; ▪ sales training materials; ▪ customer reference agreement; ▪ customer appreciation letter; ▪ management dashboards to report and track progress.
Programme management	• Monitor progress and results. • Assess gaps in customer reference coverage: geography, sector/industry and training product/curriculum.

DISRUPTIVE BUSINESS GROWTH

Any form of innovation that creates a new market and value proposition, be it product, service or business execution, will be disruptive by nature. When it is implemented, it initially tends to be a slow burner and then expand rapidly, often leaving the competition well behind.

Technical training is no different. Harvard, MIT and Stanford universities introduced massive open online courses (MOOCs) that provided content for free and tuition for a fee, which rapidly undermined the smaller colleges (Selingo 2014).

The Council for Adult and Experiential Learning (CAEL) proposed that what someone has actually learned in the execution of their job is far more important than time spent sitting in a classroom, which led to the introduction of prior learning assessments (PLAs) allowing employees with experience to get recognition without attending a training course (www.cael.org/). This in itself led to the concept of badges as a way of building credentials over time rather than attending a series of courses followed by certification.

The same is true regarding the selling of training. While transactional single course selling is lucrative and highly contributive to the bottom line, subscription-based selling offers cost-effectiveness to the customer and long-term committed revenues for the training provider. In a competitive environment, this can be disruptive in terms of forcing a change in the training delivery and a change in how revenue is recognised.

The old adage of investing a little to learn a lot holds true when contemplating disruptive business growth. Basically, it is about not being complacent and instead focusing on improving existing core training business. By allocating a small amount of money and time, good progress can be made in initiating innovative and effective disruption.

SUMMARY

Business development and marketing management are key components in establishing, growing and maintaining the training business as it moves forward.

On the business development side, consideration has to be given to competitive and tactical strategies, which in turn need to be supported with documented policies and guidelines such as discount management, attach rate objectives and adherence to VSOE or equivalent requirements.

Marketing needs to assist growth in providing demand and lead generation to enable sales to develop a pipeline of revenue opportunities and indirect promotional and influential activities via customer, advisory and reference programmes to maintain ongoing market interest.

The business development manager's (BDM's) main objective is to identify new business opportunities, expand market share and develop partnerships to generate new and increased revenue opportunities.

Defining value propositions assists in demonstrating to potential customers why they should purchase training, which helps to minimise the risk of a no sale.

To ensure a training group maximises its revenue opportunity, clear expectations regarding allowable discounts and how revenue will be best attained via attach or inclusion rates needs to be defined and agreed. As does the expectation on marketing to drive demand via well-crafted messages and campaigns, typically measured in terms of the percentage of leads that result in sales-based revenue generation opportunities.

As digital marketing techniques are standard practice, the importance of SEO to expand visibility in search engine results is fundamental to driving customer-related traffic to engage with the training organisation.

Promotional materials, whether digital or paper-based, provide quick summaries and reinforcement of what a customer actually requires by way of facts sheets, catalogues and course schedules.

Through the use of customer and partner advisory meetings, the training business development and marketing teams can both gain insights into new and existing markets that can be used to their advantage.

Opportunities to be disruptive for positive business growth should not be ignored but, equally, should be given careful consideration before implementing if the organisation is seeking to gain competitive commercial advantage.

6 REVENUE GENERATION
Making money in the mixed modality world of technical training

Revenue income can be achieved from two main sources, direct and indirect. On the direct side, it includes training sales, professional services and product sales teams. On the indirect side, it includes authorised training partners, channel partners and strategic alliances.

This chapter looks at the various pricing models that a training department might support, including how revenue can be generated via royalty payments, kit sales and revenue share schemes. It also considers the challenges associated with geographic pricing and how to maximise and protect revenue.

The final sections cover renewals and the role of a customer success manager in maintaining regular contact with existing customers, to assist in maximising their use of training and their associated investment in it.

GROSS VERSUS NET REVENUE CONSIDERATIONS

From an accounting perspective, whenever revenue is received, it will be recognised and analysed as gross revenue, net revenue and net income. Gross revenue is the price charged before discounts and any applied reimbursements, whereas net revenue is the price after the sale has been concluded. Net income, also known as net profit, is the contribution after total costs have been deducted from the net revenue.

Why is this important? In the first instance, net versus gross revenue provides an insight into the number of discounts being granted and a view on sales efficiency, including any potential VSOE issues. Net income assists in the analysis of operational and delivery efficiency.

The training department has many costs to consider and educating the sales team on how negotiating activities can influence the profit line can lead to a more aligned approach to revenue generation.

Primarily the approach that sales should consider is:

- acquiring new customers by selling the right training for the right need (fitness for purpose);
- increasing the transaction amount by minimising discounts;

- developing trusted customer relationships to encourage adoption of additional modalities in line with longer-term training needs.

PRICING MODEL CONSIDERATIONS

There are pricing models and pricing strategies. Chapter 3 compared typical strategies that can be adopted by a training group. In this section, the focus will be on pricing models that are specific to the selling of training. Table 6.1 summarises those that can be used to sell direct to customers.

Table 6.1 Pricing models

Pricing model	Sales method	Description	Example pricing
Single ILT course attended at vendor training centre	Transactional. Typically sold by an inside sales specialist or taken as an order over the phone.	Instructor-led course requiring attendance at a training centre.	Dependent upon the training provider, either priced on a per course or per day basis. Pricing varies by geographic region.
Onsite or customer-specific ILT course	Consultative. Sold by a training sales specialist or product/services sales representative.	Instructor-led course where the customer requires attendance of multiple students. Content can be standard or tailored to specific needs. Option for the course to be delivered at the customer's site or at the vendor training centre.	Pricing varies as follows: • For a standard course run at a vendor training centre, pricing is at day rate, unless agreed discount for students attending over a certain number. • If run at a customer's site, pricing is at day rate unless agreed discount for students attending over a certain number. If equipment is required, this is an additional cost. Instructor travel and expenditure (T&E) is also in addition. • Tailored content is charged at an agreed content developer day rate.

(Continued)

Table 6.1 (Continued)

Pricing model	Sales method	Description	Example pricing
Single VILT course	Transactional. Typically sold by an inside sales specialist or taken as an order over the phone.	Virtual instructor-led course accessed virtually via students' own PC or tablet devices.	Dependent upon the training provider, priced on a course or per day basis. Pricing varies by geographic region.
Onsite or customer-specific VILT course	Consultative. Sold by a training sales specialist or product/ services sales representative.	Virtual instructor-led course where the customer requires attendance of multiple students. Content can be standard or tailored to specific needs.	Pricing varies as follows: • For a standard virtual course, pricing is at day rate unless agreed discount for students attending over a certain number. • If run at a customer site, pricing is at day rate unless agreed discount for students attending over a certain number. Note that in some instances pricing may be more complex, depending upon whether the instructor can be fully utilised during the day or not.
eLearning single subscriber	Transactional. Typically sold by an inside sales specialist or taken as an order over the phone.	Self-paced course(s) that can be purchased as a subscription for a period of one year.	Pricing is subscription-based and is typically 10–20% of an ILT course.
eLearning multiple course/ subscribers	Transactional/ consultative. Sold by a training sales specialist or product/ services sales representative.	Self-paced course(s) that can be purchased as a multiple subscription for a period of one year.	Pricing is subscription-based and banded, based on volume. Pricing is reduced based on the specific volume band being purchased; for low volume bands (<10) typically 10–20% of an ILT course, for higher bands (>1,000) could be 1–2% of an ILT course.

(Continued)

Table 6.1 (Continued)

Pricing model	Sales method	Description	Example pricing
Subscription	Consultative. Sold by a training sales specialist or product/ services sales representative.	Subscription models vary by vendor. Some are based on eLearning access only. Others factor in access to VILT, labs and asynchronous training support. Subscription annual payment based.	Pricing is per student based and calculated on assumed consumption.
Custom solution	Consultative. Sold by a training sales specialist or product/ services sales representative.	Content is specifically customised to student needs. May be delivered using different training modalities.	Pricing is based on: • Amount of content to be developed. • Number of training days to be delivered. • Modality type. • Level of equipment provision.
Managed training service	Consultative. Sold by a training sales specialist or product/ services sales representative.	The customer requiring training effectively outsources their training need to the training provider. Service provision includes access to content via various modalities, operational support and training guidance. Normally the customer is supported via a learning management system (LMS) or dedicated portal.	Pricing is based on a fixed price per employee basis and assumed usage.

(Continued)

Table 6.1 (Continued)

Pricing model	Sales method	Description	Example pricing
Training credits	Transactional/consultative. Sold by a training sales specialist or product/services sales representative.	Training credits offer maximum flexibility for the purchasing customer. An agreed budget is allocated and drawn down over an agreed period, typically one year.	The incentive for investing in a training credit is that of budget protection. When the customer requests training, the cost of the training is deducted at the normal rate, unless by an agreed discount.
Training days	Transactional/consultative. Sold by a training sales specialist or product/services sales representative.	Training days relate to ILT or VILT student days delivered at a vendor training centre, or at the customer's site.	Pricing is based on a per student day rate paid in advance. When the customer requires training, they draw down on their prepaid training day allocation. T&E is charged as extras.

CHANNEL-RELATED ROYALTY, KIT SALES AND REVENUE SHARE

Revenue income and growth is achievable from several sources, including direct and indirect sales activities. Direct sales activities result from training being sold and delivered by the training organisation, whereas indirect is sold and delivered through partners.

Indirect revenue income can be royalty, kit sales or revenue share-based, depending upon the business model in force at the time. Some training organisations will focus on one, and others on a combination of all three. The decision comes down to the question of how important training is to the vendor, when compared to cost allocation, and other areas of the business that may generate greater income. In some instances, greater coverage can be achieved by using channel partners and trading revenue for higher percentage-based profitability.

Royalty-based income

Royalty-based income is derived from training delivery partners who sell direct to their customer base. They have prior access to training content and print copies for consumption by the students who attend their courses. The partner then reports the number of course places delivered and pays an agreed royalty amount, normally monthly.

The advantage to the training vendor is that the royalty payment is pure revenue with zero cost, and hence maximised profitability. Another advantage is that no upfront investment is required in supporting emerging markets and countries with low training opportunities; local training partners provide the required coverage.

Offering partners a royalty option does not restrict their entry into the market. A slight disadvantage is the requirement for close and trusted monitoring. When market conditions start to show consistent growth, other pricing models may need to be considered.

Kit sales

Kit sales is different from royalty income, whereby the training partner purchases the training content (kit) upfront based on the number of course places sold. This model provides an increased level of vendor income with high profit level contribution. Many leading training partners prefer this model as it maximises their profitability. It also removes responsibility for printing and provides access to vendor branded materials. Typical kit costs purchased from the vendor represent 15–18 per cent of the student course fee.

For the training vendor, it minimises cost of entry into both low- and high-volume markets, especially those with local language needs. For example, if operating in Europe, it is expensive to hire instructors, establish dedicated training centres and ensure access is available across multiple locations. It also reduces the costs associated with providing technical training infrastructure and local operational and administrative support.

Revenue share

Revenue share becomes important when a vendor requires the training group to maximise revenue and minimise investment costs. It is similar to that of the kit model. The training partner purchases the kit and can gain an added advantage if the training group elects to sell into their schedule. The difference is the cost of the kit, which is based on a percentage of the overall course price being charged. Typically, a vendor charges 35–45 per cent of the sale price, plus an additional 15 per cent if they sell a place on the course.

It can be difficult to position and gain agreement with a training partner on these terms. However, it does provide access to the market with minimal competition. It is advantageous to those training partners who have authorised status with other vendors and market opportunities with medium to large customers.

Whether a training group adopts one or all of the above models depends on a variety of factors, including entry costs into new markets, ability to scale its operation to cater for growth, or alignment with the commercial contribution needs of the vendor.

All three modes require coordination between training product management and the business development team to ensure expectation alignment.

GEOGRAPHIC PRICING AND CURRENCY IMPLICATIONS

When operating on a multinational basis, pricing structures are required to reflect market variations in terms of geographical training demand, cost of doing business and the gross domestic product (at purchasing power parity) per capita, known as GDP (PPP). All of these have an effect on pricing and profitability, making it difficult to achieve the same level across all countries that the training group covers.

GDP (PPP) is the primary factor that needs consideration as it reflects the economic performance of a country and provides a basis by which to make international comparisons. It is useful as it factors in cost of living and inflation rates. By using the GDP (PPP) factor for the country of the parent company, pricing for all other countries can be based in relation to it. For example:

Parent company based in USA with a GDP of $57,300 might price a technical course at $1,000 per day. For the countries where it provides training, the price is modified to reflect the actual purchasing power:

- UK: the GDP is $42,500, resulting in a purchasing power price of $740 per day (42,500/57,300 = 74% of US day rate).

- Germany: the GDP is $48,200, resulting in a purchasing power price of $840 per day.

- South Africa: the GDP is $13,200, resulting on a purchasing power price of $230 per day.

Clearly, advice should be sought from the finance and legal departments to ensure local law and trading rules are being applied correctly before implementation.

This would be further modified in terms of factoring in local costs and expected training volumes and applying the normal marketing pricing analysis to come to an agreed pricing framework for the countries of operation.

Currency fluctuations impact all companies who have an international profile. For most training groups, the company will fix an agreed set of annual rates to provide a way of tracking business progress in a fair and consistent manner. This means the training group is neither penalised nor rewarded for currency variation.

At the company level, the finance team looks at implementing a number of options to assess and address the impact of currency fluctuations on the overall business. Some typical options are:

- Monitoring changes and keeping a watching brief if they are not particularly vulnerable to high-risk exchange rate fluctuations.

- Negotiating a fixed exchange rate for an agreed period.

- Managing currency exposure through business practices; for example, building flexibility into contracts by establishing clauses to protect against currency changes, or setting up contracts in local currency.

MAXIMISING AND PROTECTING REVENUE

From a sales perspective, maintaining good customer records and relationships is vital, as is understanding the routes to market within the organisation. For example, customer support representatives deal with technical problems that may be disguising a training need, or product sales engineers may be spending time educating customers on the benefits of the technology when perhaps positioning training may enhance the customer experience, leading to a broader solution opportunity.

With the sales management emphasis often being placed on quarterly revenue attainment, it is often the case that sales representatives will move towards high-volume transactional selling and minimise the consultative technique, thereby losing out on the opportunity to develop stronger customer relationships and ongoing revenue streams.

The key to maximising and protecting revenue is to establish a best practice approach within the training sales and training group communities that encompasses both sales activity and its management. The following points are worth considering to aid in the establishment of an effective sales process.

- Assist in maintaining the sales pipeline.
  - Prospecting for new business on a regular basis is vital. The training team, be it administrators, instructors or marketing staff, have access and insight into opportunities the sales team may not be aware of. By establishing a regular update meeting, all prospects can be fed into the pipeline to ensure it is continually being topped up. Doing this helps to address any peaks and troughs that may occur in sales activity.
  - Instructors in particular can be a very effective lead generation and sales channel. Students (customers) often share their problems with them and seek advice. By engaging instructors in regular update meetings and encouraging them to share information, additional sales opportunities can be found. However, it is worth implementing some form of reward programme to ensure they get recognition, otherwise they may not be so inclined to share new opportunities when the sales team get the benefit and not them.
- Ensure the sales team is dealing directly with actual decision makers. Often, significant time is lost with a customer by talking to the wrong person.
- Ensure that selling training is not a one-time activity. It should involve others within the training team. A good customer experience is one that all members of staff can contribute to. Sales does open doors, but keeping them open requires support from all, and a robust customer care programme. Keeping the training group's name in the customer's mind assists in maintaining a positive, ongoing relationship.
- When implementing a customer care programme, consider incorporating the following:
  - Market research to understand customers' needs and requirements.
  - Capturing customer information (including instructor and administrator feedback) and insights to assist in the development of ongoing business relationships.
  - Regularly assessing and looking for opportunities to sell additional training offerings.

- Providing good levels of service and value throughout all customer contact points.

- Obtaining and documenting testimonials, recommendations and referrals.

- Consider establishing a customer reward and incentive programme.

And finally, always credit-check target customers to protect revenue. A customer is not a customer if they default on payment!

RENEWALS

Customer retention is crucial to the health of any business, regardless of size or industry. Within the technology sector the main focus will be on retention with respect to the product and certain elements within professional services, for example technical support and consulting. Training renewals can be challenging because training is often seen as a single event rather than a recurring one.

To improve training potential and develop more opportunities after the initial sale, consideration should be given to implementing a renewal strategy factoring in:

- Use of an adoption dashboard.

- Understanding of what might affect a renewal (risks).

- Predictive analysis regarding the nature and type of support calls customers have been placing, and the relevance and suitability of offering advanced training or selected workshops and its effect on training revenue.

The use of an adoption dashboard provides insight into which customers are considering renewal. Typically, it provides data regarding the size of contract, number of users, technology complexity and level and nature of training undertaken previously. An extract of a typical dashboard is shown in Figure 6.1. The first pie chart shows the number of customers who are looking to renew their product licences. This provides an insight into the potential number of customers who could renew their training. The second pie chart displays the percentage of customers who have renewed, and the third chart displays the orders received in pounds sterling.

This type of information provides an insight into sales and marketing activities that need to be undertaken to maximise the renewal rate. More detailed and granulated charts are required in order to understand the nature of the renewal opportunity. For example, five customers may represent a revenue opportunity of £5,000 between them and two customers may represent revenue opportunities of £20,000 and £15,000 respectively. In this instance, different strategies and time allocation to obtain the renewal is required. The low revenue opportunities can be covered by email requests to renew, whereas the potentially high revenue opportunities require personal account management.

Factor into this what might prevent a customer from renewing, which could be:

- cost of training;
- net promoter score (NPS) reduction.

Figure 6.1 Simplified adoption dashboard

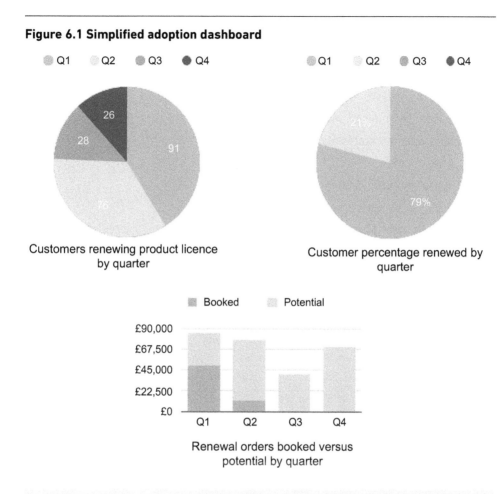

Customers renewing product licence
by quarter

Customer percentage renewed by
quarter

Renewal orders booked versus
potential by quarter

NPS is a management tool used to measure how an organisation is maintaining its customer relationships and loyalty. It is an alternative to traditional customer satisfaction research and has been widely adopted by Fortune 500 companies.[1]

Increase in support calls or complexity of the calls provides an insight into the prediction and analysis of how at risk the account is with respect to customer satisfaction issues and non-renewals.

Establishing an adoption dashboard will require the support of sales operations and feedback from the technical support team. The data should be readily at hand and standard in nature. The important message to instil in the minds of the sales renewal team and senior management is that a well-trained customer contributes to the overall

---

1   The Fortune 500 is an annual list compiled and published by *Fortune* magazine that ranks 500 of the largest US corporations by total revenue and NPS for their respective fiscal years.

benefits of the product, which in turn can assist in improved renewal rates and ultimately long-term retention of the customer.

Equally important is the establishment of an agreed process; for example:

- Ensure the adoption dashboard is kept up to date (quarterly).
- Check on the status of any unused prepaid training and address accordingly.
- Obtain customer status updates from:
  - sales teams;
  - customer success managers;
  - professional services.
- Develop a value statement per renewing customer based on predicted analysis findings (in many instances this will be standard in nature).
- Set up notification alerts to advise on data points that have not been achieved, such as target bookings and order rate. The data points might trigger at 30 per cent, 70 per cent and 90 per cent of the required target. Shortfalls can then be addressed with an appropriate action plan at:
  - six months;
  - three months;
  - one month.
- Work closely with the renewals team.
- Automatically attach relevant training offerings and supporting value statements to customer product related renewal prospects. Removal by the renewal or sales team would generate notifications, prompting internal discussion.

In a subscription-based environment, the renewal process needs very close monitoring as it can significantly affect recurring revenue streams.

CUSTOMER SUCCESS MANAGEMENT

Customer success management is growing in popularity, specifically in the technical arena. It encompasses several areas: technical support, professional services, training and sales. This requires a dedicated customer success manager to be in regular contact with existing customers to help them not just solve problems, but find new ways to use and apply the product, and for the customer success manager to gain feedback on how it can be improved for later development.

From the training perspective, the role is primarily about understanding the needs of the customer and using this to develop a shared vision, establish joint accountability, prioritise their long-term success and drive incremental and ongoing revenue streams. It is also about customer retention, which is where the training and technical support side of the role plays a key part in aligning provider and customer in a homogeneous manner. With continuous pressure from competitors, staying one step ahead is a key factor for continued success. For a technical training manager, alignment with the customer success management team is as vital as that of sales account management.

It is financially astute to assess which customers are crucial to overall company success and what type of attention to them is required. A decision can then be made on how many customer success training practitioners to allocate to support the company's dedicated customer success managers, and how best to ensure the full alignment of corporate and customer need.

SUMMARY

Training revenue income can be achieved from direct and indirect sales-based activities. On the direct side, this includes training sales, professional services and product sales teams. On the indirect side, it includes authorised training partners, channel partners and strategic alliances.

Both channels produce revenue, which has to be recognised and analysed as gross revenue, net revenue and net income from an accounting perspective. All three are important, although net versus gross revenue provides an insight into the number of discounts being granted and sales efficiency, including any potential VSOE issues.

The training department has many costs to consider, so educating the sales team on how their negotiating activities can influence the profit line will lead to a more aligned approach to revenue generation.

Pricing models for VILT, eLearning and customised offerings all affect the training revenue achieved and so need to be fully understood in terms of how to offer them in relation to market need and financial requirements.

Another factor affecting the generation of revenue is the go-to-market (GTM) activity, which can be direct or indirect. The direct side involves sales activities that maximise revenue attainment, whereas indirect revenue generation will be royalty, kit sales or revenue share-based, which dilutes the percentage of revenue received. The advantage, and hence trade-off, of using the indirect model is its ability to provide greater coverage, which satisfies market need, but reduces overall revenue income.

Other factors affecting revenue are geographic pricing and currency implications when a training group is operating on a multinational basis. The pricing structures required need to reflect market variations in terms of geographical training demand, cost of doing business and the gross domestic product implications.

In order to maximise and protect revenue, maintaining good customer records and relationships is vital, as is understanding the routes to market within the organisation. This can be achieved by establishing a best practice approach encompassing both sales activity and metric-based management. Implementing a renewals policy protects medium- to long-term revenue and can be further enhanced with the establishment of a customer success management programme.

7 SALES
Developing strategies and metrics to manage sales goals

Buying and selling is a transaction where both the seller and the buyer engage in a process of negotiation resulting in value being obtained on both sides. The seller gains revenue and the buyer gains a training offering enabling them to be more knowledgeable, gain skills and ultimately be competent in what they do.

The selling process has implied rules and identifiable stages that require strategies, operating processes and metrics to be established to achieve the business goals of the training department.

The role of sales management is to ensure that a systematic approach to the sales process is implemented (see Figure 7.1), guaranteeing that sales personnel remain focused, motivated and incentivised to achieve their sales targets.

Figure 7.1 Systematic sales process

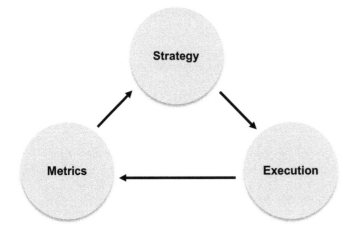

This chapter introduces the components required to establish a sales strategy, leading to the development of a sales operating model and the metrics required to manage the team and produce the expected results. The final section covers the development of compensation and incentive plans.

STRATEGY

There are four components to the establishment of an overall training business strategy, of which sales is a part. However, the sales team will require its own strategy to be defined, which needs to include input from:

- the training strategy and business execution plan;
- the training product management strategy;
- the marketing strategy.

Figure 7.2 Sales strategy

The sales strategy should comprise the four components shown in Figure 7.2. These are:

- **Strategic intent** to establish overall direction and goals by:
  - establishing priorities for the achievement of strategic advantage;
  - factoring and combining the sales strategic intent with that of the training business.
- **Marketplace knowledge** focusing on understanding the needs of the customer base (in terms of training, services and products), training partners, key competitors and their actions, and market trends. This is a fact-gathering analytical exercise, with the objective to specify in detail what is happening in the training and target marketplace, including how commercial success factors are shifting and the implications for target customers.
- **Innovation focus** challenging the training sales team to actively explore and try new modes of working and selling to the target customer base.

- **Business design** interprets the strategic intent in terms of how training sales will execute the go-to-market requirements by considering the five points below and factoring in the output from the innovation focus exercise.

  - **Customer selection:** the customer segments to be focused on versus those which should be ignored.

  - **Value proposition:** what offerings will be sold and how they will be differentiated from competitors, and why customers would purchase or engage with them.

  - **Value capture:** how money will be made, what strategic advantage can be gained and how the success of the offerings will be measured.

  - **Partnerships:** what can be done internally and what activities will sales rely on by working with external partners.

  - **Sustainability:** how offerings and investments will be protected and grown within the customer base.

These five key go-to-market elements within business design, along with the innovation and strategic intent recommendations, form the input into the sales execution stage. These are then assessed and converted into key critical tasks and subsequent sales-related operational needs, which are mapped to quarterly, monthly and weekly activities.

A well-structured sales strategy helps the sales force to focus on its target market customers and communicate with them in relevant and meaningful ways. It is a key ingredient to ensuring that the sales force spends time targeting the correct customers at the right time.

In addition to the sales core strategy, the sales manager should work closely with product management and marketing to ensure product placement, promotion and testimonials are in place. Product placement and promotion help to create brand awareness. By working with both the training and corporate marketing teams, all RTM channels can be used, such as social media networks, where broader company-wide integration messages can be sent to increase the opportunity base.

Creating an effective sales strategy requires one final and very important component: metrics, namely key performance indicators (KPIs). These allow for the strategy to be measured for progress and provide an insight into any adjustments required to either address or accelerate the results.

EXECUTION (SALES OPERATING MODEL)

The sales operating model is, in essence, the execution activities associated with the conversion of the strategy into actual results. Many organisations view the operating model as a high priority due to increasing business complexity, changing customer experience requirements, technology changes and business boundary changes, all of which affect the ability of a training sales team to be successful.

Operating model

The operating model itself is a blueprint for how employees, resources and critical tasks are combined to address and maximise the business climate they are focused on. It also encompasses decisions around the nature of the business, where to draw the boundaries, and how staff work together within and across these boundaries.

After the completion of the training sales strategy (see Strategy section in this chapter), the design of the operating model can begin. The first stage is to interpret the strategy in terms of design principles, for example: 'Expand sales coverage via training partners in emerging markets'; 'Increase sales of training subscriptions'; 'Reduce the level of discounts on standard training offerings'.

Based on the design principles (see Figure 7.3), the training sales operating model can be completed, using the following approach:

Figure 7.3 Operating model

Formal organisation and structure: describes the interactions and dependencies on other departments, including shared service needs such as staff development, sales enablement and training team support. It also includes the dependencies on other groups, such as product sales and marketing, to assist with leverage and expertise. Following this, the training sales team organisational structure can be defined.

Accountabilities: describes the roles and responsibilities of the training sales team, including ownership of sales targets, fiscal management considerations, critical tasks and customer engagement guidelines.

Governance: refers to the management processes that need to be established to enable decisions to be made regarding strategic priorities, resource allocation and sales performance management, including management and reporting of key metrics.

Climate and culture: sets the required expectations regarding how staff should behave and operate with others in the training team and broader community to support the accomplishment of the critical tasks.

Capabilities: defines how sales management combines people, process and technology in a repeatable manner to deliver the desired outcomes.

The final stage of the operational model is that of execution, which should entail the establishment of an activity road map, development of the capability plan, enforcement of key behaviours, implementation of performance management and mitigation of risk.

Challenges

On the complexity front, changes in training modalities, customer buying preferences and geographical and cultural requirements have created the need to consider customers in multiple ways. For example, the one-size-fits-all approach to sales is no longer viable. The training sales team needs to consider growth around new customer segments, products and geographies, and within these dynamics how best to maximise reach via partners and strategic alliances.

From the customer experience perspective, many leading organisations are making a shift in relation to the way they engage and build meaningful and trusted long-term relationships. It is not simply a case of the sales team owning the relationship any more, but, rather, a combined training team relationship. This means the output from the sales strategy must involve all customer-facing employees regarding their level of involvement and ability to enhance the customer experience without losing sight of their responsibility to align and liaise fully with sales.

Digital technology is changing every aspect of business operations. This includes how and where companies interact with customers. For the training sales team, this represents both opportunity and threat. With increasing information flowing into and around a company every day, many potential opportunities can be lost. For example, customers searching technical support knowledge portals, having technical discussions on company social media sites or placing enquiries for new product information can result in training revenue growth being lost due to an inability to view customer activity that could lead to a meaningful training sales-related discussion.

Business boundaries change all the time, especially when a company is expanding and becoming global in nature. This can affect the selling model and, if handled incorrectly, result in lost orders; for example, tax implications or subsidies where the customer is penalised if they purchased training directly rather than in their home location. Changes like these can easily outdate an operating model and place it out of synchronisation with the training sales strategy. It is therefore important when developing the strategy and associated operational model that all business variables are factored in.

SALES MANAGEMENT AND METRICS

Managing a sales team requires metrics to be meaningful, relevant and aligned to the needs of the training business. This includes alignment between all parties associated with the development, support and delivery of the training offering.

Roles

Managing a sales team is no different from any other team in the sense that if you can't measure it, you can't manage it. It is true to say that sales, marketing, product management and training delivery also need to be fully aligned in terms of what each other is measuring and dependent upon (see Figure 7.4).

Figure 7.4 Role alignment

Product management is responsible for specifying what content should be developed for which target audience and for setting revenue targets based on market understanding and potential. Marketing takes this information and develops lead and demand generation activities to assist sales in locating and converting opportunities. Training delivery services converts these opportunities through course provision based on appropriate levels of student attendance to sustain or achieve required targets. Sales needs to be aware that if student numbers are at lower than expected levels it can have an adverse effect on planned ROI requirements.

Sales-related metrics

Regarding specific sales-related metrics, sales managers need to consider the points below to ensure that the focus goes beyond just revenue achievement to include improvement and maintenance of overall sales performance:

- **Revenue attainment:** some training groups may accept bookings as a key metric; however, in a service-based business, revenue is not normally recognised until delivered. This can create motivational issues for sales staff if service delivery is on hold past their quota and compensation recognition period.

- **Selling time related to time spent with customers versus other non-related sales activities:** this can help to identify aspects of a sales person's role that could be undertaken by alternative means.

- **Lead activity and response time:** marketing lead and demand generation activities provide opportunities for sales teams to expand revenue potential. It is important they are followed up quickly owing to lead lifespan being comparatively short. A quick response time can improve sales performance and the overachievement of revenue.

- **Average deal size:** identifying whether the sales person is focused on transactional (high volume, lower value; e.g. course places) or consultative (low volume, high value; e.g. customised training solution) selling will provide sales managers with information on how to ensure the team is selling in a productive manner.

- **Pipeline effectiveness:** monitoring how opportunities move from one stage to another provides sales managers with vital information on how effective, competent and proficient sales staff are at progressing opportunities through to an actual sale. It enables the managers to assess if there is sufficient pipeline to reach quota, based on known or historical conversion ratios. A typical sales pipeline set of metrics is:

  - Number of unqualified opportunities to focus on and their value.

  - Number of qualified leads and their potential value.

  - Number of deals and value being progressed through the pipeline.

  - Number of deals and value with a sales commitment to close.

  - Actual deals closed and their value.

- **RTM activity based on geographic and training channel partner sales activity:** when investment decisions have been made regarding where to sell and what sales channels to use, it is important to measure how they are progressing and what actions need to be taken to address or accelerate sales activity.

In addition to the metrics mentioned above, other goals or KPIs can be set at the individual sales person level to drive and improve specific behaviours, such as:

- Number of lead or demand generation follow up calls made.
- Number of meetings scheduled and undertaken.
- Number of proposals sent.

The metrics shown in Figure 7.5 provide an insight into the health of training sales activities. Pipeline effectiveness records the percentage of opportunities that resulted in an order being sold. Lead time provides an insight into how long it took on average to close a deal. Average deal size reflects the value and revenue that was sold and delivered in a quarter. It is also important to monitor employee satisfaction. Failure to do so can result in loss of sales team motivation and ultimately failure to achieve the sales goals.

SALES COMPENSATION AND INCENTIVES

A key component regarding the development of compensation and incentive plans for staff is to ensure that all the training sales objectives are factored in. These can include

Figure 7.5 Typical sales metrics

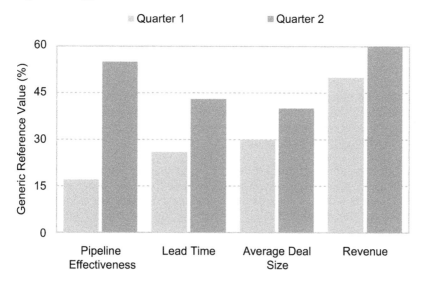

revenue attainment, average order size, selling specific offerings to agreed targets and minimising discounts.

Another component is to understand what industry competitors are paying. This is particularly important when hiring new staff or encouraging more, senior sales personnel to join the company. This can also affect staff retention when compensation plans are not attractive enough, and create difficulties for maintenance of customer loyalty when sales staff leave.

Understanding the cost of implementing a compensation and incentive programme must be factored into the overall training business plan, especially as it is part of the cost of sales (CoS) expense line. To factor CoS into the overall business plan requires decisions to be made regarding the nature of the compensation plan to be adopted. Compensation plans vary from one company to another. Those shown below are typical:

- **Margin-based:** commission paid on margin attainment above an agreed minimum level. Additional incentives can include commission rate change as profit levels increase.

- **Revenue/quota:** compensation paid on revenue attainment over an agreed minimum level.

- **Balanced:** compensation is based on margin and revenue attainment and that of an additional component, such as revenue growth in an emerging market.

- **Team:** bonuses go to all sales team members when quarterly sales goals are achieved.

Where possible, consideration should be given to implementing accelerators, where increased commission rates are paid to sales staff who overachieve their agreed targets.

Before putting proposed compensation plans into action, it is good practice to run 'what if?' scenarios to pressure-test how the plans would work in reality. There are many examples of compensation plans designed to achieve a specific behaviour that have resulted in quite the opposite!

Incentive plans can be separate from compensation plans or in addition to them. Typically, incentive plans are put in place to drive KPI achievements or specific sales goals, such as selling new courses in emerging markets, and are often sponsored by other departments within the training group.

A specialised product incentive fund (SPIFF), which is a specific form of incentive, is an immediate bonus for a sale. Typically, they are paid by the training department to encourage product sales teams to include training as part of their overall deals. The origin of SPIFF is from the world of drapers, where inferior clothing carried an extra sales percentage if sold.

SUMMARY

The selling process has rules and identifiable stages that require strategies, operating processes and metrics to be established to achieve the business goals of the training department.

The role of sales management is to ensure that a systematic approach to the sales process is established and implemented. This involves understanding the overarching training business strategy and extracting a relevant and meaningful sales strategy to be converted into a sales execution plan and operating model.

After the model has been approved and accepted by the business management team, relevant metrics need to defined and aligned to the needs of the training business, supported by a funded sales compensation and incentive plan.

8 SCHEDULE AND RESOURCE MANAGEMENT
Planning to deliver on the training market opportunity

Selling to an opportunity is in itself a business challenge. However, it is catastrophic not to have the capability to deliver. This is where understanding and interpreting demand is key, especially in relation to managing the business for both commercial and product success.

This chapter discusses the main tasks associated with scheduling and resourcing training courses together with understanding and interpreting demand, including how to cater for regional variance by way of enhancing or minimising the curriculum on offer. Practical challenges covering scheduling the right modality for the right market need, managing the delivery resource in an efficient manner, managing cost and revenue expectations, and factoring in international needs are then outlined and a scheduling checklist provided for reference and consideration.

UNDERSTANDING AND INTERPRETING DEMAND

As discussed previously, part of a product manager's role is to decide what marketing strategies should be used to launch a training offering onto the market, with the marketing department assessing who to sell to, what to sell and how to offer it in terms of maximising the training offering penetration.

From a delivery perspective, the scheduling and resource management side of the business needs to be aligned to the opportunity, but also needs to reflect the realities of supporting the anticipated market need. To do this, the team responsible for scheduling and resource management needs to understand the following:

- The nature of the training modality being offered:
  - ILT will require instructor resource as well as classrooms, lab equipment (dedicated or cloud-based) and catering.
  - VILT will require instructor resource, a conference phone or VoIP and a virtual training lab with 24-hour access for the duration of the course.
  - eLearning requires access to a training portal where students download subject matter content via the internet.
- The level of student engagement and interaction being offered outside the standard training offering:

- access to an electronic performance support system (EPSS) (see Chapter 11 for more details) to enhance the learning experience of students;
- social learning support via a dedicated portal to encourage student interaction between themselves and the instructors.

- The availability of resources:
  - instructors with relevant skills and knowledge;
  - classroom availability;
  - training partner availability and the nature of the commercial relationship;
  - technical infrastructure in support of VoIP, dedicated and virtual labs, training portals, EPSS and social learning.

- Geographic coverage requirements:
  - countries;
  - language requirements.

- Commercial needs:
  - country pricing and revenue requirements;
  - discount policies to cater for internal, customer or partner bookings, including discounts for multiple student orders;
  - costing guidelines to allow decisions to be made regarding the engagement of resources that do not impinge on course or training department profitability.

- Target student volumes:
  - by training offering;
  - by country;
  - by student type to ensure the mix of partners, internal employees and customers is balanced according to financial need.

Once these six points have been understood, the team responsible for scheduling can start to assess how best to plan and implement the provision of the training. Typically, they assess resource gaps in relation to revenue and target market goals, and work with the training delivery team to plan how to address any shortfalls.

Once the resource needs have been addressed, scheduling of courses can commence, with the team assessing and analysing the following on a weekly basis:

- Course booking rate, sometimes known as order rate or run rate.
- Cancellation rates regarding students who booked and then cancelled prior to the running of the course.
- Fill rates regarding the level of places sold on a course; for example, a 12-seat training class with nine students booked on it is a fill rate of 75 per cent.
- Standby rates regarding the number of students waiting to book on a course when it is fully booked.

- Rolling forecast of advanced booking rates, which relates to how far ahead courses are booked and to what level. For example, a course may be scheduled to run once every two weeks for six months. If the course was fully booked one month ahead, 50 per cent two months ahead, 20 per cent three months ahead and 10 per cent four months ahead, by monitoring on a weekly basis, a view can be obtained regarding the market demand on a short-, medium- and long-term basis. This allows decisions to be made regarding increasing or decreasing the frequency of courses and provides useful advance information about the need to implement additional sales or marketing activities.

- Cost of sales forecast where specific course offerings can be assessed in terms of costs to run the course versus the revenue generated. This is especially important when external resources are required to run a course, which can affect the profitability on low fill rate courses quite significantly.

The ability to monitor, report and forecast on a regular basis provides an excellent vehicle for making decisions regarding frequency of provision, level of discounts and whether to use internal or contracted resources. It also provides an insight into demand, whereby an ILT course could be substituted with a VILT, which increases profitability and does not require multiple classrooms to be tied up when demand is split across multiple locations.

ENHANCING THE CURRICULUM TO SUIT LOCAL CUSTOMER NEED

There is an old saying, 'Content is king!', which is true to a certain extent. However, the level of support and the nature of engagement can also significantly enhance its value.

Most training delivery teams rely on the output from product management and curriculum development teams to provide a curriculum that supports their customers' needs and provides a means to generate revenue in line with corporate and business unit requirements.

The reality can be different at the local level, with regional and geographic differences forcing a different mindset. What works at headquarters level does not always work locally because of differing market conditions and product sales opportunities. In some industries the **standard** training offering may not suffice. The financial sector, for example, may have differing training needs from that of the manufacturing sector, due to legal statute requirements.

Therefore, local training delivery teams may need to consider enhancing the existing corporate curriculum to ensure they hit their specific goals, or overachieve based on their market opportunity, or satisfy specific needs in their region of operation.

The technical training curriculum can be enhanced by local delivery teams in several ways:

- Offer advanced training on a workshop demand basis to minimise the need for content to be developed as a formal course and to be delivered by subject matter experts.

- Offer industry-specific content for private training opportunities.
- Offer post-training support via a local training portal with asynchronous access to an instructor.
- Engage authorised training partners to provide access to content they have developed.
- Work with strategic product partners and offer their complementary courses.
- Offer skill gap analysis to customers requiring private training.
- Offer boot camps and re-skilling sessions.

MINIMISING THE CURRICULUM OFFERED TO SUIT LOCAL CUSTOMER NEED

Delivery teams, especially those covering complex and diverse geographical and language-based regions, may elect to schedule a minimum curriculum based on market demand, ability to resource and expected returns.

Companies with headquarters in the USA often produce English-only material and require the geographic-based subsidiaries to fund translations. From the European and Asia Pacific perspective, cost of translation may be far outweighed by the sheer number of languages to be translated in relation to the market opportunity. In these instances, the delivery teams will schedule a minimum curriculum to ensure basic training only is provided.

SCHEDULING THE RIGHT MODALITY TO THE RIGHT MARKET CONDITIONS

Training has to reflect the ongoing changes taking place culturally, economically, socially and technologically in the way it is delivered.

Global economic growth is accelerating and the work ethic is becoming more centred around commercial success and improved productivity. This places increased demands on employers to minimise training expense and the time their employees spend away from the office.

For training providers, alternative modals need to be considered outside the traditional ILT, as does the need to balance training provision against the pressures of satisfying variable demand in a commercially viable manner. Table 8.1 provides an overview of alternative approaches that can be adopted for different market conditions and commercial needs.

SIZING, SCALING AND MANAGING THE DELIVERY RESOURCE

One of the many challenges facing a training delivery manager is how to assess the business in terms of expected training volume and number of staff required to support it, and how to manage the resource pool so that variations in demand are handled in an effective, productive and cost-efficient manner.

Table 8.1 Scheduling the right modality for the right market conditions

Delivery modality	Description	Market condition advantages	Market condition disadvantages
Instructor-led training	• Taught by a subject matter expert who is also a specialist in instructional techniques. • Provides a dedicated classroom and lab environment for learning interactions between the instructor and student, and between the students themselves.	• For the students, dedicated training environment with minimal interruptions and maximised interaction with the instructor. • Maximises profitability, especially if fill rates are above 40%.	• For the students' employers, it is time-consuming and costly in terms of lost productivity and travel expenses. • If student fill rates are low, revenues often don't cover overall costs.
Virtual instructor-led training	• Taught by a subject matter expert who is also a specialist in instructional techniques. • Provides a VoIP or phone dial-up facility to allow remote training with access to a remote or cloud-based lab environment.	• For employers, reduced time employees spend away from the working environment. • Employers have no student travel and hotel costs. • Minimises the delivery costs and maximises the ability to run a course across multiple locations. • Assists in the scheduling of low volume courses across multiple regions and countries. • Students can undertake practical lab work in their own time.	• Not conducive to student interactions due to the remote nature of the training. • Requires national language speakers for it to be effective across multiple country attendees. • Care required regarding instructor time management when delivering across multiple time zones. • Can suffer from internet bandwidth constraints, resulting in poor transmission of digital content and lab work.

(Continued)

Table 8.1 (Continued)

Delivery modality	Description	Market condition advantages	Market condition disadvantages
eLearning	• eLearning is based on the use of technology to enable students to learn where they want and when they want. • Typically involves the downloading of subject matter via the internet, accessing dedicated training via intranets or extranets, and using CDs or videos.	• eLearning is an on-demand environment allowing students to access material in line with their actual need and thus benefit by applying what they have learned immediately. • Can be included in a learning management system, where it provides students with the ability to define their own programme of individual asynchronous training activities. • For employers it reduces the overall cost of training.	• Little or no ability to interact with an instructor. • Requires the content to be translated into multiple languages, which can be costly due to cultural and language construct issues.
Independent lab sessions	• Complement the theory sessions and build on prior knowledge, leading to confidence in a student's ability to apply it in reality. • Can be used to support eLearning or to provide a sandbox environment for students to practise at their own pace and reinforce their learning.	• Cloud computing provides an alternative solution to on-premise labs, reducing overall fixed cost investment. This provides a simple way to access resources over the internet and support scalability by allowing access to as many labs as required on a pay-as-you-go basis. • From a training business perspective, this provides a number of advantages: ▪ Initial capital expenditure is minimised due to no upfront investment in lab equipment.	• The ability to scale an on-premise lab environment, especially if it is required to support authorised training partners, can result in large investments in hardware, software, development and support. This is further compounded if student volumes and market need is increasing. • Requires active marketing and understanding of how customers purchase and implement training if not sold with an ILT course.

(Continued)

Table 8.1 (Continued)

Delivery modality	Description	Market condition advantages	Market condition disadvantages
		▪ Operational costs are aligned to student run rates as a consequence of the pay-as-you-go model. ▪ Training schedules and lab management is less restrictive, with the ability to access infinite technology resource effectively. ▪ Minimises investment costs and provides a vehicle for exploring alternative ways of delivering training, such as blended, flipped classroom and moving towards a subscription-based offering. • Provides a safe environment for students to practise without jeopardising a live environment.	
Social learning	• Social learning is about students learning through observing others' behaviour, attitudes and outcomes, both directly and through reciprocal interactions. • Social learning platforms provide: ▪ Live chat as a communication vehicle between students and instructors.	• Introducing or providing social learning has a number of benefits: ▪ It extends the formal training by providing an environment where students can discuss how they applied it in relation to their actual job, and the lessons they learned as a consequence. It also provides the opportunity to share experiences in a collaborative manner, reinforcing what they have learned and assisting in the better retention of information.	• From the training group point of view, it requires investment in a social learning infrastructure. • Requires strong understanding of target market customer needs and industry knowledge in order to provide and position a viable offer.

(Continued)

Table 8.1 (Continued)

Delivery modality	Description	Market condition advantages	Market condition disadvantages
	▪ Streaming where news, updates, announcements and broadcasts can be communicated on a regular or daily basis. ▪ Focus groups to encourage discussion and engagement on specific and relevant topics, which also reinforces collaboration. ▪ Curation to support the aggregation and search of content from within the social learning site and broader website references.	▪ With employees moving away from job-specific roles to more task-based activities, it encourages and supports the sharing of best practices irrespective of location and time zones. ▪ Productivity improvements can be obtained, with training and support being available when and where customers need it. ▪ From a vendor training perspective, the opportunity to extend training from formal skills-based training to value add performance-based support, is significantly enhanced.	
Bootcamps	• Taught by a subject matter expert who is also a specialist in instructional techniques. • Provides a classroom with minimal lab involvement, which tends to be based around demonstrations only. • Provides a good vehicle for learning interactions between the instructor and student, and between the students themselves.	• Suitable for advanced training for technical specialists who have limited time to study. • Typically used for training channel partners as part of an overall enablement programme.	• Not suitable for teaching new concepts or products to audiences with no prior experience.

Sizing a training business requires an understanding of what the training product management team views as the market opportunity, and how and where the business development managers and sales teams intend to position and sell the training.

The product management team can provide an overview of the following:

- training offerings;
- training modalities;
- market opportunity by industry sector and geographic region;
- pricing by geography.

Whereas business development managers can provide the following:

- target revenue or volume by offering and modality;
- target revenue or volume by geography;
- budgetary guidance based on costs and expected profitability, depending on the business model in force at the time;
- route to market contact points and expected revenue requirements.

The sales manager, whose main focus is on guiding the sales team to sell to the target market opportunity, can provide the following key information:

- sales bookings forecast by offering, modality, location and time to convert from prospecting to closure;
- the level and size of discounts granted, which need to be monitored to ensure overall margins are not compromised.

With this level of information, the training delivery manager and administration team can construct a meaningful schedule of training offerings, based on the business development manager's view of the market opportunity balanced against the realities of the sales team's activities.

The first stage is sizing the opportunity in terms of how many courses to offer and where they should be located. The next stage is aligning appropriate delivery resource, taking into account any language requirements and the frequency of the offering.

If the frequency is low – for example, offering one or two courses instead of a normal expectation of four or five – consideration should be given to establishing relationships with either authorised training partners or independent instructors. This is also a typical consideration when factoring in language variance, when the permanent instructor pool may be limited in its language proficiency.

Establishing access to a pool of temporary resources allows the training delivery team to scale without commitment to expanding the permanent delivery resources. One of the major challenges is sizing the actual number of permanent delivery staff required to support the offerings and ensuring that they generate the right level of financial return to justify the investment in them. One approach that can be considered is:

- Assess if the number of courses an instructor can support, in line with market opportunity and assumed sales success, achieves the following:

  - agreed annual instructor utilisation (typically 180 teaching days, depending on annual leave and public holiday allocations);

  - desired class fill rate; note that class size is a function of course complexity, so will vary from one course to another;

  - average revenue per class after discounts, which provides a gross margin (after instructor, classroom, lab, course materials and refreshment costs are removed) of 60–70 per cent.

On a class size of 12, for instance, the business model should be based on a 70 per cent fill rate (typically eight to nine paying students).

- Assess if the level of investment in instructor development and infrastructure resource will deliver the required return on investment over an acceptable period of time. For example, if the main market interest is spread across multiple countries, and hence languages, then the use of contractor resource is more financially viable. On a course by course basis, it provides a lower gross margin but does not adversely affect the fixed cost margin contribution where permanent instructors are unable to deliver the revenue.

- Assess any seasonal impact; for example, in Europe the summer season can have a major influence on revenue and margins due to customer vacations. Therefore, when sizing the number of permanent instructors and classrooms required, consideration should be given to factoring this into the decision process. This is where the use of authorised training providers and contractors can be an effective solution, allowing the training to be supported on an on-demand basis.

When looking to scale a training business in terms of supporting training volume fluctuation, be it expansion or contraction, the following should be considered:

- Assess the benefits of increasing the permanent resources versus overall exposure to the business should the forecasted growth decline.

- Develop an authorised training partner network in regions where language or cultural issues can be best supported by local expertise, or where the training partner network has an established market presence and penetration.

- Use training contractors to accommodate growth, or provide coverage for permanent instructors who may be undergoing re-training in preparation for new product and training offering releases.

- Develop VILT offerings that allow broader coverage and reach without requiring training rooms to be allocated.

Managing the training resource overall requires a good understanding of the capability and availability of the fixed and temporary resource pools. It also requires constant assessment of the way in which the market opportunity is developing.

Market and sales analysis is an important function that all training delivery managers need to be competent in. It forms the basis by which all decisions around sizing and scaling the business are made. Understanding the sales forecast and being personally accountable is fundamental to training delivery success. Whether the sales bookings are below, on target or above, it is important to know why and be able to challenge, encourage and motivate interaction and engagement with sales facing staff. In other words, take control: no sale equates to no delivery!

Training delivery can also act as a controlling agent with views on what the market needs, what the market is buying and how it provides signals on changes that may impact the success of training moving forward.

RESOURCING EFFICIENCY (CONTRACT OR EMPLOY)

In the previous section, sizing and scalability were two key factors a training delivery manager needs to consider in order to decide how best to resource the delivery team's headcount. Of course, the underlying factor is cost. For a training organisation based on profit, cost control is as important as it is for a cost centre-based group.

With one of the main costs being headcount, it is important to ensure instructor efficiency and effectiveness is achieved. Making decisions on headcount comes down to:

- How many training days can an instructor deliver without affecting the quality of service provided?
- How much does it cost to train an instructor on a new training offering before they become productive and what is the ROI?
- How versatile are the instructors? Can they deliver different courses, and can they teach in multiple languages?
- What is the training demand and requirement to support the headcount?
- For profit-centred training groups, are the finances measured and reported annually or quarterly?
- What alternatives are there to increasing the training volume and level of profitability without loading the organisation with increased headcount?

One of the many considerations a training product manager and training manager need to look at is that of employing or contracting instructors to balance expected customer demand versus cost of providing the training and maximising the profit contribution. Table 8.2 highlights the pros and cons of this conundrum.

Table 8.2 Employ versus contract considerations

Considerations	Employ	Contract
Training days an instructor can deliver	**Pros:** • dedicated resource and known fixed cost; • cost per training day approximately 45% of a contractor; • teach days typically 180, with maximum being 230. **Cons:** • restricted number of courses an individual can teach, depending upon product(s) complexity; • unable to teach when preparing for new courses; • normally cannot accommodate multiple languages.	**Pros:** • unlimited resource, especially if using a pool of contract instructors or authorised training partners; • can accommodate different languages. **Cons:** • cost per training day is 50%+ more expensive than dedicated resource; • not dedicated and therefore may not be well-versed in broader vendor knowledge; • may have to commit to a dedicated number of training days to gain flexibility for booking their time on an ad hoc basis.
Cost to train an instructor and time to gain ROI	**Pros:** • broadens and protects brand image via dedicated instructors who are viewed by customers as subject matter experts; • can teach the customer with a broader level and depth of knowledge; • quality of training is high. **Cons:** • loss of revenue; • lowered billable utilisation; • ROI can vary, depending on training volume market opportunity.	**Pros:** • cost of training absorbed by contractor or authorised training partner in return for agreed number of courses to deliver; • no loss of utilisation and therefore ROI is improved due to no instructor training costs. **Cons:** • not as well-versed in broader vendor knowledge, and hence quality of delivery maybe jeopardised; • may have difficulties representing and protecting the brand image; • limited linkage and communication with course developers or subject matter experts.

(Continued)

Table 8.2 (Continued)

Considerations	Employ	Contract
Instructor versatility	**Pros:** • versatile / able to accommodate requirements to customise specific course content and deliver to the customer's needs. **Cons:** • restricted regarding number of different courses an individual can teach, depending on product(s) complexity; • travelling abroad may be restricted due to family commitments; • normally cannot accommodate multiple languages.	**Pros:** • can cover multiple courses; • can teach in multiple languages; • can cover multiple geographies. **Cons:** • limited ability to customise training content; • cost per training day is 50%+ more expensive than dedicated resource.
Training demand and ability to supply	**Pros:** • can focus on volume growth in key offering areas, maximising revenue and profit generated per instructor head. **Cons:** • can be difficult to scale and accommodate volume growth due to resource restrictions; • growth in one course area may imbalance ability to support other courses, which may minimise revenue and profit growth.	**Pros:** • can accommodate and grow with the demand; • minimises the need to hire extra instructor resources; • provides a flexible and more manageable approach to cost management. **Cons:** • reduces the margin return per course delivered.

(Continued)

Table 8.2 (Continued)

Considerations	Employ	Contract
Effect on profit-centred training organisations	**Pros:** • fixed and known delivery costs; • maximised per course delivered margins; • if reporting financial results annually, the training delivery manager can balance costs and revenue over the full 12-month period. **Cons:** • if reporting financial results quarterly, the training delivery manager may have difficulties justifying headcount in those quarters where seasonal fluctuations affect revenue and profit margins.	**Pros:** • provides a means for supporting increased revenues and actual bottom line margin contribution in pure monetary terms; • provides a more flexible fiscal model to be implemented on a month by month basis. **Cons:** • percentage profit reduced, due to the cost per training day being 50%+ more expensive than dedicated resources.
Increasing training volume without affecting increased headcount costs	**Pros:** • none once the optimum level of fixed resource has been hired. **Cons:** • can be difficult to scale and accommodate volume growth due to resource restrictions.	**Pros:** • accommodates growth without incurring an increase in fixed headcount costs; • scalable in a way that does not risk the training business due to overstaffing to support business growth; **Cons:** • skill sets are being developed external to the vendor.

CONTRACT INSTRUCTORS

When engaging contract instructors, it is important to ensure that there is a legally binding contract in place to clearly define the business relationship, delivery expectations, expected modes of behaviour and required metrics, including predefined quality expectations. It also protects the aspects of customer and training group confidentiality.

SCHEDULER'S CHECKLIST

The checklist in Table 8.3 highlights some of the more common tasks a training coordinator or training administrator is involved with regarding the scheduling of courses in a commercial training environment. Note that some elements of the checklist may be undertaken by multiple administrators as some may focus on scheduling resources only and others deal with the booking and billing side, depending on the business volumes they are supporting.

Table 8.3 Scheduling checklist

	Activity	Staff involvement
6–9 months before ILT or VILT courses are scheduled to run	Assess training course demand by offering and geography.	Training administrator working with training delivery management, sales teams and authorised training partner management teams.
	Draw up schedule of offerings in accordance with forecast and business plan needs.	Training administrator.
	Assign internal training room resource requirements. If VILT, reserve virtual lab environment.	Training administrator.
	Contact authorised training partners and agree on training schedule and room and instructor resource requirements.	Training administrator and training partner administrator.
	Obtain authorised training partner resource schedule.	Training administrator and training partner administrator.
	Assign training instructors according to availability. Where training group instructors not available, assign contract instructors.	Training administrator.

(Continued)

Table 8.3 (Continued)

	Activity	Staff involvement
	Review training resource costs versus forecast revenue and address accordingly.	Training administrator working with training delivery manager.
	Assess schedule and cross-check for resource conflicts.	Training administrator.
	Finalise schedules and reserve catering facilities.	Training administrator.
3–6 months before ILT or VILT courses are scheduled to run	Develop schedule and publish on training website.	Training administrator and web marketing team.
	Develop PDF flyers and schedules to assist in promotion to existing customers.	Training administrator and marketing.
	Accept bookings and send student joining instructions.	Training administrator.
	Produce daily report on bookings and course seats still available to be sold and send to training and sales management.	Training administrator, training delivery manager and sales teams.
	Produce student waiting list report for overbooked courses and send to training manager. Assess the need to schedule additional training courses.	Training administrator working with training delivery manager.
	Obtain authorised training partner bookings report and produce weekly report to be sent to training management.	Training administrator, training partner administrator and training management.
Two weeks before ILT or VILT courses are scheduled to run	Produce report on courses at risk due to low enrolments and make decisions with training delivery manager to cancel or replace with VILT if low volumes are observed in other similar courses across geographies.	Training administrator working with training delivery manager.
	Send cancellation letters if required regarding cancelled courses.	Training administrator.
	Book and confirm catering needs.	Training administrator.

(Continued)

Table 8.3 (Continued)

	Activity	Staff involvement
	Request printing of course materials or send PDF course content if policy is to provide electronic materials.	Training administrator.
	Confirm virtual lab resources with external provider if course requires access to virtual equipment.	Training administrator.
	For VILT courses, send instructions regarding VoIP and virtual lab access to students.	Training administrator.
	Confirm catering facilities.	Training administrator.
	Send printed course content or enable access to PDF copy for authorised training partners running scheduled courses to known student volumes.	Training administrator.
	Request instructor checks training room resources.	Training administrator and Instructor.
Day of ILT or VILT course that is scheduled to run	Printed materials and other student specific materials are provided in the classroom, including customer satisfaction and student attendance sign-off sheets.	Training administrator and instructor.
	Send electronic copy of customer satisfaction sheets and student attendance sign-off sheet to VILT course instructor.	Training administrator and instructor.
Duration of ILT or VILT course	Instructor liaison: check instructor has no issues, such as inability to complete the course, or student problems.	Training administrator and training manager.
	Training administrator establishes and maintains backup plans to address potential assumed issues.	Training administrator
End of first day of ILT or VILT course	Obtain course attendance sign-off sheets.	Training administrator and instructor.

(Continued)

129

Table 8.3 (Continued)

	Activity	Staff involvement
End of ILT or VILT course	Send invoice to students who have attended the course.	Training administrator.
	Send finance department evidence of billing (payment demand) and invoice (payment advice) for purposes of revenue reconciliation.	Training administrator and finance.
	Obtain customer satisfaction sheets from the instructor running the course and generate report.	Training administrator.
	Obtain customer satisfaction sheets from the authorised training partners running the course and generate report.	Training administrator.
	Assess and action any complaints or poor results with the training manager.	Training administrator and training manager.
	Assess customer satisfaction results and send summary to training delivery manager	Training administrator and training delivery manager.
	Send out payments to contract instructors.	Training administrator.
	Send invoice to authorised training partners for training content provided, or request payment in accordance with the financial arrangement in place at the time.	Training administrator and training partner administrator.
	Send finance evidence of billing and invoice for purposes of revenue reconciliation regarding authorised training partner training delivery.	Training administrator and finance.

INTERNATIONAL AND LANGUAGE CONSIDERATIONS

Understanding cultural differences is as important, if not more so, as translating or delivering in a country's local language. Get it wrong and the market opportunity and brand damage can be costly, especially when operating in a competitive product environment.

As training is a service, it is important that time is spent becoming culturally aware because of the significant communication element involved in training, be it instructor-led or eLearning. Therefore, the first priority of a training delivery manager supporting a cross-cultural region is to ensure that the teaching is adapted to suit the target community.

English is the international business language and one that is used extensively in the world of information technology, so in many countries it is permissible to provide English written course content that is delivered in English or in the local language. If a course is being delivered in English to a foreign audience, consideration needs to be given to the pace of the course and time for frequent local language discussions to occur between students.

Optimally, courses should be translated and presented in the local language. Several factors need to be considered in order to make decisions regarding how to proceed:

- Is it strategically important for the company to have service provision in the local language?
  - If it is, is general funding available that minimises any impact on the training department's fiscal responsibilities? If not, there will be a need to locate and negotiate with internal sponsors for funding, where they depend on the service being available.
- Does the revenue goal depend upon offering training in various countries?
  - If yes, consideration needs to be given to the effect on margin contribution regarding the following alternative strategies:
    - Content is provided in English and the instructor teaches in the local language. The cost of hiring an appropriate instructor needs to be balanced against ability to generate required revenue and margin contribution over the lifecycle of the offering.
    - Content is translated and taught in the local language, which results in both revenue and agreed margin attainment.
    - Training is undertaken by an authorised training partner, who translates and delivers in the local language. The partner could acquire the English content under licence and translate at their own expense, with revenue contribution being based on an agreed percentage of sales.

Websites, marketing and promotional material also need to be translated and factored into the overall costs of development and operational expense.

Finally, ensure that all training schedules and booking instructions clearly state when a course is available:

- in English only;
- delivered by a local language speaker using English-only content;
- delivered using translated content by a local language instructor.

MANAGING COST AND REVENUE EXPECTATIONS

As discussed previously, there are many elements to how a training business is sized in terms of its training volume, staffing levels and cost allocations. Once this has been understood and defined, the next stage is how to manage the resultant revenue and cost expectations within the agreed business plan requirements.

Whether the reporting cycle is monthly, quarterly, annually or a combination will determine the level of flexibility a training manager has regarding how best to report and manage the inevitable changes that occur during the various reporting periods.

Being held to a monthly target with no ability to correct within a quarter is difficult, and would probably result in the development of a cautious monthly plan. Alternatively, an annual target can drive a more ambitious approach with the option to deliver strong results towards the latter part of the year, sometimes referred to as a **back-loaded** plan.

Neither is particularly favourable if they are not based on reality in terms of market need and opportunity.

Assuming the plans put forward and agreed to are based on actual market need and potential, then the importance of metrics and trend analysis come into play. Order and cancellation rates can provide an insight into short- to medium-term issues or opportunities, depending upon whether they are rising or falling, as can the delay between order to actual training delivery, all of which have an effect not just on revenue but on costs too. If revenue demand is growing in an unexpected manner, decisions will need to be made as to whether to schedule additional courses, with the resultant effect on costs, or move the demand to another month or quarter.

Being able to explain with robust metrics and highlight trend changes assists the training manager not only to manage the revenue and cost aspects but also to set the right level of expectation as the plan evolves over its reporting period.

Table 8.4 provides some examples of how to manage cost and revenue expectations for several situations that might arise over a reporting period.

SUMMARY

Training delivery managers need to assess their business in terms of expected training volume, number of staff required to support it and how to manage the resource pool so that variations in demand are handled in an effective, productive and cost-efficient manner.

Understanding and interpreting demand is an important activity, allowing for effective planning to be undertaken. It covers the training offerings, the environment to support them, allocation of resources and financial management in terms of revenue, cost control and profits.

Table 8.4 Managing cost and revenue expectations

Cost or revenue challenge	Description	Possible approach	Considerations
Increased revenue demand	Revenue growing above the agreed business plan. This is good news. However, it is important to explain why and its impact on the forecast, both revenue- and cost-wise.	• Assess market metrics and validate. • Assess whether growth is based on deal size. Is the opportunity moving from transactional to consultative? • Assess impact on delivery expenses. • Is the demand due to seasonal or other market fluctuations?	• Market metrics can provide an insight into why demand has increased (such as recent marketing campaign). • Changes in buying characteristics can affect the public schedule offering, which could be detrimental to class fill rates and overall profitability. • Can require additional courses to be run, which will need additional resources. Initially may require third-party instructors and hence additional cost. • If seasonal, consideration should be given to using training partners. If related to other factors, such as increased marketing or sales activity, consider aligning planning activities earlier in the business cycle.
Revenue growth in smaller regions or countries	Growth may arise because of new or emerging markets.	• Assess market opportunity and whether the revenue is sustainable. • Assess the viability of offering dedicated training classes or using third-party instructors or training partners. • As an interim solution, consider offering virtual training.	• Caution is required in these situations as the revenue may be intermittent and therefore clarity of training delivery approach is important. • If demand justifies a regular schedule, balance costs, profitability and availability to justify using dedicated staff or third-party/training partners. • If volume or frequency of delivery is low, consider offering virtual training access, which improves profitability due to its low-cost base.

(Continued)

Table 8.4 (Continued)

Cost or revenue challenge	Description	Possible approach	Considerations
Increased cancellation rates	Customer cancellation rates increasing beyond an acceptable level, resulting in loss of revenue and potentially overall course cancellations due to profitability pressures.	• Assess if specific to courses, regions or dates. • Analyse the sales method and process used on those customers who cancelled. • Consider establishing a waiting list that may help to minimise the cancellation impact on high-demand courses.	• Assess relevancy of offering and how the course is being sold. • Assess how the customer is being validated and how the order is being taken. Consider changing the customer cancellation terms to protect the business.
Revenue fluctuations across the training offering portfolio	Demand for offerings may vary, which affects both revenue and costs.	• Assess available metrics, including market conditions and sales method. • Granulate assessment by region, country and product growth.	• Fluctuations may arise due to changes in exchange rates if operating across geographies or other outside influences. • Demand may be fluctuating due to other influences within the parent company that require further investigation and alignment.
Costs increasing at higher rate than that of revenue	Costs may be increasing due to use of third-party instructors or supporting courses in non-profitable regions.	• Analyse the training business model to assess which element(s) is creating the increased expenditure.	• Typically associated with variable costs, which can be addressed once the nature of the overspend is understood. • Costs may increase when revenue is lower than expected on a fixed level of employees. In many European countries, the summer months result in lower revenues. Therefore, when hiring staff it is important to hire to a lower level and substitute with third-party contractors, which helps to minimise seasonal fiscal challenges.

The ability to monitor, report and forecast enables decisions to be made regarding the frequency of offering, level of discounts, enhancing or minimising the curriculum, and whether to use internal or contracted resources.

By optimising resource efficiency, decisions can be made regarding how to size and scale for growth and manage cost and revenue expectations in a controlled manner.

9 AUTHORISED TRAINING PARTNER MANAGEMENT
Expanding sales and delivery capability through qualified third parties

By establishing a training partner network, a vendor can control, monitor and expand sales and delivery coverage in a consistent and effective manner without having to commit to large investments in staff and resources.

This chapter looks at the advantages and considerations regarding the establishment of a partner network, including the different partner types such as distributors, resellers and training partners. It also outlines the decisions that have to be made regarding the type of business relationship required, contractual needs, how revenue will be recognised, quality control, territory management and how partners will be rewarded.

WHY USE AUTHORISED TRAINING PARTNERS?

With many sales going through distribution and channel partners, vendor visibility can be lost in terms of knowing who, how and why products have been purchased. This results in both lost revenue and an inability to train customers on how to be effective in the deployment of the technology purchased.

Successful businesses invest not just in technology, but processes and people. Often, the people aspect is the last element to be focused on. Many studies have been done that show customers are more likely to purchase training at the point of sale. If positioned correctly, this will be solution-based and cover the product and associated professional services.

Many channel partners focus on selling products and look to engage the vendor directly or training partners to help them craft and deliver a broader solution. From the vendor perspective, if dealing with multiple geographies and regions, it is not always viable to establish a direct training presence in all countries.

By establishing a training partner network, a vendor can control, monitor and expand coverage in a consistent and effective manner. Control and consistency is important not just for the training group but also for the customer. Consistency on the sales front guarantees that training is sold correctly, to the right person, for the right reason and the customers know what they will receive irrespective of where they purchase it. On the delivery side, consistency is about ensuring the training delivered is of high quality and covers specific topics at the right level and right depth.

The training partner, whether selling, delivering or providing both, needs to be seen in the eyes of the customer as an extension of the training vendor. The customer should not be able to discern the difference and hence will have the confidence to invest in authorised training.

Training partners enable vendors and the training group to balance costs, revenue, profits and resources against opportunity, irrespective of where in the world the training need arises.

One of the many challenges facing training organisations is how best to support countries in their regions with varying cultures, languages and delivery costs. Some countries will favour one or more products over another, with variable demand and volume.

Being able to assess and analyse demand to ensure maximised use of fixed resource and available budget allows the selection of authorised training partners to accommodate the variable demand and delivery in local languages without having to establish remote training centres. This allows the training team to focus on business development, working with partners to jointly expand the opportunity and share in the wealth creation.

AUTHORISED TRAINING PARTNER TYPES

These come in all shapes and sizes from multinational to single city providers. Many training partners focus purely on providing authorised training for multiple vendors. This provides a distinct commercial advantage whereby they can offer a comprehensive managed training service to their customer base. Quality and service levels tend to be very high, with brand recognition and trust being central to sustaining and growing training as their core business.

Some training partners specialise in particular vendor product lines and often provide broader professional service support as well. This has a distinct advantage as the prospective customer can align training with the technology deployment in a fairly seamless manner.

Distributors also offer training that their product-based channel partners sell into. This removes channel conflict and reduces the need for channel partners to provide training directly, which in turn minimises the risk of students transferring their product business to the partner providing training.

Of course, there are many examples where channel partners do in fact provide training as well, which, from the vendor training perspective, requires careful management by working with them and the vendor channel management team directly to minimise business conflicts. Table 9.1 lists the main types of authorised training partners.

SALES VERSUS DELIVERY PARTNERSHIPS (OR BOTH)

The preference for most vendors is to have a business relationship with a partner that sells and delivers the training, mainly because it shows commitment. However, it does not always provide comprehensive sales coverage.

Table 9.1 Authorised training partner types

Authorised training partner type	Description	Benefits	Considerations
Distributor	Resells products and services via channel partners including the selling and provision of training.	• Training offered to channel partners to sell. • Channel partner does not have to establish own training centre. • Allows channel partner to sell low volume without concerning themselves about classroom utilisation.	• Sales commission is reduced due to splits between channel and distributor. • Distributor may dictate what courses to offer, which may impede channel partners from supporting training. • Can make vendor entry into the market difficult to implement.
Channel partner	Sells and provides training in support of a broader product and service-based offering.	• Establishes a strong and trusted business link with the customer. • Provides broader local coverage. • Accommodates market need with training supporting actual customer need. • Profitable for partner and vendor.	• When setting up channel partners as training providers, be aware that custom or tailored solutions may not result in income. • Can create channel conflict.
Multinational training partner	Dedicated training organisation providing and selling multi-vendor training offerings internationally.	• Can support multinational customers with a single contract and guarantee consistency of offerings. • Ability to offer additional value-add training solutions complementing standard vendor training courses.	• Can demand better financial terms from the vendor. • Managed training services can inhibit some vendor training from being offered to customers.

(Continued)

Table 9.1 (Continued)

Authorised training partner type	Description	Benefits	Considerations
National training partner	Dedicated training company providing and selling multi-vendor training offering within a dedicated country.	• Strong understanding of local market needs. • Specialises in local language training provision.	• Requires thought regarding market growth and expansion in terms of taking on additional national-based training providers.
Product-specific training partner	Dedicated to the selling and provision of training for a specific vendor only, often providing additional support services.	• Specialist skills dedicated to the provision of product-specific training. • Enables closer relationships to be developed between partner and vendor.	• May limit vendor training growth, if skills or product coverage is not continuously developed.

Therefore, channel partners that prefer to sell products only, do in fact de-risk their business significantly by not investing in or supporting training infrastructure costs and headcount resources. However, customers do look for partners to have the ability to provide guidance and consultation support on how to maximise the investment in the technology. To do this, the reseller partner needs to establish relationships with the trusted supplier, which is the vendor.

In these types of partnerships, there is a tight bond of trust formed between supplier, partner and customer. The customer gains partner confidence through the alignment with the vendor regarding training provision, which has the advantage of differentiating the partner in their particular competitive marketplace. From the vendor perspective, the training group has broader sales coverage, comprising a combination of transactional and consultative selling.

Transactional selling is quicker and easier to close as it tends to be solving an immediate customer need and is short term in nature. From this point of view, it tends to drive and support high-volume training sales. If you introduce an incentive to sell training, the channel partner can add value to the customer and increase their sales.

With consultative selling being broader in scope and addressing both the immediate and long-term needs of a customer, the sales time frame is long and usually requires an ongoing sales cycle, with the collaboration of many people. For many partners focused on product sales, this is too time-consuming and of minimal interest.

Sales-only relationships are best kept to transactional activities that assist in the growth of the public, scheduled training business. Authorised training sales partners are able to engender confidence with customers, because they are selling bona fide training. The training group is confident, because the training is being sold correctly to the right audience and need.

Consultative selling is best supported by partners who both sell and deliver training. These types of partners recognise the business potential of training offers by establishing longer-term business relationships with their customers. As a consequence, they invest in both technical and people-based infrastructure. Focus is on transactional selling for driving attendance in their public scheduled classes. Consultative selling for ensuring customer investment in technology achieves business goals and performance needs.

As a training partner, they provide flexibility for the training vendor in terms of minimising investment in classrooms and teaching staff across multiple locations and regions. They have the ability to add value and integrate other training offerings to provide a richer overall solution.

This type of training partner relationship can maximise customer coverage, but will tend to minimise top line vendor revenue growth in terms of not being able to recognise the final end user price. However, profitability percentage-wise can increase due to significantly reduced delivery costs.

Partners who deliver training only help to supplement those vendor training groups who have strong aligned sales coverage through their product sales teams and want to minimise investment in training infrastructure. Or, they may use these partners to enter a marketplace or region where they do not want to invest in additional services until market conditions allow.

The decision to use training partners as sales only, delivery only or both depends upon various factors. In some instances, it might make sense to utilise all three, depending upon market and fiscal need.

REVENUE AND REWARD

When looking to enter the market, all vendor training groups focus their attention on how they satisfy and address the following business criteria:

- market potential and growth prospects;
- market coverage (customers and students);
- revenue attainment and growth;
- investment justification;
- profit;
- customer satisfaction.

For a training partner, there is another: reward. Let's consider these.

When motivating training partners to engage with a vendor, the first criterion the potential partners will request information on is the market potential and prospects in the short to long term to grow the business. This is particularly relevant regarding expected product sales penetration.

For training partners who either deliver or sell and deliver, investment decisions regarding equipment, train the trainer, trainer salaries, marketing and sales require an understanding of what potential is out there in the market. The size and nature of the opportunity will dictate their initial level of interest and engagement.

Assuming market potential opportunities are good, the next criterion will be the expected level of market coverage, based on the number of potential customers requiring training and the average number of employees (students) they can expect to deliver training to.

Once the market opportunity has been understood, the all-important fiscal aspects apply. How much revenue can be generated and what level of profitability can be returned based on the investment (cost) requirements?

The sixth criterion is customer satisfaction in terms of what the training vendor is offering from the training perspective (content, labs and certification, for instance) compared to what the partner can provide.

The final criterion that is extremely relevant to the partner is reward. Certainly, revenue and profit are key drivers; however, the way in which these are delivered and aligned with their expectation is of key importance. Reward requires careful consideration. Satisfying the partner may inhibit fiscal progress or corporate requirements at the training vendor level, or prevent committed engagement for the partner. Table 9.2 highlights some typical approaches to reward.

Table 9.2 Training channel rewards

Reward type	Description	Partner benefits and challenges	Vendor training group benefits and challenges
15–20% resell fee (sales only)	• Commission payment as a percentage of actual sale price. • May be restricted with an agreed maximum discount level.	• Agreed payment amount. • May be penalised if discounts applied. For example, if the discount exceeds guidelines, a reduction in sales fee may apply. • Does not require investment in training infrastructure. Does, however, allow partner to maintain customer relationship control.	• Can be seen as incremental revenue and therefore 15–20% is in line with industry norm sales costs. • Care needs to be taken regarding agreed level of discounts and implication to the resell fee payable. Discounts above a certain level could be penalised with a similar lowered payment value.

(Continued)

Table 9.2 (Continued)

Reward type	Description	Partner benefits and challenges	Vendor training group benefits and challenges
Revenue share – partner sells and delivers	• Resell fee is paid at agreed rate, typically 15% of actual fee paid. • Delivery fee paid at agreed rate of 40–45% of sold value.	• Partner gets paid for selling and delivering. • Partner has to pass the order direct to the vendor training group to fulfil. • Partner paid agreed delivery fee on course completion. • Provides access to broader customer base with opportunities to sell other training offerings.	• Training group recognises actual end user revenue. • Profitability after sales and delivery payments 40–45%. Note that not all training partners will agree to revenue share, due to customer billing arrangements.
Revenue share – vendor sells and partner delivers	• Delivery fee paid at agreed rate of 40–45% of sold value.	• Partner paid agreed delivery fee on course completion. • The vendor training group selling assists partner fill rates and profitability. • Partner is recognised as a trusted delivery source for the vendor. • Partner does not need to spend money on selling or marketing into a market where customer base is not known.	• Training group recognises actual end user revenue. • Profitability after delivery payments is 55–60%. • Minimises and de-risks vendor requirement to provide direct training in low volume or merging markets.
Agreed delivery rate	• Partner receives agreed fee irrespective of sold value.	• Partner receives a guaranteed amount per delegate. Partner may request a minimal student number to protect against financial loss.	• Option available to vendors if training partners in new or emerging markets not comfortable with percentage of sale splits.

(Continued)

Table 9.2 (Continued)

Reward type	Description	Partner benefits and challenges	Vendor training group benefits and challenges
Book model	• Training partner purchases the course contents (book) either under licence to print terms or on a piece by piece basis.	• Increases overall profitability. • Reduced cost of entry and can support lower breakeven student numbers.	• High gross and net profits, especially if provided under licence to print terms. • Revenue per student is lower. • Opens up broader market opportunities, especially in high-volume markets. • Vendor can focus on content production and significantly reduce sales and delivery costs.

TERRITORY MANAGEMENT (EXCLUSIVE VERSUS NON-EXCLUSIVE)

Territory management can be a legal minefield, depending on where the training organisation wishes to establish a partner presence. For instance, there are anti-trust laws in the USA and exclusive distribution laws in the European Union (EU) to consider.

In general, it is about whether the exclusivity is competitive or anti-competitive. In the EU, the laws tend to be applied in a more lenient way if the so-called exclusivity does not exceed 30 per cent market share or enforce resale price maintenance or absolute territorial protection. In the USA, the application of legality is whether the exclusivity restraint acts as a regulator to help promote competition or whether it suppresses or damages competition.

With the commercial goal being to maximise overall market penetration, it is important to assess how best to allocate training partner territory coverage. Maximising their revenue without creating undue competitive stress is the main requirement. From a training group perspective, guidance should be requested from the legal department or commercial trading specialist before embarking on the introduction of territory management. Table 9.3 highlights key questions and concerns that should be considered when looking to operate an exclusive or non-exclusive territory with a partner.

CUSTOMER OWNERSHIP DILEMMA

Most companies partner in order to deliver customer value. The dilemma, however, is who owns the customer experience when multiple organisations are involved.

Table 9.3 Territory management exclusive versus non-exclusive considerations

Key questions and concerns	Partner view	General notes
Will the territory be exclusive or non-exclusive?	• If allocated sufficient territory, partners can generate revenue without undue competition. • Non-exclusive territories allow partners to work more effectively with customers without being restricted regarding where they are based.	• Additional training partners can reduce course attendance and result in price cutting and reduced financial gain. • From the vendor perspective, non-exclusive relationships remove market restrictions and partners may not have the relevant skills or appropriate sales coverage.
How will the territories be determined?	• Partners may want to select territories based on customer coverage and courses they can teach. • Multiple partners in the same territory may cause confusion with customers if they specialise in different courses.	• Partners may want to re-negotiate based on progress.
Will the territory be based on sales quota and student volume attainment?	• Concerns may be raised regarding attainment expectations and time limits to address shortfalls.	• Careful consideration should be given to required metrics for success before embarking on a territory-based strategy.
Can partners establish training centres in other regions or territories?	• Independent training companies may have a footprint in other countries and request additional provision.	• Can be advantageous. However, independent training companies may subcontract to smaller training companies. This can create local issues.
How should customer training requests from other territories be handled?	• Customers may contact training partners from outside their allocated territory and request permission to service.	• Clear guidelines and rules of engagement need to be defined by the vendor.
Will non-exclusive territories minimise market coverage?	• Larger training partners will not favour non-exclusivity. • Smaller partners may prefer this as it minimises contractual obligations.	• Non-exclusivity provides less vendor control and partner commitment. • Consideration can be given to combining exclusive and non-exclusive when dealing with mature and emerging territories, respectively.

From the training perspective, the ultimate owner should be the vendor training group. The experience a customer has will decide the nature of the ongoing relationship with not just training, but the product and other associated services also.

When establishing a training partner network, the processes and organisational needs required to ensure all stages of the customer experience are effective need to be defined and in place before customers are engaged. In some instances, issues will not surface until an actual customer training engagement commences. Therefore, it is important to put in place guidelines that both the training vendor and partner agree to. Listed below are some guiding principles that can be considered:

- Agree who is responsible for selling to customers, and how they receive information to complete the sale and answer questions regarding training provision.

- Agree clear guidelines on how customer communications will be undertaken and where customers go to find out how the training partnership operates.

- Understand how vendor key accounts are supported and communicated with.

- Decide who owns the ultimate resolution of customer issues.

- Define and agree how issues requiring customer reimbursement, eLearning returns and other requests are to be handled prior to the establishment of a partner and vendor relationship.

- Agree who the ultimate arbiter will be if there is a dispute with a training partner about how to resolve a customer training-related issue.

When a customer buys from a training partner, they are assuming the partner is reflecting the values and customer care policies of the vendor. The customer must come first, and ownership issues are secondary to ensuring good resolution and service levels are maintained.

Training partnerships can prosper by offering customers a complete solution. Establishing and agreeing on the guiding principles before customers are engaged is key to success.

QUALITY MANAGEMENT

Quality is important in all business ventures, and training is no different. Being able to provide the required skills and competencies to manage, administer, teach, sell and develop training content to an agreed quality standard is vital to success and customer confidence.

While some companies develop their own standards, increasingly training providers are adopting the ISO 9001 standard, which provides a framework to develop and maintain their own quality management system, and is certified and recognised internationally.

Customers expect training to be relevant, fit for purpose and serviced in a competent manner. With the growing demand for training, it is important that authorised training partners can demonstrate how they provide a high level of quality service. ISO 9001 enables training vendors to assess a training partner's capabilities with confidence. The key elements that should be covered and documented include:

- Customer focus and processes.
- A defined quality policy.
- An agreed responsibility, authority and communication framework.
- Resource provision and management.
- Staff competent in the delivery and selling of training.
- Training infrastructure and working business environment.
- Training product planning and implementation.
- Content design and development.
- Sales and marketing process.
- Customer care and satisfaction with documented metrics.

Not all training partners will be applying ISO 9001, and so training vendors should look to specify a standard that is similar in essence before signing partners up. This ensures that their best interests and those of their customers are being looked after. It is difficult to build a brand image, but easy to destroy it!

CONTRACTUAL REQUIREMENTS

The old adage 'get it in writing' still holds true today. When establishing a training partner relationship, one of the most common mistakes is not having a good written agreement in place. It is important therefore to consider what aspects need to be included to ensure the business relationship delivers to expectations and is understood by both parties and protected by a legally binding contract. The guidelines in Table 9.4 should be considered when deciding what to include in a training-related partner agreement.

Training partner management is the process of systematically and efficiently managing partner creation and execution and analysing for maximum operational and financial performance while minimising risk to the organisation.

SUMMARY

A training partner network provides vendors with the ability to expand both sales and delivery coverage in a consistent and effective manner without having to commit to large investments in staff and resources. It should, whether selling or delivering, be seen in the eyes of the customer as an extension of the training vendor.

Table 9.4 Typical training partner contractual requirements

Agreement terms	Description	Training partner relevancy		
		Training reseller only	Training delivery only	Training delivery and reseller
Purpose	To appoint as a training partner and grant authorisation to use the title, and sell and/or provide licenced authorised courses, subject to the provisions of the agreement.	Yes	Yes	Yes
Definitions	Words or phrases used in the agreement with definitions and descriptions.	Yes	Yes	Yes
	Typically covering: authorised course; licensor materials covering student kits, instructor kits and certificates; partner portal for accessing information; certified instructor; effective date of the agreement; programme defining terms and conditions; trademarks and usage; programme documents relevant to the agreement, such as instructor programme guide and application request forms; price lists.			
Appointment	Defines the term of the agreement and its scope in terms of resell, delivery or both, including use and restrictions of materials provided and trademarks, whether the appointment is exclusive or non-exclusive.	Yes	Yes	Yes
Training partner programme	Includes the programme documents, which the licensor can change and typically make binding upon giving written notice after an agreed number of days. Should a partner not agree, then a termination request can be entered by the partner.	Yes	Yes	Yes
Use of qualified certified instructors	Partner instructors must comply with the certified instructor guidelines, with partners ensuring any person teaching is a certified to teach the particular course.	No	Yes	Yes

(Continued)

Table 9.4 (Continued)

Agreement terms	Description	Training partner relevancy		
		Training reseller only	Training delivery only	Training delivery and reseller
Course delivery	The training partner delivers authorised courses in a professional and competent manner using a certified instructor at approved partner facilities. Each student must be supplied with a student kit.	No	Yes	Yes
Portal access and policy compliance	Partner must access the training portal on an agreed basis regarding vendor updates, and annually to ensure compliance with vendor policy and programme changes.	Yes	Yes	Yes
Anti-piracy	The training partner agrees not to sell any vendor content obtained from non-authorised sources.	Yes	Yes	Yes
Unauthorised courses	During the term of the agreement, the authorised training partner may only offer authorised courses and will not distribute, offer or sell any training course that competes directly with the vendor.	Yes	Yes	Yes
Facilities and equipment	The training partner must meet the requirements for facilities and equipment as defined in the relevant classroom requirements for the delivery of courses.	No	Yes	Yes
Classroom requirements	The training partner must maintain its equipment in good working order and procure the appropriate version and number of copies of the technology product for each specific course as required.	No	Yes	Yes
	Onsite courses at a customer location must be pre-approved to ensure course quality and delivery.			

(Continued)

Table 9.4 (Continued)

Agreement terms	Description	Training partner relevancy		
		Training reseller only	Training delivery only	Training delivery and reseller
Course documentation	The training partner must order and use the authorised contents that are applicable to the course.	No	Yes	Yes
	No reproduction of content is allowed unless a licence royalty model is in place.			
	Supplemental materials cannot be used without prior vendor approval.			
	Each student who successfully completes an authorised course should receive a certificate of attendance and completion.			
Customer satisfaction	The training partner agrees to maintain and achieve high student satisfaction as a condition of their continued authorisation, the scope of which includes teaching standards, facilities, service levels and mode of practice.	No	Yes	Yes
Use of trademarks	The licensor (vendor) typically grants the training partner a non-exclusive, non-transferable licence to use the current trademarks as outlined in the agreement, for the sole use of marketing and advertising of the partner's training services.	Yes	Yes	Yes
	Trademarks must be used only in accordance with the current vendor trademark usage policies.			

(Continued)

Table 9.4 (Continued)

Agreement terms	Description	Training partner relevancy		
		Training reseller only	Training delivery only	Training delivery and reseller
Sales and marketing activities	The training partner agrees to use reasonable efforts to market, distribute and promote the licensor services. In so doing, the training partner agrees that its marketing and advertising efforts will be of high quality and preserve its professional image and reputation.	Yes	No	Yes
	The vendor sales organisation will normally require the training partner to participate in quarterly operations reviews and agree to attend sales enablement training as required.			
Ordering and payment terms	Training partners can order course materials direct or via an authorised distributor, depending upon channel sales structures in existence at the time of operation.	Yes	Yes	Yes
	Typical payment terms for training content or services provided to the training partner tend to be within the agreed number of days of invoice, after which any unpaid invoices could be subject to late payment charges and ultimately termination of the agreement.			
	Taxes and duties remain the responsibility of the training partner.			
Quality compliance	During the agreement, and typically for one year afterwards, the licensor (vendor) may, at its own expense and with prior written notice, audit the training partner's facilities and records to determine compliance with the agreement terms.	Yes	Yes	Yes
	Any issues or concerns not addressed can result in termination of the training agreement.			

(Continued)

Table 9.4 (Continued)

Agreement terms	Description	Training partner relevancy		
		Training reseller only	Training delivery only	Training delivery and reseller
Term and termination	Training partner agreements can be set up as fixed term or renewable on request.	Yes	Yes	Yes
	Termination can be instigated by either party upon written notice for a number of reasons:			
	• breach of contract by either party, for instance, which, if not addressed within an agreed period, can proceed to termination;			
	• termination for convenience where either party may terminate by giving the other party an agreed period of prior written notice.			
	Upon termination of a training partner agreement, all rights and licences granted immediately cease, with all related training activities suspended and use of licensor materials returned.			
Warranties and indemnification	Licensor (vendor) warrants it has the right and title to provide the training materials to the partner for use in the delivery of authorised courses. Any mistakes in the course materials remains the vendor's responsibility.	No	Yes	Yes
	Regarding licensor (vendor) indemnification, the licensor defends any third-party claim brought against the training partner when it is based on an allegation of copyright or trademark infringement by the licensor materials. The licensor agrees to indemnify and hold the partner harmless from any damages, liabilities, and costs finally awarded.			
	Training partner indemnification is where the partner agrees to			

(Continued)

Table 9.4 (Continued)

Agreement terms	Description	Training partner relevancy		
		Training reseller only	Training delivery only	Training delivery and reseller
	indemnify, defend and hold the licensor harmless from any and all damages, liabilities and costs incurred by the licensor as a result of any claim against the licensor by any third party resulting from the partner's delivery of services.			
Limitation of liability	Protects either party from liability to each other. Where there are liabilities on the licensor's side that affect the training partner, those damage payments are limited to a defined amount.	No	Yes	Yes
General provisions	Can cover a number of categories: • Confidential Information where each party agrees to protect the confidentiality of each other's information in a manner consistent with the way a reasonable person protects similar confidential information. • *Force majeure* protects either party from legal action in the event that either party is prevented from performing any portion of the training agreement by causes beyond its control, including labour disputes, civil commotion, war, governmental regulations or controls, casualty or acts of God. • Each party will, at its own expense, comply with any applicable law, statute, ordinance, administrative order, rule and regulation prevailing in the country or economic region where they are based. • Survival of terms requires that all obligations by either party are completed even after contract termination.	Yes	Yes	Yes

Training partners vary, from multinational to single city providers, and can be independent training companies or distributors and resellers of products. The nature of the business relationship depends upon whether the vendor training company wants a delivery and selling relationship or simply a delivery-based one.

Depending upon the region where the relationship is being established, territory management considerations have to be factored in. In the USA, there are anti-trust laws to consider and in the European Union there are exclusive distribution laws. Other factors, such as customer ownership, also come into play; it is therefore important that agreement is reached allowing the vendor training group to maintain a relationship that allows for product and other associated services to be discussed.

The final element when establishing a training partner network is to have a written agreement in place defining service level agreements, quality requirements and commercial terms in a legally binding contract.

10 CONSULTING SERVICES
Expanding the training offering with broader customer-aligned services

Training organisations who provide consulting services gain the ability to assist customers in maximising the effectiveness of their investment in the technology purchased, and that of their employees.

Establishing trust and respect enables the building of strong and long-lasting business relationships. Consulting provides the means to positively influence the customer's experience by applying their skills in strategy, planning, implementation and execution to ensure the achievement of desired goals.

This chapter outlines the service offering and details the main steps that a training group needs to consider if looking to offer consulting as a service to their customers.

THE CONSULTING SERVICES PROFILE

Training is a service-based business with chargeable elements comprising design, development, delivery, managed training and consulting. In this section, the focus will be on consulting services. Table 10.1 provides a description of some of the possible offerings a training group could consider providing to its customer base.

Table 10.1 Training consulting service offerings

Consulting service offering	Description
Training needs analysis	Typically forms part of an overall training and evaluation exercise to understand the requirements to address employee knowledge, skills, competency or performance needs related to the adoption of a new technology or more efficient use of a current technology.
	The process involves the assessment of:
	• Business goals and behaviours required in relation to the technology being deployed.
	• Impact on employees and their job roles.
	• Required competencies and performance needs.

(Continued)

Table 10.1 (Continued)

Consulting service offering	Description
	• Preferred and current learning styles.
	• Timelines and deployment schedules.
	• Budgetary restrictions.
	• Success metrics.
	• How the training momentum will be maintained after technology deployment.
	• Transformational change requirement needs.
	• Quality and regulatory requirements.
	• Employee assessment requirements.
	Following this, a high-level recommendation is produced and presented to the customer for comment, modification and approval.
Training solution design	A training solution being recommended for design needs to factor in learning styles and preferences, modalities, job roles and tasks, content objectives and use of relevant learning-based technologies.
	Following the recommendations, the training consulting team, on obtaining customer approval, proceeds with the design.
Transformation change management	Implementing a new training solution inevitably involves change management, which the customer or a suitably qualified training consulting team take responsibility for undertaking. Assessing the impact of the solution and how to address change management should be discussed with the customer sponsor. Failure to undertake and address this can have an impact on the effectiveness of the overall training solution's success.
	The output from a change management recommendation covers the creation of actionable plans and activities that positively affect the learning and student experience.
Job task analysis	Assessing employee job roles and associated tasks regarding the required level of knowledge, skills, competencies and performance needs. This level of analysis assists in defining a higher level of granularity, leading to more modular and reusable course content. It provides greater choice regarding which learning modality can be offered to customers and their employees.

(Continued)

Table 10.1 (Continued)

Consulting service offering	Description
Content design and review	Depending upon the nature of the training solution design being put forward, the content design is focused on how to ensure the content objectives and target audience needs are accommodated in an interactive, engaging and pedagogically sound training manner.
	Content design therefore has to factor in whether the content is to be consumed as an instructor-led course, a hybrid or accessed via on-demand modules accessible from within a learning management system. As a consequence, the content and design review needs to ensure that:
	• The content can be delivered in a manner that suits the customer's learning environment.
	• Instructional design best practices are applied in relation to the modality being used.
	• High-quality and industry recognised design standards are adhered to.
	• Content is accessible to users with disabilities.
	• Review processes are established at critical milestone points between the development team and the customer sponsors.
Learning technology assessment, recommendations and adoption	Learning technologies are constantly and rapidly changing. Assessing which ones are relevant, cost-effective and provide the ability to maximise the use and financial benefits of alternative and new learning modalities is crucial. This level of service helps to provide customers with choices, whether on-premise or cloud-based solutions, to ensure the technology provides them with a solution that best fits their needs.
Metrics and analysis	In order to measure and control the effectiveness and success of a training solution, it is important to identify and define the trends and metrics required, and to analyse and deliver on the required training solution outcomes.
Regulatory compliance	When designing a new training solution, the training consulting team factors into their activities relevant country or industry-specific regulatory laws.
Usability testing	Employees using new learning technologies need to be able to access, use and take advantage of the functionality. A training consulting team assesses suitability and relevancy to ensure the adopted learning technologies are fit for purpose.

CONSULTING AND ACCOUNT MANAGEMENT

Technical training is primarily focused on ensuring that those attending training gain knowledge and skills which enable them to be competent in the use or application of a technical product when put into practice.

This is a desired outcome that the technical training product management team defines and specifies at a generic level. Training consultancy expands the benefits even further by assisting customers to identify and tackle the more complex business challenges that the technology being adopted provides.

Typically, an investigative approach is used to understand the nature of customer challenges and what the best solutions might be. Taking a prescriptive approach to consulting will not achieve a desired customer business outcome. Based on a sound understanding of how the technology links to people and process, training consultants need to provide advice in alignment with the customer's business strategy, enabling them to develop a training solution that can be implemented and measured for joint success.

A typical approach to undertaking a consultancy engagement involves:

- **Assessment:** discussing and exploring why the technology has been purchased and what effect it may have on achieving the key objectives for the customer's business, including the main challenges users are faced with. This is normally undertaken in conjunction with the customer's key sponsors.

- **Diagnosis:** following on from the assessment phase, training consultants work in collaboration with other groups within the customer's organisation. They obtain more in-depth and pertinent information to assist in analysing and diagnosing any people, process, culture and cost-based issues that need to be factored into a recommendation for adoption.

- **Initial recommendation:** having completed the assessment and diagnosis phases, recommendations are presented to key sponsors and interested parties to ensure that overall alignment of the solution being proposed is agreed. Using an iterative approach, any issues are resolved before proceeding to the solution development phase.

- **Solution development:** following acceptance of the proposed solution, the training consultants working in conjunction with the rest of the training team design and develop the solution. The solution can be a mix of learning modalities, approaches and interactions, depending upon the analysis of the customer's requirements and desired end results.

- **Delivery:** the training solution is delivered according to agreed timelines and costs. Metrics and check points are defined to ensure desired results are being achieved.

- **Reinforcement:** customers investing in training consulting services will require a process to be established to ensure that momentum is maintained. This momentum can be undertaken by the consultants, but is normally passed on to the customer after guidance has been provided on how best to implement it in a practical and efficient manner.

Training consultants are normally introduced to a customer via a sales or strategic account manager. The account managers are responsible for all customer relationships and they develop strong business ties on behalf of the company they work for. Their main remit is to serve as the face of the company and act as an interface between the customer and all other sales-related departments, including that of the training group. They are strategically important as they maintain ongoing customer relationships and ensure the customer continues to use the company for its business needs.

From the consulting perspective, sales account managers provide an important conduit by which to add value and assistance in further account penetration. In situations where account managers are not available, training consultants, if versed in business strategy, can fulfil a similar role and significantly enhance the growth of the training business within a known customer base.

The training management team should always look to work closely with, and establish strong personal relationships with, the sales account management team to maximise influence and effectiveness within accounts. This should include bringing them up to speed on any issues, conflicts and the potential to introduce new training offerings. Table 10.2 highlights the roles of training consultants and sales account managers.

Table 10.2 Training consultant and account manager roles

Training consultant	Sales account manager
Liaise with sales account managers to establish annual activity plans, opportunities and revenue goals.	Set and agree financial budgets with the customer, company and training department.
Assess key account plans for the potential to open up new training opportunities.	Determine new sales opportunities with existing customers by up-selling and cross-selling.
Undertake training and business needs analysis, strategy design, training modality design, process design, culture change and value proposition development.	Manage and resolve conflicts with customers in a timely and efficient manner to maintain client loyalty.
Design training solutions based on analysis, and the training group or training partner's ability to deliver.	Interact and coordinate strategies with sales and the training department team that are working on the same customer accounts.
Develop the training group's customer base.	Generate sales across defined key accounts to achieve required sales target goals.

(Continued)

Table 10.2 (Continued)

Training consultant	Sales account manager
Undertake problem solving, coaching and mentoring within the training group and that of the customer.	Develop annual account plans and account activity across the various sales teams and training group.
Be the face of training regarding influence across sales and other service lines, including the representation of what value training brings to overall customer success.	Undertake quarterly reviews.

TRAINING AND BUSINESS NEEDS ANALYSIS

Training needs analysis, sometimes referred to as TNA, involves a process of activities regarding the identification of knowledge, skills, competencies or performance gaps that may exist when a new technology is being deployed to employees in a company, the output of which is used to help design and develop a training solution.

Most organisations invest in technology to gain a business benefit. It is therefore important when a TNA is undertaken to include the business requirements and findings in the results. If omitted, the training solution could be operating in isolation and fail to deliver on its expectations.

TNA is the first stage in the consulting training process and should preferably be included within an overall technology solution offering. To achieve this, the training group needs to align its activities with the technical sales and professional services groups within its own vendor organisation. This ensures a more successful and aligned solution. In some instances, training may operate independently for a number of reasons, such as customers purchasing training after deployment or simply looking for a new approach to developing skills.

TNA, apart from identifying knowledge, skills, competencies and performance gaps, needs to factor in cultural issues, learning style preferences, budgetary implications, employee geographic distribution, employee availability, expected business outcomes and the level of commitment management will be providing to their employees.

Figure 10.1 shows the stages that need to be implemented from an overall training solution perspective.

Planning stage

Table 10.3 represents a typical approach from the planning perspective.

Figure 10.1 Training solution design process

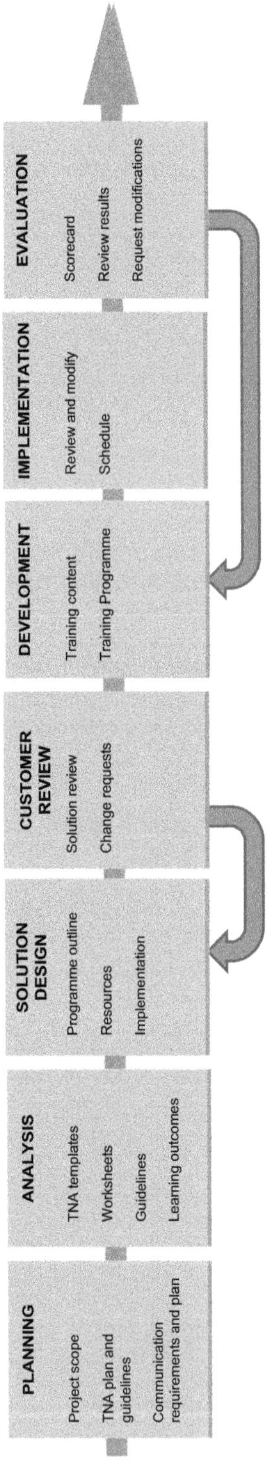

PLANNING	ANALYSIS	SOLUTION DESIGN	CUSTOMER REVIEW	DEVELOPMENT	IMPLEMENTATION	EVALUATION
Project scope	TNA templates	Programme outline	Solution review	Training content	Review and modify	Scorecard
TNA plan and guidelines	Worksheets	Resources	Change requests	Training Programme	Schedule	Review results
Communication requirements and plan	Guidelines	Implementation				Request modifications
	Learning outcomes					

Table 10.3 Project planning stage activities

Key activities	General description
Develop templates for capturing and documenting the overall training solution project, including appropriate guidelines	All projects require a definition of the nature of the project, which is agreed with all the key stakeholders. Templates help to clarify the training project's objectives, approach, scope, deliverables, roles, risks, resources and important timelines.
Develop project plan, including guidance on how to apply and use	The training project plan assists in guiding nominated resources on how to undertake the various tasks. It provides guidance on how to undertake the various tasks, for example, objectives development, liaising and working with stakeholders, defining and scheduling times to specific tasks and understanding what is required regarding risk assessment, change control, communication and budget management.
Develop programme communication plan and appropriate guidelines	All stakeholders must be kept informed regarding all aspects of training programme activities and development in a manner appropriate to them and in a way they understand.

Analysis stage

Following on from the planning stage, Tables 10.4, 10.5 and 10.6 represent a typical approach to undertaking the analysis stage. The first table is an initial high-level investigation of need; the second table covers more specific individual departmental needs; and the third table covers additional requirements at the specific individual employee level.

Table 10.4 High-level training needs assessment

Key activities and needs	General description
Locate sponsor(s)	Obtaining sponsor support is vital to validating the nature and scope of the opportunity and ensuring budgets are available.
Locate key contacts	Key contacts are those involved in the deployment and success of the training.
Investigate reasons for the request	It is crucial to understand at sponsor and manager levels why training is required. Sponsors normally have high-level business outcomes and performance-based needs. Managers tend to have a mixture of training and departmental-based needs.

(Continued)

Table 10.4 (Continued)

Key activities and needs	General description
Business rationale	Depending upon the nature of the technology being adopted, the business rationale for the investment will vary. It could be related to process improvements, employee productivity improvements or other requirements. It is important to understand what it is and how it relates to the technology and its effect on employees.
Understand the specific business and organisational objectives	Primarily, this is granulating the business rationale and understanding what the implications are at lower levels within the organisation. Departments will have different needs for the technology being deployed. For example, a technical support department may be required to provide end user support, whereas a finance department may be minimally effected at the end user level.
Number of employees requiring training and their geographic location	To size and cost out a training solution, understanding how many employees are involved and their geographic location is important, especially if instructor-led training is required or remote locations have low numbers of employees that may require alternative learning modalities to be deployed.
Employee roles affected	Organisations have many and varied roles. It is therefore important to understand what they are and how the technology being deployed affects them. Training is not a one-size-fits-all approach; it is about fitness for purpose and maximising the use of an employee's time and the customer's training budget.
Budgetary considerations	Understanding what budget is being allocated or considered is crucial. There is nothing worse than scoping out and positioning the ultimate training solution only to disappoint the customer and lose credibility due to lack of funding. Training consultants should be able to position alternatives that allow the customer to understand what choices they have and what they may need to forego.
Technology deployment timelines	The training solution needs to align with the technology deployment schedule; otherwise the overall solution will be jeopardised due to mis-timed training.

Table 10.5 Individual departmental training needs assessment

Key activity and needs	General description
Departmental business needs and initial employee overview	Each department will have different business requirements that will need to be assessed and understood in relation to how the technology being deployed supports and assists them in the achievement of their goals, including a summary of how the proposed technology changes may affect employees.
Employee distribution	Understanding how many employees there are and where they are located plus language(s), culture and criticality of availability also needs to be captured. For example, some roles require the employee to always be available at particular times.
Role-specific needs	Each employee role and their associated job tasks will need to be assessed to understand what specific knowledge, skills and competency requirements are needed. This allows content to be tailored to specific job roles and improves training solution relevancy.

Mapping employee roles to business performance needs	Sponsors will normally want to see a return on investment. One of the best ways to show this is to map the training as follows:
	
	• Specific job role tasks aligned to specific business performance needs.
	
	• Analysis of how the technology being deployed and its recommended training maps to performance in terms of:
	
	  ▪ required level of knowledge;
	
	  ▪ associated skills;
	
	  ▪ key competencies gained because of the skills developed;
	
	  ▪ how the competencies contribute to specific and overall performance improvement.
	
	As part of the ROI process, the training consultant recommends what performance improvement training ought to be undertaken, but leaves it to the sponsor to decide as to whether it should be included in an ongoing employee development programme that most large companies undertake themselves.

(Continued)

Table 10.5 (Continued)

Key activity and needs	General description
Language requirements	When dealing with international customers, local language translations may be required. If the technology itself is developed in American or British English, technical staff may be amenable to training documentation being in English and the oral presentation in a local language. For end user communities, language translation will typically need to be undertaken.
Learning preference styles	Investigate preferred learning styles at individual and organisational level. It is important to understand and factor this into the overall assessment and recommendations to ensure that any inhibitors to learning adoption are minimised.
Employee availability including utilisation criticality	Training must be planned in line with employee availability and may have to be phased to ensure the customer can continue with existing business demands. For employees who are paid and measured on utilisation rates, alternative approaches to training delivery will need to be considered.
Training locations	Depending upon learning preferences, physical training locations may be required at the customer's locations or alternative delivery methods used.

Table 10.6 Employee specific training needs assessment

Key activity and needs	General description
Employee assessment	To enable specific training to be designed at the employee level, data collected at the departmental level regarding roles, required skills and competencies can be cross-correlated against individual employee needs. Depending on the organisation, badges may have been introduced or adopted by employees to recognise skills gained previously. These should be factored in.
	This level of TNA provides organisations with choices in terms of selecting a generic training solution or one customised to the individual. Both have advantages and it often comes down to budget availability versus the need to include training within specific employee performance plans. If the latter is a requirement, it is normal to engage with the HR department to discover possible sensitivities and requirements outside the TNA remit.
Employee behaviours	The nature of the technology being deployed and its bearing on behavioural change should be factored into the TNA with assistance from the customer's HR department.

Solution design stage

The findings from the TNA are used to define and document a high-level programme design that factors in the customer's departmental and the individuals' needs. Using a structured approach, the solution design will provide information and guidance on the following:

- training and programme scope;
- purpose;
- resource requirements;
- design parameters;
- implementation requirements.

Customer review stage

The purpose of the customer review is to ensure that the solution design and its associated recommendations align with the key requirements obtained from the TNA and the needs of the sponsors. Following the review, further analysis or tweaks to the solution design may be required before continuing. Once this has been agreed, it is normal practice to obtain sign off from the sponsor before continuing to the next stage: development.

Development stage

Table 10.7 summarises the key activities to be undertaken in this stage.

Table 10.7 Content development

Key activity and needs	General description
Course objectives by target audience	Define the course objectives for the specific audience types, typically based on their roles. Details on the target audience that are known, such as background, experience, level of technical expertise and job function, will help to provide more clarity on the nature and depth of the course objectives.
Course outline and prerequisites	Create a course outline based on the course objectives, target audience needs and prerequisites. The course outline should describe the modules that are required to be covered and their duration. Prerequisites assist in defining what prior knowledge and skills are required prior to attending the course.

(Continued)

Table 10.7 (Continued)

Key activity and needs	General description
Select appropriate modality	Based on the findings from the TNA and solution design recommendations, select the modality to be used to deliver the content.
Develop content and lab sessions where relevant	Using the course outlines, develop the course content, labs, demonstrations and reference materials.
Course duration	In those situations where the duration is deemed to be too long, prerequisites can be defined to help minimise the length and depth of specific modules.
Develop assessment and examination questions	To reinforce that learning has taken place, including the transfer of knowledge and skills development, assessment and examination questions should be developed to validate the achievement of the course objectives.
Develop instructional guides	Develop an instructor guide to assist in the running of the course, covering objectives, key points and timings.

Implementation stage

Having developed the content, the next stage is implementation. This is where delivery schedules, communication messages regarding the rationale for the training and promotional activities are put in place to encourage target audience attendance.

Evaluation stage

The final stage is that of evaluation, where scorecards are used to measure how the training has progressed, what level of feedback has been obtained and whether the required learning outcomes have been achieved. Following a review of the results, changes may be requested that result in recommendations for content or training programme modification.

Successful TNA service provision is underpinned by tools to aid the overall process, which typically comprise the following:

- training project definition templates;
- key sponsor and contacts templates;
- interview questionnaire worksheets;
- training needs analysis questionnaires;
- communication needs assessment and promotion templates;
- evaluation technique guidelines.

CUSTOM VERSUS TAILORED SOLUTIONS

By definition, a custom course is one that has been specifically designed following a TNA for a specific customer, whereas a tailored course is one where standard training content has been modified to satisfy the broad-based needs of a customer.

Whether to steer the customer decision towards tailored or custom-built training should be assessed using the points shown in Table 10.8.

Table 10.8 Custom versus tailored training

Decision points	Tailored solution	Custom solution
Training needs assessment	• Basic TNA indicates minor changes to an existing standard offering. • Standard training is relevant to most of the customer's employee roles.	• Comprehensive TNA indicates substantial content development that reflects the specific needs of the customer. • Standard training is not relevant to target customer employee roles.
Training content development	• Standard training content requires minor changes or deletions. • Changes to content can be undertaken by an instructor or content developer with minimal effect on other training-related commitments.	• Content must be developed based on TNA findings. • Requires dedicated project management and content development resources.
Training delivery and instructor preparation	• Training can be delivered with minimal instructor preparation. • Training can be delivered at the customer's or training group's classroom if instructor-based. • Requires a specific print run.	• Training requires dedicated instructor resources to be allocated sufficient time to prepare. • Requires print resources to be allocated. • Training can be delivered at the customer's or training group's classroom if instructor-based.

(Continued)

167

Table 10.8 (Continued)

Decision points	Tailored solution	Custom solution
Costs and ROI	• Additional charges for the tailoring are minimal, depending upon the level of involvement. • ROI for the training group is good as it will predominately uses existing material.	• Charges are substantial. • ROI for training should be in accordance with defined requirements for private projects. However, as the content will not be eligible for reuse, the ROI is not as high as the tailored option, which can extend beyond the delivery of the specific requested customer course.

When deciding to support a request for customised or tailored training, resource availability and potential to maximise profitability will be fundamental questions to be answered. As most training is based on reusable content, customisation can lessen the potential for maximising profit due to lack of reusability, whereas tailoring increases the potential. Conversely, tailoring generates lower revenue and customisation higher revenue.

Trends in the technical training marketplace constantly change as customers try to keep their costs down, so the demands of employees regarding the way they prefer to learn forces training providers to offer more customised and effective solutions. Modular and task-based development linked to more reusable content can help customised training to become a more regular and viable option.

MANAGED TRAINING SERVICES

Managed training services refers to any training activity that has been outsourced. This can be as simple as handling the printing of course material, or as comprehensive as managing the entire learning and development function.

For many vendors, technical training is a professional service, where the training element is limited to the company product portfolio being produced. However, if the product portfolio is broad, requiring technical training that has a broad effect on customers' end users and the way business is run, there may be opportunities to consider expanding the service remit into that of managed training services provision.

Managed training services has emerged as a fast-growing industry, in part driven by large organisations recognising that while learning and development does maximise the skills and competencies of staff, it comes with an overhead in terms of additional resources and cost.

The main advantages for a company considering the transition to managed training services are:

- Access to a professional service set up to focus purely on training with a commitment to provide relevant and effective services, designed to drive overall business success via state-of-the-art delivery methods, high quality content and seamless administration with best practice execution.

- Improved organisational efficiency, with a company's workforce being able to focus on its core competencies, while simultaneously working with the managed training service provider to align business objectives via defined training programmes. This level of alignment greatly enhances the opportunity to maximise and validate the training ROI.

- Minimising and controlling the training cost while maximising expenditure value. Training departments require regular investment in equipment, technology, systems and resources. Due to its scalability, a managed training service provider can spread its cost base among its other customers, hence providing a lower cost base and access to additional resources at fractions of the total cost.

- Access to broad-based training and subject matter expertise.

Managed training service provision can be simple or complex. In its simplest form, it can involve the provision of printing services, booking and administration, or training delivery. Depending upon the nature of the organisation looking at outsourcing its training functions, it can be very comprehensive and include TNA, content development, learning management system provision or full management of the entire training group.

Table 10.9 highlights a more comprehensive view of the types of managed training services that can be provided. These depend on the business model and range of services a vendor-based training group may want to consider when broadening its professional services footprint.

Table 10.9 Managed training services

Managed training service	Description	Key elements
Training administration and management	Provision of administration services that cover all aspects associated with the promotion, booking, billing and organisation of course attendance or content access.	• Training schedule planning and management. • Training resource planning (instructors, training rooms, labs). • Customer training-related enquiries. • Order taking and confirmations of attendance, including student joining instructions. • Booking and billing.

(Continued)

Table 10.9 (Continued)

Managed training service	Description	Key elements
		• Organising access and distribution of course materials.
		• Classroom and lab set-up.
		• Student hospitality.
		• Student evaluations, collection and statistical reporting.
Training delivery and management	Management and provision of all training delivery resources, including instructors, materials, training delivery technologies and associated technical support.	• Instructor management and skills development. • Training facilities maintenance and provision. • Training material production and quality control. • Training partner management and selection. • Training delivery technology provision and maintenance. • Training delivery governance and reporting.
Content design and development	Management and provision of content development and design services, including print and modality production.	• Instructional design. • Content creation (all modalities). • Project management. • Language translation and cultural corrections. • Content maintenance. • Quality control. • Print production.
Training systems management	Management and provision of LMS and other training-related systems, such as portals and websites.	• 24×7 technical and end user support. • LMS platform provision, development and content creation. • Custom application development. • System maintenance.

SUMMARY

Training consultancy offers broader opportunities for a training group to identify and provide advice on how technology links people and process with alignment to the customer's business strategy. This enables a training solution to be developed, implemented and measured for joint success.

The process starts with a training needs analysis (TNA), involving a series of activities to identify knowledge, skills, competencies and performance gaps, which is then used to assist in the design and development of the training solution.

The next stage after the TNA is solution design. The findings from the TNA are used to define and document a high-level programme that factors in both the departmental and the individual needs of the customer. This is then reviewed with the customer and tweaked accordingly before moving on to the development stage, when the content and training programme is built. After this, delivery schedules, communication messages and promotional activities are developed to encourage target audience attendance as part of the implementation phase.

The final stage is evaluation, which is used to measure how the training has progressed, what level of feedback has been obtained and whether the required learning outcomes have been achieved.

The solution can either be customised or comprise existing content that can be tailored according to the needs of the customer.

Some customers may be interested in outsourcing not just their TNA requirements but all of their training activities through a managed training service offering. This can be as simple as handling the printing of course material, or as comprehensive as managing the entire learning and development function.

Managed training services has emerged as a fast-growing industry, but one that needs careful consideration when it comes to overhead in terms of additional costs and resources.

11 OFFERINGS AND MODALITIES
An insight into what they are

A training offering can be considered in terms of what is being taught, whereas a training modality is the way in which the training is delivered. Many training organisations will provide a training offering on product XYZ, which students can enrol on to suit their preferred learning style; whether that offering is instructor-led or eLearning can then be referred to as a learning modality option.

This chapter explains in more detail what training offerings and modalities are available or under future consideration within the industry.

INTRODUCTION TO ILT, VILT AND ELEARNING (INTERACTIVE AND GAMIFICATION)

Instructor-led training (ILT) and virtual instructor-led training (VILT) both require an instructor to present and engage with an audience. Where they differ is the location of the students. ILT students are physically present in a classroom, whereas with VILT, they are remotely connected via the internet. eLearning removes the requirement for an instructor to be physically or remotely connected because the training depends purely on electronic media, with the emphasis being on the student to access the course through technology and to be responsible for participating in the course at their own pace.

Instructor-led training

This method has been in existence for many years and is still currently the most popular modality requested to date. ILT comprises an instructor who presents and explains concepts by way of a projector, screen and whiteboard. They demonstrate the technology, answer student questions and motivate the attendees to actively participate. The students themselves are provided with course materials, equipment to practise on and an environment in which to learn, namely a dedicated classroom. The main advantages of ILT are:

- Taught by a subject matter expert who also specialises in instructional techniques.
- Provides an environment for learning interactions between the instructor and students, and between the students themselves.
- Develops a camaraderie between students that is often continued after the course has been completed.

- Allows the instructor to tailor the content according to the needs and capabilities of the students.

- When courses achieve a fill rate above 35–40 per cent, gross profitably can be high, in the order of 75 per cent or more.

The disadvantages of ILT are:

- Can be expensive in terms of providing classrooms and associated infrastructure.

- For employers it is time-consuming and costly in terms of lost productivity and travel expenses.

- If student fill rates are low, revenues often don't cover overall costs.

- Industry insight suggests that, without further reinforcement, only 10–30 per cent of what is learned by the student is retained after the course has been completed. There are many factors that come into play with this, such as age, interest in the topic and experience, which have an effect on a more precise value. However, the retention rate is low.

From a learning perspective, ILT provides a high-quality experience for the student with the ability to ask questions in real time, obtain one to one tuition with the instructor and network with other attendees. For the training provider, it can be lucrative when market volume and need is high. However, it's not without its challenges.

Making logistical decisions on where to run a course, how many to offer, what approach to take when student interest is multicultural or how to accommodate language needs complicates the investment and operational aspects of ILT.

Virtual instructor-led training

VILT does not require the student to attend a physical classroom. They participate by being connected via phone or VoIP and viewing the instructor content via a dedicated training portal that forms a virtual training room.

The virtual training room provides the student with the ability to remotely view and interact with the instructor, other students, presentations and practical sessions from their own office or home.

It does require a slightly different approach from the ILT in order to maintain student interest and engagement. As the physical classroom element is missing, students can be easily distracted by external influences and so more motivational and engagement activities on the part of the instructor could be needed.

A key advantage is that practical hands-on sessions can be set and then carried out in the student's own time. Many training organisations provide a virtual hands-on training lab that can be accessed on a 24-hour basis for the duration of the course.

For the training vendor, VILT does require staff dedicated to managing the environment, but there is increased coverage from a single delivery location. The instructor running the course can be located in a training office, while enrolled students can access the VILT from multiple locations. This helps to ease scheduling challenges, when it is difficult to get sufficient students to attend specific locations. VILT, if planned right, can significantly increase overall course profitability.

eLearning

eLearning is based on the use of technology to enable students to learn where they want and when they want. This can involve downloading subject matter via the internet, accessing dedicated training websites and using CDs or videos.

Often, eLearning can be on-demand, allowing the student to access learning material according to their actual need and benefiting by applying what they have learned immediately.

A number of training providers reinforce the benefits of eLearning by providing students access to a LMS. The LMS provides an environment where the student can access a series of additional learning activities designed to enhance their information retention. In addition, asynchronous access to instructor support and engagement with other learners can be provided to reinforce the overall learning process.

Interactive training

Students learn in many different ways and respond to different stimuli when they receive information, such as what they hear, see and interact with.

ILT and VILT accommodates all of these, whereas eLearning may or may not, depending upon how it has been constructed. Incorporating the use of audio, visual and physical involvement with content helps to enhance the overall effectiveness of training.

eLearning interactivity can be as simple as incorporating multiple choice questions or as complex as requiring students to participate in some form of simulation. Either way, interactivity is important to ensure knowledge and skills are imparted in a manner that improves training effectiveness.

Gamification

Interactivity, when applied within the context of work or based on some form of competitive activity, can help to motivate students to be more engaged with the training.

From a games perspective, participants need to be motivated, engaged and enjoy their involvement with it. When interactivity and gaming philosophy are combined with some form of behavioural change, this becomes known as gamification.

The technique of gamification as applied to learning can be extremely effective when designed into an eLearning offering. Gamification uses the techniques of game design to aid student engagement, motivation and problem solving.

When developing a gamification eLearning-based solution, consideration should be given to:

- Designing increasing levels of active engagement.
- Designing real-life activities and challenges to aid knowledge retention.
- Providing instant feedback to reinforce what has or has not been learned, to encourage student involvement and motivation.
- Using the technique of continued repetition to reinforce the learning; by using the principles of game play, topics can be reintroduced under slightly different challenges, and can include the use of leaderboards and badge awards.
- Applying the principles of repeated retrieval to reinforce memory retention through the use of variable testing; this is where the test questions and scenarios are slightly different every time the student undertakes them, but on the same topics.
- Building a reward mechanism to aid motivation and encourage active engagement; this could be point-based or provide access to a new tool that can assist the student in their everyday role.

In principle, gamification supports people's natural desire to learn, compete and achieve. For it to be successful, the six points above need to be factored in, along with a strong course design strategy that takes into account the need to educate, engage, challenge and maintain ongoing student interest.

ELECTRONIC PERFORMANCE SUPPORT SYSTEMS

Electronic performance support systems (EPSSs) can enhance students' learning experience by increasing their productivity and performance. They are typically used to support an employee in their working environment.

Irrespective of whether the initial training was ILT- or VILT-based, the content can be stored in an EPSS in an eLearning format for easier search-based retrieval. The EPSS can also hold extra content and reference material provided by training vendors to aid the learning process. Content can be further enhanced by employers adding additional material to reflect the way technology is being applied within their environment. The process of continuous learning can be supported by inclusion of ongoing synchronous and asynchronous subject matter support, further enhancing the value of the training provided.

From the training vendor perspective, an EPSS is an optional service to be provided, especially when target customer employees require knowledge, skills and competency development to achieve improved ongoing individual performance in their business environment. It can also be considered when full training is impractical or constrained. For example, technical staff employed in the financial sector are often limited in terms of the time they can spend away from the financial systems they are responsible for.

A typical EPSS comprises a user interface with log in to provide validation and registration, a support layer consisting of help, documentation, text retrieval, tutoring support and communications, and an application layer with company-specific support tools.

The key advantages for a student and their employer are:

- Information required to perform a technical task is readily at hand.
- Technical tasks can be achieved quicker from the ability to search on demand.
- Content can be added to reflect specific application-based needs.

The key advantages for a technical training provider are:

- Extends the training offering and maintains contact with the customer.
- Provides an extended revenue stream after initial ILT, VILT or eLearning user training has been completed.
- Increases customer loyalty.
- Provides an insight into the future training needs of the customer.

SOCIAL LEARNING

Social learning theory, which was developed by Bandura and Walters in 1963 and revised later in 1977 (Bandura and Walters, 1963), concluded that people learn through observing others' behaviour, attitudes and outcomes of those behaviours, both directly and through reciprocal interactions.

When this is compared with the 70:20:10 learning model created back in the 1980s (see Lombardo and Eichinger, 2000), which defines that 70 per cent of learning is gained through real-life job experiences, 20 per cent from interactions with other employees and 10 per cent through formal training, it is clear that social learning theory aligns well with the 20 per cent through its link to coaching, mentoring, collaborative learning and general interaction with others. With the continuous progress in the development of learning technologies in general, the informal side of the 70:20:10 model is well supported regarding social learning platforms.

There are many social learning platforms on the market, some specifically designed for learning and others evolving through indirect use. YouTube is a good example of indirect use, with videos and comments for how to do tasks on practical and theoretical levels being shared among many. Another example is LinkedIn, the employee and employer professional relationship website, which provides access to shared files on business and technical topics that are useful when undertaking specific roles or job tasks.

One example where a social network has been specifically targeted at direct learning is Udemy, which provides access to free tools and applications to support the collaborative sharing of information for teaching and learning.

Social learning and the technology surrounding it is evolving. When considering this type of environment, a training group should consider including the following:

- Live Chat functionality as a communications vehicle to support interaction between students and instructors.

- Streaming, where news, updates, announcements and broadcasts can be communicated to all on a regular or daily basis, to maintain awareness and active engagement.

- Focus groups to encourage discussion and engagement on specific and relevant topics, which also reinforces collaboration.

- Curation to support the aggregation and search of content from within the social learning site and broader website references.

- Task or team-based learning, providing the ability to plan and orchestrate tasks in a structured manner.

- Tracking to monitor and report on progress.

- Access to subject matter experts and knowledge bases to enable interaction with key information and resources.

- Social walk-in areas and blogs to encourage the sharing of information and the ability to support requests from others.

- Feedback and survey tools to obtain ongoing views on how to improve and maintain social learning interaction.

Introducing or providing social learning has a number of benefits. It extends the formal training by providing an environment where students can discuss how they applied it in relation to their actual job and the lessons they learned as a consequence. It also provides the opportunity to share experiences in a collaborative manner, reinforcing what they have learned, and assists in the better retention of information.

With employees moving away from job-specific roles to more task-based activities, social learning encourages and supports the sharing of best practices irrespective of location and time zones. Productivity improves when training and support is readily available when and where customers need it.

Social learning enables closer and more meaningful collaboration. From a vendor training perspective, opportunities abound to provide this as part of an extended and meaningful service, moving from formal skills-based training to value-adding, performance-based support.

LABS AND SIMULATIONS

'Practice makes perfect' is an old adage that holds true today. Theory on its own does not develop skills or help in the reinforcement of knowledge. Being able to undertake a task or exercise puts the theory into context.

Practical sessions should represent, on average, 60 per cent of the time spent in attendance on a technical course. These sessions can be lab- or simulation-based or a combination of the two.

Lab sessions

To be effective, a training lab environment should reflect a real system as near as possible. The labs themselves should complement the theory sessions and build on prior knowledge, leading to confidence in the student's ability to apply it in reality.

A major challenge for technical training departments is the ability to scale the lab environment, especially if it is required to support a broader network of authorised training partners. Computing systems require large investments in hardware, software, development and support costs. This is further compounded if student volumes and market need increases.

Cloud computing provides an alternative solution to on-premise labs, enabling a training group to be independent of the internal IT department. It provides a simple way to access resources over the internet in terms of servers, storage, lab management and student enrolments. It also provides the all-important scalability by allowing access to as many labs as required on a pay-as-you-go basis.

From a business management perspective, cloud provides a number of advantages: initial capital expenditure is minimised as there is no upfront investment in lab equipment; operational costs are aligned to student run rates as a consequence of the pay-as-you-go model; and training schedules and lab management is less restrictive, with the ability to access almost infinite technology resource.

Depending upon the vendor, technical training tends to be defined as non-core business and can often be restricted in terms of investment regarding its growth and requirement to run the latest technologies. Cloud computing minimises these investment costs and provides a vehicle for exploring alternative ways of delivering training, such as blended, flipped classroom and moving towards a subscription-based offering.

Simulations

Students sometimes find it difficult to grasp how technical systems operate and interact. Because of the tendency to teach in a linear fashion, they obtain a view of the independent elements and then struggle to understand how all the different parts are combined.

Simulation is a technique for practise and learning, and replaces the actual system environment with a replica, enabling students to immerse and interact with it in a more effective manner.

Simulation is a powerful tool as it encourages learning and experimentation in a safe environment. If designed in the right manner, simulated situations and scenarios can give students exposure to realistic and challenging problems, with any incorrect actions resulting in guidance and reinforcement of key learning points.

Simulation also supports eLearning whereby interactive animations and complex theories can be included in the course. By using web-based simulation and cloud technology, very complex visualisation simulations can be undertaken and supported. For less complex simulations using a combination of Java and Flash animations, local client-side devices can run the simulations directly, allowing students to study without connection to the internet.

When considering the inclusion of simulation, it is important to factor in what benefits it brings to facilitating and enhancing the learning process, such as:

- ability to support the development of problem-solving and decision-making skills;
- ability to provide feedback, guidance and reinforcement;
- repetitive practise;
- ability to support increasingly difficult levels to accommodate advanced skills development;
- encouragement for students to experiment without fear of damaging a live system.

MOOC: IS IT RIGHT FOR YOU?

The MOOC movement was initiated by a number of US-based universities in 2006. It essentially comprised a series of online courses with no restriction on attendance size where interested parties could sign up via the web in an open and unrestricted manner. As the reality of the financial implications became known, a number of MOOC providers reassessed and moved towards a more commercially based model.

MOOC content is primarily lecture-led material, recorded for access via streaming or video download and supported by interactive user forums to encourage interaction and collaboration between students and teaching staff.

It can be seen as a form of blended learning. One example is the so-called flipped classroom. This is where content is viewed and studied online, and practical work and interaction with the instructor provided later in the classroom. The advantage for the training provider is increased classroom productivity; for the learner, there is a potential increase in performance due to the ability to study and discuss with peers via forums and then consolidate learning with practical sessions in person with the tutor.

MOOCs do offer the potential to cover large numbers of students, in the order of tens of thousands. The downside is that completion rates are approximately 10 per cent. The MOOC movement can be viewed as a training disruptor by providing access to free training leading to certification. The main issue is converting the attendance into revenue.

A number of commercial MOOC providers (such as Coursera and Udacity) have been considering establishing models whereby the content is free and the practical, tutor support and certification is charged at a fee.

For a vendor-specific technical training group to adopt a MOOC model, it requires careful financial modelling and assessment of its market position to provide a blended solution with access to content for free and value-add services, such as remote lab access and social learning support, for a fee. Bundling training based on the MOOC model into its overall solution offering can provide an advantage for a company wanting to gain product-related market share. However, the main issue with this approach is how to balance the cost versus the benefits. Consideration should be given to:

- The additional costs for:
  - supporting a blended learning infrastructure (social learning platform, registration, remote labs);
  - developing content to accommodate the blended learning model;
  - developing and managing certification;
  - supporting 24×7 remote instructor access;
  - accommodating scalability.
- The benefits to the company regarding:
  - enabling the sale of solutions rather than products;
  - differentiating itself from the competition, with training being seen as an integral rather than an additional cost;
  - increasing overall product sales.

For technical training groups looking to adopt a MOOC model but not bundle it in with the product, then a blended subscription-based approach is worthy of consideration where students are:

- Invited to register interest in a particular course.
- Given free access to content fundamentals.
- Given access to additional support, for a graduated fee, including
  - access to remote instructor resources;
  - access to remote labs;
  - access to advanced topics;
  - certification.

While this is, in principle, a variation on the theme of blended solutions, it has the ability to broaden market interest and could be integrated within other commercial and non-commercial MOOC offerings.

PUBLIC, PRIVATE, ONSITE AND WORKSHOPS

Public, private, onsite and workshops are all forms of instructor-led content delivery. The nature of the delivery being offered depends upon market need, opportunity, cost of development and expected return on investment.

Focusing on market need, Table 11.1 summarises the differences and benefits of the four delivery types.

Table 11.1 Public, private, onsite and workshop summary

Delivery type	Description	Attributes	Pricing model	Key benefits
Public	Scheduled course open to the general public to enrol and attend at either the vendor training centre or the authorised training partner.	• Instructor-led. • Defined student prerequisites. • Defined training objectives. • Fixed duration. • Designated location. • Provision of course manual with access to equipment resources.	• Normally fixed price, based on course duration.	• Standardised course content and quality of delivery irrespective of location or audience attendance. • With high student fill rates, profitability is maximised.
Private	A course dedicated to a specific company where they are sending their own employees to either the vendor training centre or the authorised training partner. There are two types: 1. The course is standard as per the public offering.	• Instructor-led. • The standard offering is the same as the public offering. • For the tailored option, training objectives and content are modified or removed to align with the employer's objectives.	• The standard offering is typically priced at the public rate less an agreed discount, which can be in the range of 10–20%. • Customised training incurs costs associated with TNA, content development and training delivery. Typically, £1,000–1,200 or £600–800 delivery rate as per the above, respectively.	• For the standard offering, the employer has a dedicated class where students can discuss topics openly without fear of compromising company confidentiality. • For the tailored or customised option, content is relevant to the customer's unique needs.

(Continued)

181

Table 11.1 (Continued)

Delivery type	Description	Attributes	Pricing model	Key benefits
	2. The course has been tailored or customised to suit the specific needs of the customer.	• For the customised option, the training is developed and delivered based on the customer's actual needs.	• Tailored training incurs two costs: delivery as per the above, and content development at an agreed daily rate of £600 to £800, depending upon content developer rates in force at the time.	• For the standard offering, the employer has a dedicated class where students can discuss topics openly without fear of compromising company confidentiality.
Onsite	A course dedicated to a specific company where the employees are trained at their own site. There are two types: 1. The course is standard as per the public offering 2. The course has been tailored or customised to suit the specific needs of the customer.	• Instructor-led. • The standard offering is the same as the public offering. • For the tailored option, training objectives and content are modified or removed to align with the employer's objectives. • For the customised option, the training is developed and delivered based on the customer's actual needs.	• The standard offering is typically priced at the public rate less an agreed discount, which could be in the range of 10–20%. • Customised training incurs costs associated with TNA, content development and training delivery. Typically, £1,000–1,200 or £600–800 delivery rate as per the above, respectively. • Tailored training incurs two costs: delivery as above, and content development at an agreed daily rate of £600 to £800, depending upon content developer rates in force at the time.	• For the tailored or customised option, content is especially relevant to the customer's unique needs. • Employer saves on student travel and expenses.

(Continued)

Table 11.1 (Continued)

Delivery type	Description	Attributes	Pricing model	Key benefits

		• Training equipment provided as an optional extra.	• In addition, charges apply for the following:
			
			  ▪ training equipment hire and transportation where relevant;
			
			  ▪ instructor travel and expenses.
				• Course can be attended in line with employer timelines or technology deployment needs.

Workshops	Normally offered where either demand does not justify investment in a fully specified course, or the training is targeted at subject matter experts, such as support sales engineers who require a high-level overview.	• Instructor- or subject matter expert-led. • Theory and demonstration only. • Workshop duration typically 50% of a normal public class. • Handout materials only.	• Depends upon the target audience, where it can be free for partners, or chargeable for customers at a rate of approximately 50% of a daily public class.	• High-level training. • Quick and cheap to develop. • Good for supporting beta product releases and early adopter customers.

CAPITALISING ON LEARNING MODALITIES

The world of training has evolved, particularly in the use and application of technology. However, the various learning modalities, although supporting learning style preferences, have not always kept pace with commercial reality and the changes taking place regarding the way people are expected to work. Time away from the office, deployment timing not aligned with the training schedule, content not specific to job task requirements, budgetary restrictions and balancing learning style preferences of millennials to that of baby boomers have all become factors creating a complicated view of what the market needs.

Positioning and differentiating one modality over another certainly provides student choice, and training providers with a guide for what to offer or focus on. To some extent, it is still a prescriptive model for the student: look at the choices and select the one preferred. A better approach is to offer a mix and match option and let the customer define their own solution.

This is what blended training is all about. Its restriction is that many providers only offer it as a custom solution. If linked with a subscription model, there is the potential to capitalise on the learning modalities offered in a more controllable and commercial manner.

The blended learning model set out in Figure 11.1 progresses from formal to informal and in principle is based on the 70:20:10 model, allowing a training provider to capitalise on available learning modalities.

Figure 11.1 Blended learning (typical elements)

Commercial control and access can be provided via the subscription access interface, which provides registration, billing and control access level on a student by student basis.

ILT is for students who need formal training at a dedicated training centre; for those with limitations on travel, access can be via VILT. eLearning provides the ability to support on-demand training needs and access to learning bytes (small audio-visual recordings similar to the YouTube principle), which can be customised to specific employee requirements. EPSS can hold additional, advanced content and reference material provided by vendor-based subject matter experts, with mobile and tablet support to optimise learning on the job; and social media can assist with information sharing across broader learning communities.

This type of model enables training providers to repurpose and enhance content in line with the learning needs of their customers. It provides a legitimate way to engage in long-term business relationships and offers an insight into how and what customers actually require. As the customer grows in confidence, the informal social and EPSS elements provide meaningful feedback on market need and direction, which training vendors can assess regarding supplemental services.

NEXT GENERATION LEARNING

All generations carry a label; as a rough example, the Baby Boomers were born between 1946 and 1964; Generation X were born between 1965 and 1984; Millennials from 1985 to 2000; Generation Z were born after the Millennials, and those following them are Generation Alpha. But what does that mean for training?

Well, it tends to reflect the cultural, economic, social and technological progress made at the time. For the Baby Boomers, technology was in its infancy and employment was longer term and therefore the approach to training was more along the traditional instructor-led lines. For the Millennials, it was about accessing knowledge via laptops and mobile devices, and consuming training when they required it.

As technology changed, economic growth accelerated, social attitudes changed and the work ethic became more dominated by commercial success and improved productivity. Education has always and will continue to be seen as fundamental to a nation's success. However, the challenge is how to keep ahead of this rapid rate of change, a challenge that is requiring educationalists and training providers to look at alternative, more effective and relevant ways of providing the right training at the right time in the right manner for the right reason.

Over the years, training has been shifting from a total dependency on ILT to that of social consumption, where collaboration, just-in-time learning and coaching have become the norm. Technology improvements have played a major part in driving the change within the training industry, allowing it to satisfy traditional delivery vehicles and accelerate the need to support employee development in new and effective ways.

To continue with this rate of change, the next generation learning has to capitalise on current blended learning models, social models and the recent advancements in augmented reality, Big Data and machine learning.

Augmented reality provides massive potential, with portable head-up display units being able to show data, information, images and guidance while employees are taking on tasks in real time in the real world. Machine learning, which is an expansion of artificial intelligence, provides an environment where the learners of tomorrow will need to understand how to coexist and obtain guidance from machines in order to do their roles. In today's fast moving world there is data being generated everywhere. The abundance of data, if captured and interpreted in the right manner, can be used to observe end users' online behaviours, as is the case with Google and Amazon. With the onset of Big Data and the ability to execute algorithms designed to interpret user knowledge, actions and interests, models can be created to predict future training needs and preferred learning modalities.

Next generation learning models will have many inputs. Training vendors will need to understand what part their products play in the overall activity of the student as an employee, and how they will need to access and engage with the product. Standalone training will still have a part to play, but its real impact will be how it can be integrated into a broader working and intelligent learning environment.

BECOMING A DISRUPTIVE LEARNING LEADER!

In their own way, wikis, blogs, social networks, mobile devices, MOOCs, anytime and anywhere eLearning training, creative commons, instant messaging supporting synchronous and asynchronous instructor communication, YouTube and VILT have all been disruptive in the training world. For how long has depended on how quickly and efficiently they were brought to market.

Of course, not everyone needs to be disruptive. Some training providers, especially those operating in niche markets, may simply follow those trends if it is effective and efficient for them to do so in terms of productivity and profitability.

It is a different matter for others, when commercial advantage, customer reach and influence is important. This is where disruption can be broader than just providing content. It can be GTM- or RTM-based. Both provide many opportunities to be disruptive, for example:

- Targeting a competitor by offering a packaged training solution that includes both formal and informal training for a cheaper combined price point.
- Providing industry sector-specific training rather than generic training.
- Promoting training into new channels, such as YouTube, by pricing foundation level training for free, a common trick used by gaming providers, who only charge for advanced features.
- Offering subscriptions using 'freemium' pricing models,[1] similar to the YouTube approach.
- Providing training for free on successful completion of a certification examination, which increases interest at the expense of other competitors.

Disruption can simply be about being a driver for change and not about creating friction. Social learning was disruptive in terms of making people aware that training could be continued beyond the formal classroom and provide a platform for continuous and collaborative learning.

---

1   A business strategy where the basic product or service is free of charge and additional elements are charged at a premium rate; the term is a play on the words 'free' and 'premium'.

SUMMARY

Training offerings can be considered in terms of what is being taught, whereas a training modality is the way in which the training is delivered. This allows training organisations to provide a training offering on a particular product to be delivered, for example, as an ILT, VILT or eLearning course, each of which is classified as a learning modality option.

Learning modalities come in several forms. The most well-known one being ILT, where an instructor is physically present in the classroom presenting and explaining concepts by way of a projector, screen and whiteboard. The VILT modality does not require students to attend a physical classroom because they participate via phone or VoIP and view instructor content via a dedicated training portal. eLearning technology-based modalities allow students to learn where they want and when they want, and typically involves downloading subject matter via the internet and accessing dedicated training websites.

As everyone knows, theory does not develop skills, so being able to undertake a task or exercise puts the theory into context. By using lab sessions or simulators, students complement the theory sessions and build on prior knowledge, leading to confidence in their ability to apply it in reality.

Social learning platforms enable closer and more meaningful collaboration with others and take advantage of the 70:20:10 learning model, in particular the 20 per cent, with its linkage to coaching, mentoring and collaborative learning and its general interaction with others. Examples of this include YouTube and LinkedIn.

With technology constantly changing, being able to offer a mix and match of training modalities is a better option for a customer looking for a blended training solution. When linked with a subscription model, there is the potential to capitalise on all the learning modalities offered in a more controllable and commercial manner.

Staying abreast of next generation learning models is important if training vendors want to understand what part their products play in the overall activity of the student as an employee, and how they will access and engage in training in their working environment. Standalone training will have a part to play, but its real impact will be how it can be integrated into a broader working and intelligent learning environment.

12 CURRICULUM DEVELOPMENT AND MANAGEMENT
Designing and managing the training offering

When a new technology is being introduced, the product training management team will assess, discuss and specify high level aims to ensure customers can install, configure and deploy the technology successfully. These initial aims form the basis of the overall curriculum.

This chapter introduces the main activities and considerations regarding the development and management of a training curriculum, starting with how to define curriculum objectives, understanding what a minimum curriculum is and how to define audience types. This is followed by an introduction to the content development models, ranging from the traditional Analyse, Design, Develop, Implement, Evaluate (ADDIE) through to the latest rapid development method known as AGILE (Align, Get set, Iterate and implement, Leverage, Evaluate)[1].

Lifecycle management, covering content development and content shelf life, is then outlined and discussed, followed by an introduction to the costs associated in developing different modalities and how to defend investments made in curriculum development.

The final section of the chapter looks at authoring tools and the selection criteria that needs to be considered in choosing one of them.

DEFINING CURRICULUM OBJECTIVES

Developing a curriculum requires a number of stages that need thought, consideration and definition. These stages are recognisable by all who purchase training as they significantly affect the buying decision. They are the aims, goals and objectives of the training offering (see Bloom, 1956). Table 12.1 assists in clarifying the three terms.

Table 12.1 Aims, goals and objectives

	Description	Example
Aims	Aims are general statements outlining the direction and intent of the overall training activity.	Students will understand and become proficient in the use and application of the TRITON database.

(Continued)

---

1   ADDIE was created by the Center for Educational Technology at Florida State University for the US Army and adapted by all the US Armed Forces (Branson et al., 1975; Watson, 1981).

Table 12.1 (Continued)

	Description	Example
	Normally written using words such as: learn, understand, know and appreciate. They are not measurable, but do state an intent.	
Goals	Goals are more specific than aims, and define the purpose of the training in a more granulated manner. However, they do not provide guidance on how they will be achieved.	Students will be shown how to identify and use the TRITON database reporting tool. Students will be shown how to use entity relationship modelling to build simple relational databases.
Objectives	Learning objectives are predictive statements that describe specific outcomes the training session is intended to achieve.	Students using the reporting tool will be able to: link multiple tables together; create simple reports using multiple related tables.

These curriculum aims are then further assessed and grouped into meaningful course categories, after which they are granulated into specific goals and associated objectives. The level of course categorisation will depend upon technology complexity, audience need and estimated duration for the overall curriculum. Figure 12.1 shows a graphical representation of a curriculum and the process of converting aims to objectives.

The aims and goals for a course should be small in number and written in a concise manner, whereas objectives need to be detailed and written in a way to ensure that the outcome stated is achievable within the context of the training being developed. Table 12.2 provides guidance and advice on how to consider constructing and defining objectives.

Figure 12.1 Aims, goals and objectives

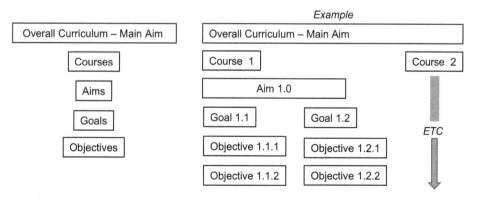

Table 12.2 Objectives writing recommendations

Objectives must be:	Objectives must use words that describe observable activities, such as:
Clear and concise	state, describe, explain
Learner centric	identify, analyse, compare
Specific to an outcome that can be observed or measured	demonstrate, plan, develop
Realistic and achievable	use, apply, configure

The example below shows an extract of a set of aims, goals and objectives for an end user database course:

Aim: To provide an introduction to the functionality and use of the database system for inputting and searching customer records.

Goals: Students will be able to:

- access and navigate the individual functions of the database;
- search, locate and query records;
- provide reports.

Objectives: Upon completion of the database system course, students will be able to:

- search, sort and filter records in a table;
- add records to a new table;
- create simple and effective queries;
- create meaningful reports from tables.

WHAT IS A MINIMUM CURRICULUM?

A curriculum is a framework used to design and provide training offerings that meet particular needs regarding what a target customer base requires to be proficient in the use and application of its product offering.

The framework adopted by most providers is based around competency and task analysis and typically structured as follows:

- assessment of needs;
- definition of the learning objectives;
- development of the content;
- content structure;

- delivery modality;
- evaluation method.

Depending upon the level of granulation required, the output could be a collection of independent modules, an individual course or a series of related courses.

From the product management perspective, they will assess the needs of the target audience in relation to what training is required to ensure the product or service being sold by the vendor is adequately catered for. The key factors are customer satisfaction, repeat business and brand protection from the vendor perspective.

From the training department's point of view, the output will be based on its ability to support the needs of the company and provide a level of service the customers require and are prepared to pay for.

The Pareto principle, or 80/20 rule, is the one that product management teams will normally subscribe to, in terms of what content to develop and which modality to provide in relation to the volume the opportunity supports. For example, a product may require basic, intermediate and advanced training content to be produced to support the full scope of competencies required in order to be 100 per cent proficient in the use and application of a product. In reality, 100 per cent of the target audience will attend basic training, whereas only 70 per cent will attend intermediate and around 10 per cent the advanced offerings. Therefore, a minimum curriculum from the product management perspective may involve the basic and intermediate levels being developed as ILT courses, and the advanced topics being covered by eLearning or possibly an on-demand workshop that a delivery team develops locally.

DEFINING AUDIENCE TYPES

A target audience comprises individuals and groups of people who have a specific need for training, which must be explored and defined by undertaking a TNA. Chapter 10 provides a more detailed description.

The output from a TNA, if undertaken correctly, assists in providing relevant information sufficient to categorise and define target audience types. For example, a vendor may be releasing a new technology to the market, requiring the training group to develop offerings to assist in supporting the adoption and application of the technology. A TNA is undertaken to assess the following across the target customer and partner profile:

- How will the technology be deployed in the target customer base and what are the required competencies?
  - Will it require installation, configuration, implementation?
  - Can the technology be used to design and develop process and business-based solutions?
- What roles are affected by the deployment of the technology?

- Are they customer or partner-based?
- Are conventional roles applicable, or does the technology require a functional and task-based approach?

- What type of training will customers require to be successful?
- How do customers access the training and what are their learning modality preferences?

Assessing and answering these questions provides guidance on how to categorise and define the audience type, sufficient to make decisions on what level and type of training should be offered. For example, Figure 12.2 shows a graphical representation of how a TNA output could be displayed, highlighting where competencies overlap for specific roles.

On the other hand, Figure 12.3 represents how competencies could be grouped by activity type, such as Basic Support and Troubleshooting, which, rather than having to offer courses by audience role type, can be offered by general task activity.

CONTENT DEVELOPMENT MODELS

Over the past 40 years or so, many innovative instructional methods have been considered and used to develop content for courses. These have included active learning,

Figure 12.2 Role mapping and competency overlays

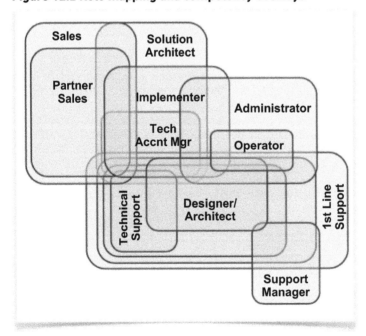

Figure 12.3 Audience type by general task activity

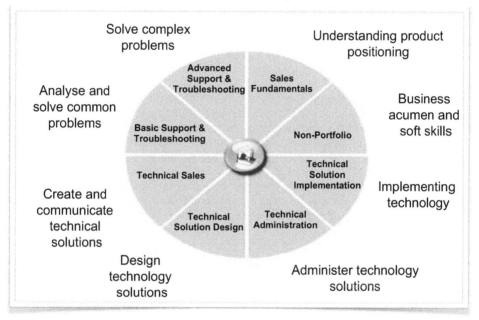

experiential learning, enquiry-based learning, discovery-based learning, problem-based learning and the ADDIE model of instructional design.

For many training developers, ADDIE has been the method most commonly adopted. It is a generic process based on the execution of five sequential phases: Analysis, Design, Development, Implementation, Evaluation. From an instructional design perspective, it is robust in terms of approach, but restricted in terms of the time and effort required to complete each phase and its inability to support iterative corrections until the evaluation phase.

As a consequence, and with the advent of eLearning, an enhanced ADDIE model was developed allowing rapid prototyping techniques to be introduced, which greatly improved the model's ability to support changes at each stage. For the development of ILT courses, it was a significant and valued improvement. However, for eLearning courses, with their high degree of complexity and need for increased modularisation, an alternative method for instructional design was required. This is where **rapid prototyping** in its true sense gained traction by way of enabling learners and subject matter experts to interact with prototypes and instructional designers in a continuous review and revision process. Rather than having to wait for a completed course, a prototype was produced first, with the design and development phases done simultaneously and evaluation provided throughout the process of iteration. Typically, the first iteration provides feedback on technical issues and effectiveness of instruction. This content is modified to reflect the feedback, before additional iterations are undertaken to achieve the final end result.

With the demands on eLearning training becoming more customer centric, the basic principles of rapid prototyping were further developed by Conrad Gottfredson and included in a new instructional design process known as **AGILE**.

The AGILE instructional design process encompasses five stages: Align, Get set, Iterate and implement, Leverage, Evaluate. It is an iterative process allowing collaboration and feedback throughout the eLearning design and development process.

The AGILE instructional design process is initiated by inviting instructional designers to meet with stakeholders, eLearning content creators and customers to define a plan for moving forward with the development of a course, followed by an agreement on its look, feel and required content, and then the content is divided into segments. The first segment is developed using rapid prototyping techniques and reviewed, followed by further iterations until the segment meets everyone's satisfaction, after which the next segment is developed following the same iterative process. A key benefit of the AGILE instructional design process is its ability to generate segments, or modules, quickly without having to wait for the course to be completed in its entirety.

ADDIE is, in essence, the science of instructional systems design (ISD) and the basis by which rapid prototyping and AGILE has evolved. eLearning development benefits significantly from the AGILE process, whereas ILT development can be improved via the adoption of the enhanced ADDIE and its alignment to rapid prototyping. As content becomes more modular and blended, AGILE instructional design will become the norm.

ADDIE summary

Figure 12.4 shows an ADDIE model.

- **Analysis phase**: in this phase, the instructional problem is clarified, the goals and objectives established, learning environment defined and target audience, prior knowledge and skills, identified.

Figure 12.4 ADDIE model

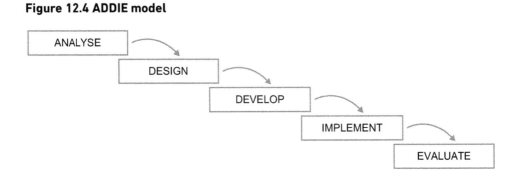

- **Design phase**: in this phase, learning objectives, course structure, contents, labs, tests and assessments, and modality choice is defined and decided.

- **Development phase**: is where content, labs and test questions are developed by content developers with support from SME's where applicable.

- **Implementation phase**: in this phase, documentation is produced to provide guidance to instructors on the method of delivery, course structure, pace and expected learning outcomes. The training administration team schedules courses and required resources.

- **Evaluation phase**: this phase provides for feedback to be provided by both instructors and students to the content development team to either enhance or correct the course.

Enhanced ADDIE summary

The enhanced ADDIE model was developed to accommodate the need for rapid prototyping techniques to be implemented to speed up the overall process and to prevent issues, problems and modifications only being addressed at the final evaluation stage.

With the enhanced ADDIE model, the process of evaluation is completed at the end of each dual-related phase (see Figure 12.5). That is, evaluations occur at the Analyse and Design phases, Design and Develop phases, Develop and Implement phases and Implement and Analyse phases. The evaluations are done by the target audiences, sponsors and designers, thus providing a more effective iterative process to be accomplished with issues, challenges and improvements being addressed before proceeding to the next phase.

Rapid prototyping summary

Rapid prototyping is used to develop eLearning content in a continual design and evaluation cycle. Training solutions can be prototyped at module and course level because the design and development phases are undertaken simultaneously. Continuous review and revision is undertaken by sponsors, developers and customers to ensure valid feedback is provided at all stages of the process.

The first stage is gathering information regarding the training requirements, after which a series of prototypes are created, initiating an early iteration loop that provides valuable review and feedback on technical issues, look and feel, and the effectiveness of the training. Following the review, further iterations and changes to the design are made. When an iteration proves to be effective and usable, the next cycle of development and implementation begins, again using the iterative process of evaluation.

With the ability to complete multiple tasks at the same time rather than sequentially, rapid prototyping results in the minimisation of time-consuming revisions and a decrease in the overall design and development time. Figure 12.6 represents a typical process.

Figure 12.5 Enhanced ADDIE model

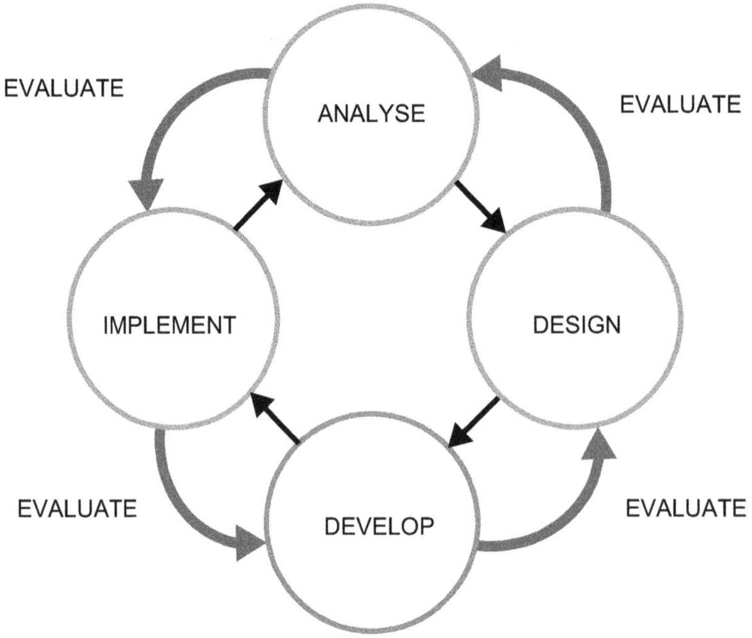

AGILE instructional design summary

The Agile software development process as defined by the Agile Manifesto and the AGILE instructional design developed by Conrad Gottfredson[2] (see Figure 12.7) are both based around the principle of rapid prototyping. While they are both grounded in similar principles, they are executed in a different manner.

AGILE is a process that supports collaboration, feedback and multiple iterations to assist in a faster design and development process than other conventional methods, such as ADDIE.

---

2   Computer Education Management Association (CEdMA) Europe Ltd would like to thank eLearning Guild and Conrad Gottfredson for allowing reference and use of the data from the article 'Agile Instructional Design: The Big Questions' referenced throughout this chapter (Neibert, 2013), and recognises that the content has been provided courtesy of eLearning Guild and Conrad Gottfredson.

Figure 12.6 Rapid prototyping model

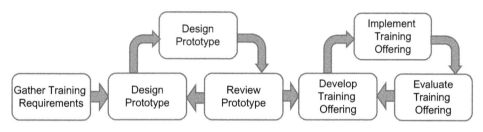

Figure 12.7 AGILE instructional design model

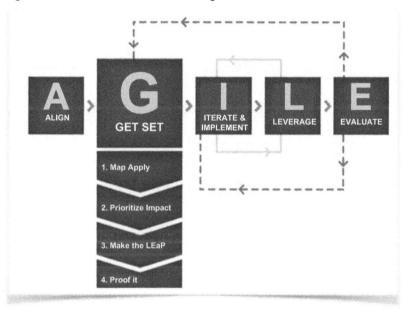

The first step in the AGILE process is Align. When developing a course, irrespective of its modality, it is important to factor in how customers will need to incorporate the product or service within their business environment. This also needs to be factored in to the second stage of Get Set.

The Get Set phase comprises the obtaining and understanding of who the audience is and how they are expected to undertake their roles in relation to the technology they are looking to get trained on. Once this information has been obtained, rapid task analysis and critical skills analysis can be undertaken and validated using an iterative process, followed by prioritisation of the recommendations. The output is then used to create a learning experience and performance (LEaP) plan.

A LEaP plan is only required when a blended solution is recommended, and outlines which modalities are required to deliver the learning experience. If the analysis indicates a single modality course, the LEaP plan is not required.

The final element of the Get Set stage is proofing, which is related to validating the use of any components from the task and critical skills analysis being included in an EPSS system.

The output from the Get Set stage, be it task and critical skills analysis with or without the inclusion of the LEaP recommendations, is fed into the third stage of Iterate and Implement and executed in the same manner as that covered in the rapid prototyping model section earlier in this chapter.

The fourth stage, Leverage, is based on being able to manipulate technology, people and research to deliver effective performance support. For many technology training providers, this may be considered as a value-add service and not developed as part of a standard offering.

The final stage, Evaluate, is similar to that undertaken in the ADDIE model and its output is used to provide feedback for corrective and maintenance purposes.

AGILE instructional design has its roots in the area of business and performance support, but as technology is increasingly impacting these areas, training providers should look to embrace its principles.

CONTENT DEVELOPMENT AND CONTENT LIFECYCLES

Content development and content lifecycles are explicitly linked. Training departments need to continually develop new offerings to replace those that are declining. Training courses have limited lifecycles, based on product market maturity, saturation levels and changes in the training demographics.

As discussed in Chapter 3, the training lifecycle comprises seven stages:

1. concept;
2. feasibility;
3. design and planning;
4. development;
5. verification;
6. release;
7. maintenance.

The content development lifecycle, whether it be ADDIE, rapid prototyping or AGILE based, maps to phases 1–6. The content lifecycle aligns to phases 6–7. Both can be represented as shown in Figure 12.8.

Figure 12.8 Content development and content lifecycles

Content Development Lifecycle				Content Lifecycle			
Content Request	Market and commercial assessment	Content design and development	Implementation and evaluation	Market introduction	Growth	Maturity	Decline

The content development lifecycle can be summarised as follows:

- **Content request**: requests for new training offerings are assessed and evaluated for business opportunity and viability.

- **Market and commercial assessment**: high-level training requirements are defined along with the RTM and the GTM offering. Once the RTM and the GTM offering is defined, ROI modelling is undertaken and balanced against the market opportunity. Following this, a business case is developed to allow stakeholders to review, approve or reject.

- **Content design and development**: in the design phase, learning objectives, assessment methods, lab exercises, content, lesson planning and media selection is undertaken and defined. In the development phase, content and labs are created for the required modality.

- **Implementation and evaluation**: procedures are established to enable the successful deployment of the course, including organisation and enablement of training department resources, followed by student evaluation and review.

The content lifecycle, also referred to as a product lifecycle, is a commercial model based on four distinct, but separate, stages, as shown in Figure 12.9, which can be summarised as follows:

- **Market introduction**: the training course is launched into the market and requires investment in marketing, advertising and distribution. Costs tend to be higher than income, with minimal or no profit being achieved during the ramp up stage of increasing sales volume.

- **Growth**: in this stage, the training course gains acceptance in the target market and sales and revenue increase. With the increase in sales, profits begin to be generated, although the breakeven point in terms of recovering development costs may be achieved in this phase or the next, depending upon volumes and the size of investment to be recovered (see Figure 12.10).

- **Maturity**: during this stage, training course growth reaches its peak and starts to decline. In some instances, it may be possible to extend the lifecycle by revising the content or adding additional modules. This stage is typically the longest and, while the ROI is maximised on an ILT course on a course by course basis, profitability may drop due to lower student numbers and classroom fill rates. For an eLearning offering, profitability will be lowered purely as a consequence of lower production volumes.

Figure 12.9 Content lifecycle

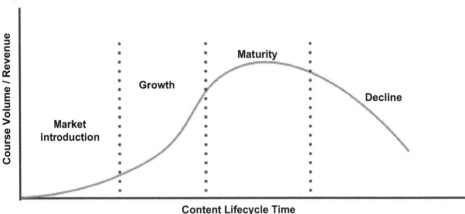

Content Lifecycle Time

- **Decline:** at this stage, the course is rapidly coming to the end of its lifecycle, with decisions being forced to cease promotion and production due to its inability to produce profit.

As a training offering moves through the content lifecycle stages, pricing, promotion, packaging and distribution should be constantly re-evaluated and changed in order to extend and maximise its revenue and profitability contribution (see Figure 12.10).

COSTING MODEL

The costing model in Table 12.3 represents a broad overview of the most common development methods currently being applied. In all organisations, there will be differences in approach and application. The duration and associated costs will depend upon skills, competencies and salaries available at the time.

Figure 12.10 Content lifecycle – commercial view

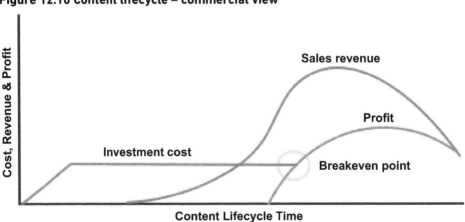

Content Lifecycle Time

The figures given in the table represent information obtained from various respondents and sources within the CEdMA community regarding how long it took to create different learning formats, including instructor-led training materials, content-based eLearning, interactive-based eLearning and simulation-based eLearning. It provides a benchmark to initially assess required development hours and salary costs before embarking on a more detailed model, depending upon required levels of complexity, time to market and investment availability. It shows the average time it takes to complete one hour of content by modality type. Time to market requirements, budgets, availability of skills and complexity of the subject matter defines whether the project will be simple and straightforward, or more complex in nature. The values shown in the middle column represent average times required to develop an hour of content, which enables an approximate assessment of costs to be done prior to more detailed analysis being undertaken.

Table 12.3 Development time per one hour of content by modality

	Simple	Average	Complex
Instructor-led training	25:1	48:1	90:1
(ILT and VILT)			
Content-based eLearning	50:1	80:1	125:1
Interactive-based eLearning	100:1	160:1	250:1
Simulation-based eLearning	200:1	500:1	700:1

Table 12.4 clarifies the differences between the three levels of eLearning content development. From a product management and training business owner perspective, the benefits and ROI need to be carefully considered when deciding on the more advanced modalities, as the time to breakeven is potentially very long.

Table 12.4 eLearning clarification

Level	Description
Content-based eLearning	Content pages comprising text, graphics, test questions and audio. Some training organisations use slide presentations (i.e. Microsoft PowerPoint).
Interactive-based eLearning	As above, including interactive exercises and the use of multimedia.
Simulation-based eLearning	Minimal use of slide-based presentations, and significant emphasis on interaction, simulation and gamification-based techniques.

DEFENDING THE CURRICULUM INVESTMENT

Training is essential for technology providers if they want partners to sell and support the product and customers to use and apply it for maximum commercial benefit. Partners who can't sell or support effect both current and future revenue generation. In a similar manner, customers who do not achieve the desired business results from their technology investment will transfer their allegiance elsewhere.

While this is a strong argument for why training is beneficial, it can still be difficult to justify the investment when it is one of many requests the corporate finance department receives at the beginning of a fiscal year, especially when training is not viewed as being core to the business.

There are two main ways to validate and defend an investment in curriculum development, which can be linked to monetary advantage from a direct and an indirect perspective: the first is being able to show a direct financial return and the second is value.

On the value side, if positioned correctly, the CEO can be won over if it is coupled with indirect corporate savings and direct training investment contributions. The key, as always, is showing tangible evidence.

Obtaining tangible evidence requires a training team to undertake direct customer surveys and interviews with management and employees from within the organisation and its channel partners. The evidence can then be constructed into a table highlighting how the value of a training investment provides indirect financial benefits (see Table 12.5).

From the example in Table 12.5, the value estimations can be used to highlight risk and model financial upside. This assists the finance department to assess indirect financial benefits in a more meaningful way and show the contribution training makes to overall company success. The value that training can provide at a broader company level is difficult to measure; therefore, the finance department will always require an absolute measurement committing the training department to an actual ROI.

Calculating the curriculum ROI is straightforward and based on the following costs:

- internal design and development days based on salary costs for the employees used;
- external design and development days based on contractor costs;
- content development tools (licences);
- copyrights where relevant (amortisation);
- equipment costs (depreciation);
- travel and expenses where relevant.

As a standalone cost, it does provide a metric by which finance can attribute a revenue stream and assess the return as a percentage of development costs. The reality is that it also requires production, sales, delivery, administration and consumable costs to be included as well to provide an absolute ROI.

Table 12.5 Justifying the value of a training investment

Value category	Description	Benefit	Estimated benefit
Repeat business	Customers who renew or purchase additional products.	Trained customers understand how to use and apply the technology for business benefit and, as a result, look favourably at other products in the company's portfolio.	Customers who take training are 4–6 times more likely to purchase additional products.
Customer loyalty	Maintaining a regular and positive relationship.	Customers who take training are significantly more satisfied with their product purchase.	Contributes to improved NPSs and customer satisfaction ratings, resulting in longer-term commercial relationships.
Brand	Distinguishes the company or product from its rivals in the eyes of the customer.	Training assists in improving image and helping to reinforce trust.	Minimises brand damage due to lack of support and training on how to maximise the customer investment. Failure to do so can be very expensive to address.
Total cost of service provision (TCOSP)	A financial estimate regarding the direct and indirect costs of providing product service support.	Customers who are trained to install, configure, deploy and use the technology are less likely to contact sales, sales engineers and the help desk for support.	40%+ improvement in productivity due to lower cost of customer service provision.
Value-add sales	The ability to add additional sales value to initial product sales activities.	Improved knowledge and skills results in sales teams being able to sell broader services and technology updates.	Sales teams demonstrate a 51%+ improvement in sales pipeline development.

(Continued)

Table 12.5 (Continued)

Value category	Description	Benefit	Estimated benefit
Reduced support calls	Reducing the level of technical support calls regarding new or existing products.	Customers who are trained are less likely to call the support desk for help on simple problems, resulting in fewer requests.	Customers are 25% less likely to contact the help desk resulting in productivity improvements and minimised headcount.
Channel effectiveness	Ability to influence and increase channel sales and support activities.	Trained channel partners are more successful at selling, implementing and supporting customers.	Every £1 spent on training a channel partner can generate £345 in product and service sales.
Solution expansion	Ability to provide and sell integrated solutions rather than just products.	Pre-sales engineers demonstrate improvements in closing deals.	Staff demonstrate 51%+ improvement in expanding and broadening deal size opportunities.
Service support	Improving technical support staff competency.	Technical support professionals demonstrate improvements regarding their ability to resolve complex calls.	Staff demonstrate a 51%+ improvement in solving problems, resulting in improved productivity.

The advantage of assessing the ROI at curriculum development level is that it allows alternative approaches to be considered, such as:

- off-shoring the development;
- outsourcing the development;
- considering alternative modalities with lower-cost development points.

Curriculum lifecycle and re-development investment

Curriculum lifecycle plays a part in justifying the investment. Longer lifecycles provide a greater opportunity to turn the investment into a substantial cash generator.

When economic conditions are changing, and companies look to reduce training costs, being able to demonstrate to customers what other benefits can be gained from investing in training, beyond the value and ROI that the training department provides, becomes more crucial. This can be achieved by highlighting the impact it would have on customers and channel partners if training investment was reduced.

Highlighting at this level allows senior executives to understand the impact not just to the customer and channel, but also to the organisation. This impact can be measured and observed in terms of the following:

- **Engagement**: particularly relevant for channel partners to ensure that they are developing knowledge and skills which maintain their relevance in the promotion of products and services on behalf of the company. Failure to provide engagement can affect revenue and profit streams.
- **Application and implementation**: are customers and channel partners demonstrating the required behaviours regarding the technology? Failure to develop or enhance training can contribute to loss of productivity or ability to capitalise on the technology, resulting in brand and trust issues and minimising revenue and profit in the longer term.
- **Business impact**: customers who are not receiving the appropriate training will not be implementing, deploying and applying the technology in a manner that provides them with an expected ROI. They may well have cause to initiate excessive demands for first-line technical support, which affects both short- and long-term financial results for the company.

Being able to evaluate value, ROI and impact provides the training department with a means to defend its position and force the company and finance department to take stock and recognise its curriculum investment needs, which, if ignored, can have far-reaching effects both within and outside the company.

AUTHORING TOOLS

There are various tools that support content development authoring in terms of text, video, audio, animations and other multimedia learning environments. With the advent of LMSs and learning content management systems (LCMSs), content from multiple sources can be more easily integrated and constructed to produce a rich eLearning experience.

Although ILT is not eLearning, the content produced in many instances could be downloadable for reference via the internet, and therefore can be categorised as a form of eLearning.

The IT industry moves at an increasingly fast pace, so customers need to be kept up to date on the latest industry standard practices, emerging trends and technologies. Online training provides an environment where the learners' needs can be more readily accommodated through integrating virtual classroom interaction, individual assessment, online video and multimedia in an effective and controllable manner.

When looking to select an authoring tool, of which there are many, there are a number of considerations that can aide with the decision process and cost of ownership:

- **Balance ease of use versus creativity**: creative freedom for an instructional designer can result in a sophisticated and extremely engaging learning experience. The downside is that it will be more challenging to use, more costly and extend the time to develop. Using tools that are easier to apply and that provide pre-made templates minimises creativity, but is more convenient to use and cheaper to purchase. The decision comes down to balancing flexibility versus convenience, cost and target market expectation.

- **Assessment of current and future outcomes**: authoring functionality and fitness for purpose in terms of look and feel, student engagement and level of interaction are key decision points that need to be considered when assessing which tools to purchase and the likelihood of applying them.

- **Target audience needs**: understanding the needs of the target audience in terms of learning preference and suitability is extremely important. Providing a learning experience that is highly interactive and comprehensive in nature needs to be considered against a more simplistic approach that provides the customer with an effective solution with minimised effort and complexity.

- **Audience interactivity requirements**: authoring tools provide access to interactive and immersive elements. Understanding the level and depth required to produce an effective and efficient learning solution will enable decisions to be made regarding the need to purchase libraries of interactive templates versus more basic and limited ones. Assessing the level of required interactivity is an important criterion in the decision process.

- **Ability to track student progress and performance**: tracking student progress enables the training provider to have greater and more meaningful engagement. With pressure constantly being applied to justifying the student ROI, the progress of a learner can be tracked and determined, which enables corrective action to be offered to the student and provides data on areas requiring content improvement. Some authoring tools only provide basic user data. However, the benefits of broader feedback may be a consideration worth thinking about.

- **eLearning authoring compatibility**: authoring tools need to be compatible with other eLearning software tools and platforms in regular use. Not all authoring tools create deliverables that can be accessed on all platforms and browsers. Some of the features and design elements in an authoring tool may not be available for the desired training offering required.

- **Ability to support quiz and assessment creation**: assessments, whether simple or comprehensive, require authoring tools to provide the required level of functionality, especially if there is a need to customise.

- **Linear versus non-linear development**: there are two general types of training courses that can be developed using eLearning authoring tools: linear and non-linear. Linear courses are the most basic type and involve the navigation for the course being fixed and flowing in one direction. Students advance sequentially from one section to the next. Non-linear courses include branched navigation, often with interactive scenarios where the learner is presented with multiple choices or options. Students move forward based on their specific choice or action in a branched manner. Assess which type of navigation is best for the target audience.

- **Shareable Content Object Reference Model (SCORM) and Tin Can compliance**: SCORM is a standard in eLearning that supports the tracking and tracing of student results in an LMS. A course is SCORM compliant when the authoring tool produces a publishable version of student results and activities that can run on an LMS. SCORM allows the LMS to track eLearning progress in terms of which questions were answered correctly or incorrectly, which pages have been viewed and for how long, scores per learning objective and overall progress.

  Tin Can is a standard that makes it possible to collect data about a wide range of experiences a person has both online and offline. It captures data in a consistent format about a student's activities from many technologies by capturing and sharing activities using the Tin Can standard defined vocabulary.

- **Language support**: with the need to develop courses in multiple languages, especially when operating in Europe and Asia Pacific, it is important to assess if the authoring tool supports the development of courses in languages other than English.

- **Simulation tool support**: authoring tools designed to produce multimedia simulations with sophisticated graphics and audio require high degrees of expertise and creativity, but do provide a rich learning experience whereby the student can practice in a pseudo real-world environment without creating real-world problems. For business-critical-related training, simulation is a good option, but does need to be balanced against ROI and the ability to charge premium pricing.

- **Mobile learning**: Adobe Flash was one of the most popular authoring tools for eLearning courses due to its high level of interactivity, immersive graphics and engaging animations. However, many mobile devices were unable to support it. As a consequence, HTML5, a mark-up language used for structuring and presenting content was released in support of mobile devices. Its main strength is its ability to support the running of an eLearning course on all screen sizes and creating smart meta-tags to optimise the eLearning course experience.

The authoring tool considerations described above provide a basis by which to start assessing currently available tools. Due to the complexity and cost of these tools, it is advisable to request a demonstration of the eLearning authoring tools and an example of an already developed course before making any decisions.

Popular authoring tools

This section provides a short summary of some of the most popular authoring tools available in the market.

Articulate 360
Articulate 360 includes every single authoring tool Articulate produces. It includes apps and services for creating a wide variety of multi-device eLearning content, and collaboration tools for working in a team environment.

ActivePresenter
ActivePresenter allows the creation of software demos, training videos and HTML5 content, which can run on any device. It has a number of features, including full high definition screen recording via its webcam recording tool, free form quizzes, annotation tools and embeddable webpages.

Adobe Captivate 9
Adobe Captivate 9 provides LMS authors with seamless movement from storyboarding course concepts to designing and creating responsive eLearning content. It produces device-aware content, which, once developed, will automatically be rearranged to fit any device.

iSpring Suite 8
iSpring Suite 8 creates courses using Microsoft PowerPoint and enhances the content with voice-overs, video narrations, interactive quizzes and surveys, including dialogue training scenarios and screen capture videos.

Kitaboo
Kitaboo is a HTML5-enabled, cloud-based eLearning content authoring solution. It uses drag-and-drop features to produce engaging content and assessments. Build-once, use multiple times is the focus of the tool.

Raptivity
Raptivity provides eLearning authors with the ability to integrate a range of 'interactions' into courses, including planning cards, timelines, bullet lists, flash cards, graphic choice tests and interactive videos.

SUMMARY

When a new technology product is announced, the training management team needs to define the aims, goals and objectives of the offerings and curriculum in support of the identified audience types, while ensuring that the overall lifecycle costs are understood and funding obtained and justified.

The amount of funding required depends upon a number of factors. The first is modality, where ILT requires on average 48 hours of development time per one hour of content, versus interactive eLearning, which requires about 160 hours, and simulation-based learning, which requires 500 hours. The second is the development method used for course creation, which can be based on the traditional ADDIE model or the rapid development AGILE model. A third factor, and one the training management team needs to justify with the financial and senior executive team, is an indirect one: the cost of and loss of product revenue if training is not provided – for partners to sell and support the product, and customers to use and apply for maximum commercial benefit.

With the IT industry moving at a fast pace, customers need to be up to date on the latest industry standard practices, trends and technologies. Traditional ILT does not easily support this, whereas eLearning training does in an effective and controllable manner through the use of virtual classroom interaction, individual assessments and multimedia. The development tools required to support this are eLearning-based authoring tools designed to support rapid development methods, such as rapid prototyping and AGILE.

ILT and eLearning are both viable modalities. Any future investment in training needs to consider fitness for purpose, development method and lifecycle duration before committing to the development of content.

13 CERTIFICATION
Requirements and approach to
designing exams

Certification is used to validate the skills and competencies of an individual's level of proficiency. Most IT companies implement certification programmes to validate their channel partners and ensure that customers have the skill required to be competent in their roles.

With certification gaining broad acceptance across most industries, there are three main objectives that an organisation looks to achieve when implementing certification:

1. Ensuring customers and channel partners have access to a network of trusted training expertise and experience, which provides product knowledge and the skills required to be competent in their roles.

2. Establishing a method of testing which proves that knowledge, skills, competency and performance improvements have been gained.

3. Ensuring customers, partners and their sponsors gain a return on their technology investment.

In this chapter, the process of certification development, legal defensibility, item writing and proctored versus unproctored examinations are discussed in detail.

CERTIFICATION AND TESTING TYPES

There are three classifications and four types of testing used throughout the technical training arena, all of which reference and apply the ISO 17024 standard.[1] The key bodies behind this standard are:

- the International Organization for Standardization (ISO);

- the American National Standards Institute (ANSI);

- the United Kingdom Accreditation Service (UKAS);

- the International Accreditation Forum (IAF).

---

1 ISO 17024 is an international standard (https://en.wikipedia.org/wiki/International_Organization_for_Standardization) specifying the criteria for the operation of a personnel certification body (https://en.wikipedia.org/wiki/Personnel_certification_body) and the requirements for the development and maintenance of the certification scheme.

The main issues ISO 17024 addresses can be summarised as:

- defining what is being examined (competencies);
- exploring required knowledge, skills and personal attributes;
- ensuring examinations are independent;
- checking that examinations provide a valid test of competence.

Testing types

Testing types are:

- **Written or practical:** based on levels of understanding rather than an ability to implement competently within the working environment, and referred to as a low-stakes examination.

- **Accreditation:** accreditation and certification are often used in the same sense, but actually are not the same. Accreditation is typically used to validate that channel partners can perform their role as authorised practitioners on behalf of a vendor. These examinations are classified as medium stakes.

- **Certification:** used to validate skills and competencies and is referred to as a high-stakes examination.

- **Performance-based:** performance-based testing is defined as high stakes where it tests skills, competencies and a candidate's abilities to perform an actual role with demonstrable and measurable results.

Classifications

Examinations are classified as low, medium or high stakes. The term is derived from gambling and based on what is at stake in terms of risk level. In a high-stakes assessment, students who may have inappropriately been certified could jeopardise the stakeholders they work for, whereas those who deserve to be certified, but are turned down, may have grounds for legal action against the certifying body.

High-stakes testing is used to assess competency where it would provide a mechanism for a student to demonstrate their ability to apply knowledge, skills and attributes associated with a technology they have studied. It is normal practice for a high-stakes examination to be sat after the student has attended a course and been given the opportunity to put it into practice.

Medium stakes tend to be more skills assessment-based and in some quarters used to award accreditation, particularly for channel partners rather than customers. Low stakes are used to measure levels of understanding and often inserted at the end of a training course.

The important point to consider regarding the three stakes categories is that what is low stakes for one individual may be high for another. Therefore, legal defensibility can apply to all three levels.

ADVANTAGES AND DISADVANTAGES OF CERTIFICATION

There are plus and minus points to certification, depending upon how the value, cost and time of both developing and studying for the examinations are viewed. The two sections below provide a summary of some of the advantages and disadvantages.

Advantages

- Certification improves industry recognition.
- Certification can improve job opportunities and employee compensation.
- Certification ensures that channel partners attain recognised levels of competency, which in turn provides confidence for customers.
- Certification can be used to add value to the training content offering.

Disadvantages

- Certification is costly in terms of development time and money.
- It can be expensive for students to sit the examination.
- Not all students will undertake certification, resulting in a low return on investment.
- Every vendor has its own certification programme, which is not always aligned to a specific industry need.
- Certification can lead to loss of employees who expect increases in their compensation packages aligned with higher skill levels.
- Certification amendments and updates are costly in relation to staying abreast of the latest product releases.

THE CERTIFICATION DEVELOPMENT LIFECYCLE

To ensure compliance with ISO 17024, a robust development process must be established and implemented. Table 13.1 reflects a typical process to be followed to ensure the development of a valid certification examination to assess knowledge, skills and competencies within the context of a legally defensible framework.

DEFENSIBILITY

From an industry perspective, defensibility must ensure the ability of a testing entity (certification team within a training group) to withstand legal challenges. Challenges can come from those undertaking certification regarding the validity of the test development process. Therefore legal defensibility has to be able to prove that the process and programme of test development is valid in a court of law. It is therefore more to do with the validity of the certification examination process and not someone's, or their company's, ability to do the job.

Table 13.1 Certification development process

Process stage	Description
Job task analysis	• To ensure the examination content to be developed is valid, the knowledge, skills and competencies required to be a minimally certified professional are assessed and documented by a group of subject matter experts.
	• The knowledge, skills and competencies are typically grouped in terms of tasks, which are then validated by running a survey to gather feedback on their importance, relevance and criticality from a group of actual practitioners.
Blueprint development	• The output from the job task analysis survey is used to develop the blueprint for the examination. The tasks are assessed regarding their importance, criticality and relevance, which is then converted into an agreed number of items to be developed per task area.
	• The blueprint guides the item development and examination processes to ensure they satisfy the relative importance of the required knowledge and skills to perform the role, within the criteria of a minimally certified professional.
Item development and validation	• Item development is undertaken by subject matter experts, who need to be trained in writing, reviewing and editing questions.
	• Each item is classified by a content category, assigned a cognitive level and validated according to its relevancy to the minimally certified professional requirements.
Examination assembly	• Items from each content category, as defined in the blueprint, are reviewed and validated by subject matter experts.
	• The questions that are validated are formulated into an initial version of the examination.
Beta examination and psychometric analysis	• The initial version of the examination is released as a beta, with selected candidates invited to participate under test conditions. The questions and results are checked for technical accuracy and psychometric integrity, which can lead to further refinements of the overall examination, and assists in strengthening its accuracy and validity.
Cut score	• Based on the output from the psychometric analysis, a pass/fail mark will be agreed, which is based on a minimum competence level that is legally defensible in terms of being fair, reliable and valid.

(Continued)

Table 13.1 (Continued)

Process stage	Description
Examination administration	• A secure examination environment must be established, as well as the ability to report and document candidate results.
	• Some organisations undertake this themselves and others contract it to specialist companies, which minimises overheads associated with infrastructure, administration and security.
Examination review	• In line with the training content development process, the examination needs to be reviewed for relevancy and validity in the market as the product and job requirements change.

In relation to recorded legal cases, there are four main areas where tests are typically legally challenged:

1. **Reliability:** regarding how consistently the test measures a construct (a construct is the latent variable that is being assessed, such as mathematical ability or mechanical aptitude).

2. **Validity:** regarding whether the test is measuring what it is supposed to measure.

3. **Fairness:** regarding the test measuring the construct(s) it was designed to measure, with no unfair advantage for any given demographic group or subpopulation.

4. **Cut scores:** which are the 'pass/fail' benchmarks used to determine whether participants have demonstrated an appropriate level of knowledge or skill on a test. A test may be legally challenged if it is believed that these have been unfairly set.

The training certification group must assemble and maintain a portfolio of legal defensibility evidence to promote best practices, and document the processes and procedures that need to be followed in a consistent manner.

As certification rigour is labour and cost intensive, some training groups may find themselves fiscally challenged. In this instance, if it is important to maintain certification then any reduction in rigour needs to be documented and not have significant impact on the validity, reliability and fairness of the exam.

Regarding test question development, to have a sound basis for legal defensibility, the ISO 17024 standard needs to be applied in the following areas:

• **Reliability**: how consistently the assessment measures a student response.

• **Validity**: whether the test measures what it is supposed to measure.

• **Fairness (and bias)**: whether the test performs fairly for different groups or demographics.

- **Cut scores**: benchmarks used to determine whether students have demonstrated an appropriate level of knowledge or skill on a test. These scores are very common in high- and medium-stakes assessments and used to define pass and fail levels. There are many well-established processes and methods existing for setting pass/fail scores. One of the more popular ones, which is based on a test and question-centred approach, is the modified Angoff method (Thorndike et al., 1971), which requires:
    - SMEs to be briefed on the Angoff method and take the test with performance levels in mind.
    - SMEs to provide estimates for each question of the proportion of borderline or 'minimally acceptable' participants that they would expect to get the question correct.
    - Several rounds of assessment balanced with empirical data from a beta exam against the SME estimates.

ITEM WRITING DEVELOPMENT

As discussed, when developing questions for a low-, medium- or high-stakes examination, an important consideration is that of legal defensibility – specifically, how consistently the questions measure a student's response and measure what they are supposed to.

To achieve this, it is important to understand the structure and approach that should be followed. The first task is to access the course objectives, which allows extraction of the key concepts and learning points by topic area. From this, meaningful and valid test questions can be developed that focus on Bloom's taxonomy of higher levels of cognition (Bloom, 1956).

Bloom's taxonomy is based around three hierarchical models, which classify learning objectives into levels of complexity and specificity. They are cognitive, affective and sensory. The cognitive is where most focus has been applied in the technical training arena.

On the cognitive level, test questions are structured to measure a learner's ability to:

- remember and recall facts, terms and basic concepts from the course studied;
- apply and use the acquired knowledge to solve problems;
- analyse, examine and divide information into parts and decide how they relate to one another;
- synthesise and compile information into different solutions;
- evaluate, present and defend findings through the application of valid judgements based on access to known information.

Evaluation is the highest level, which requires critical thinking to be applied and is useful when developing performance-based tests. The other levels are more commonly used in the low-, medium- and high-stakes examination questions.

To write multiple choice items for a question requires a structure where a problem statement known as a stem is constructed. The stem needs to be written based on a definite problem that applies focus on specific learning outcomes. This is followed by the development of a list of alternative answers or solutions. One of the alternatives is correct and the others incorrect, known as distractors.

Multiple choice test items have several advantages. One of these is versatility, where the test item can assess different levels of learning outcome from basic recall and analysis, through to evaluation. The other is to do with legal defensibility.

Legal defensibility requires a test to be reliable and valid. Multiple choice items are not prone to true or false question testing and can be written to test specific aspects of a learning outcome. This significantly enhances test reliability, and validity is improved with the use of multiple choice items mainly because they cover the broader aspects of a course rather than an essay-type examination. However, to ensure multiple choice items are written well, the following approach is recommended:

- The stem needs to:
  - define a problem statement that relates to a learning outcome;
  - focus on known and relevant content covered in the course, otherwise it can be challenged as unreliable and invalid;
  - be a question allowing students to answer by applying the knowledge learned, rather than a partial statement requiring completion from one of the alternative answers.
- When writing alternative answers for the stem, there are several guidelines that should be followed:
  - Consider four options per stem. Most examinations standardise on this number, as the benefit of writing additional options does not achieve any extra level of validity or defensibility.
  - Distractor answers should be concise, comparable, plausible and, where possible, relate to common errors or misconceptions.
  - The answers should be grammatically consistent with the stem and of similar length, structure and concept.

Items in general should focus on the application of knowledge and problem solving, rather than on the recall of knowledge or facts. When developing items, a team of SMEs comprising content developers, instructors, technical support and technology design staff should be enlisted to review and assess all items against agreed criteria, including setting the pass or cut score. This enables items to be checked for validity, fairness and reliability to ensure legal defensibility criteria are satisfied.

Example stem and alternative answers:

1. Which company runs the Firefox web browser?
   a. Mozilla [correct answer]
   b. Google
   c. Yahoo
   d. Safari
2. Files included in messages are often referred to as:
   a. client-side scripts
   b. cookies
   c. attachments [correct answer]
   d. server-side scripts

Table 13.2 is an example of a sample stem with alternative answers. The purpose of the stem is to define a problem statement that relates to a learning outcome. The alternative answers comprise a correct answer and two or more incorrect answers, known as distractors, which should be plausible and relate to common misconceptions.

Table 13.2 Sample stem and alternative answers

	Poor example	Good example
Stem	California:	What is the main reason so many people moved to California in 1849?
Distractor answers	• Contains the tallest mountain in the USA • Has an eagle on its state flag • Is the second largest state in terms of area	• California land was fertile, plentiful and inexpensive • The east was preparing for civil war • It is the second largest state in terms of area
Correct answer	Was the location of the Gold Rush in 1849	Gold was discovered in central California

The modified Angoff method is a popular approach used to determine passing scores for an examination. It is based on the judgement of a panel of subject matter experts, as mentioned above, and their view on what questions a minimally qualified practitioner should be able to answer. The SMEs then consider how many practitioners in a typical cross section of 100 would be likely to answer the questions correctly. This is followed by using standard deviation calculations on a question by question basis to determine a pass score, and further ratified by running a beta examination for a selected audience of 100 participants, with the results being used to normalise the passing score before being released.

PROCTORED VERSUS UNPROCTORED EXAMINATIONS

Over the past few years there has been a transition from paper-based examinations towards internet-based ones, the majority requiring candidates to be tested in a controlled physical environment monitored by a proctor. This method ensures that every candidate takes the exam in a secure and quiet environment where the use of mobile phones, private notes, reference books or other means of accessing answers is not allowed. This helps to minimise cheating.

In the real world, employees reference their course notes and search the internet for answers to questions to assist them in the execution of their role. If this was applied to the test environment, there would be no requirement for a proctor. The main disadvantage of unproctored examinations is that there is no way of validating who the actual candidate is.

As proctored examinations are expensive to develop, run and support, consideration could be given to running a mix of the two. If the complexity of the technology being tested is high, then a proctored high-stakes exam could be developed. On the other hand, if expected volumes are low and the examination geared to testing knowledge is defined as low stakes, then the approach could be to go unproctored.

When looking to balance the training budget, decisions can be made regarding the level of importance placed on the decision to go low, medium or high stakes, which is another way of saying: develop the examination as proctored or unproctored based on its fitness for purpose.

EXAMINATION-RELATED REVENUE

Revenue from examinations, when compared to content and delivery provision, will normally be low. Most technical certification-based examinations are in the range of £100–400, depending on the level of complexity. For example, many Microsoft examinations are £100 each, whereas an Agile examination with higher complexity will be £450.

The student course to certification conversion rate will be less than 100 per cent, and will depend on vendor influence, promotional activities and relevancy to industry and the employer base. Certification revenue can be improved by the promotion of vouchers, especially if discounted, or by bundling certification in with the purchase of the course.

When vendors provide partner accreditation, conversion rates can be high because it is a requirement to gain entry into the partner programme and be eligible for discounts. Some vendors charge the same as they do for customers, others discount and some provide for free. For vendors who use third parties to provide customer and partner access to their examinations, the actual net revenue is lowered, typically by 40 to 60 per cent.

FUTURE TRENDS (BADGING, PERFORMANCE)

Many in the world of education understand the importance of the term 'lifelong learning', but what does it mean in the context of technical training?

Well, it is the process of engaging what we understand, apply and utilise with experience over time. Primarily, it is using what we have learned in the past and expanding our overall knowledge, skills and understanding to perform or interpret more effectively what is happening around us. Sometimes this is a subconscious activity, as opposed to a programmed or developmental activity.

With the shift from manufacturing to high technology, having the right attitudes, approach and skills for learning are becoming increasingly vital for survival and important for business and economic success. The technical training industry needs to understand and adapt the way it provides access to training, based on providing customers and their employees with skills leading to improved individual and corporate performance.

This is where lifelong learning and testing provision need to be aligned. Attendance at a single course and passing the examination is a small part in the overall process. What is required is a broader approach whereby technical training becomes an integral part of the overall employee developmental experience.

Employee development covers training, career development, performance management, coaching, mentoring, succession planning and assessment. For it to be successful, assessment needs to be applied and used in a manner that is progressive and reflects all aspects of employee development. This is where badges and performance assessment can be combined to measure the overall influence and growth of an employee's developmental progress.

As technology plays a major part in the success of most companies, it is incumbent upon training providers to understand how it supports the broader success of both employees and employers. From this standpoint, training providers can align their training offering in a more effective and meaningful way.

For example, for each stage of the employee's development plan, whether knowledge or skills acquisition, a badge can be issued (similar in principle to what a Boy Scout or Girl Guide would receive) to recognise and reward progress. Further badges could be awarded when specific tasks or competencies were proven. This then becomes evidence of an employee's lifelong learning journey and value to a company.

Badging can also be used to recognise specific areas of employee performance. For example, employees could demonstrate their skills by referencing projects they have completed, where actual tangible proof can be provided to verify that all requirements were met. This validation is undertaken by evaluators who would compare the project goals to the result achieved.

For technical training providers, designing a badging programme is worthy of consideration. Many employers look to hire staff who are task-based and therefore only need to be trained on the elements of the task that the technology supports. To a certain extent, this is accelerating the need for on-demand training, which requires examinations to reflect that. Badging provides a means to support this, which can be further enhanced with performance-based testing.

Mozilla's Open Badges project, which started in 2012 from funding provided by the MacArthur Foundation, has developed an infrastructure that provides companies with the ability to use and share resources globally by way of an open standard. To date, more than 1,000 organisations have issued several million badges. The Open Badge Infrastructure[2] is defined by a technical standard and a Badge Backpack, which is a service providing badge earners a way to collect and manage their awards. The standard itself defines the metadata that must be included in a badge for it to be considered OBI-compliant. This includes how it was earned, where it was earned, who earned it and when it expires. This is not too dissimilar from the certification process.

On the performance assessment side, employees are required to demonstrate or provide evidence they can undertake the task proficiently. This is more effective than traditional multi-choice certification examinations as it reflects the candidate's ability to actually do the task by way of providing proven evidence. There are three main categories of performance assessment:

1. **Project-based:** employees are required to show actual tangible proof regarding completion of a project to an expected and agreed level. Evaluators discuss and question how the project was completed and what lessons were learned.

2. **Portfolios:** especially useful for employees involved in programme management where they show evidence of how an overall programme was constructed and executed.

3. **Demonstration:** employees are required to demonstrate mastery of particular tasks. Evaluators make judgements by way of observation and questions.

As with certification examinations, badges and performance-based testing require robust, fair, reliable and valid processes to be in place to ensure that legal defensibility is maintained when the stakes for the employee are important.

SUMMARY

Training organisations that implement certification should reference and apply the ISO 17024 standard, which is controlled by four internationally recognised bodies. From a certification perspective, it is used to validate skills and competencies, referred to as high-stakes examinations, which must adhere to the ISO 17024 standard.

In order for the certification examination to be compliant with ISO 17024, a robust certification development lifecycle must be established and implemented within the context of a legally defensible framework.

---

2 The Open Badges Infrastructure (OBI) Group focuses on developing and maintaining the technical infrastructure that supports open badge systems.

Legal defensibility is a key component of certification, which must ensure that the assessment results and the testing programme are defensible in a court of law. Therefore, a training certification group must maintain a portfolio of legal defensibility evidence to promote best practices and document the processes and procedures that need to be followed in a consistent manner.

Question development also comes under legal defensibility requirements, specifically regarding how consistently the questions measure a student's response and measure what they are supposed to measure, which is where the application of Bloom's taxonomy comes into play.

The final stage of certification development is validation of the passing scores, which is determined by the application of the modified Angoff method.

Employee development tends to be progressive and reflect not just skills proficiency but also performance contribution. Many companies are looking for training providers to align their training offerings in a more effective and meaningful way. In support of this there is a move towards the adoption of badges.

As a meaningful extension to certification, the Open Badge Infrastructure (OBI), which is defined by a technical standard, provides a process by which training providers can establish project-based activities where they can award badges to students who provide demonstrable evidence of proficiency.

14 GOVERNANCE AND METRICS MANAGEMENT
Establishing control with confidence

This chapter outlines the importance of being able to track, monitor and assess the success or challenges facing a training group, including the importance of establishing quantifiable metrics and governance processes. These metrics need to reflect how the business is operating in the achievement of its long- and short-term objectives, sufficient to provide insight in order to establish relevant controls that protect and steer the business.

GOVERNANCE AND TRAINING

Irrespective of organisation size or structure, it is good practice to implement a governance process. In its broadest sense, it is about how a company or group is run, and covers the processes, systems and controls that are used to protect and develop the training assets.

The World Bank describes governance as 'promoting fairness, transparency and accountability' (World Bank, 2017) and the Organisation for Economic Co-operation and Development (OECD) describes it as 'a system by which business organisations are directed and controlled' (OECD, 2017).

At the training group level, the focus is on demonstrating how well-run and governed it is, in order to show that shareholder value is being maximised. The shareholder in this instance can be senior executives from within professional services, other sponsors from within the broader organisation, such as the product development group, or, in smaller organisations, the board of directors.

To establish a training group governance policy, the management team needs to be clear on the current state of the business, where it intends to go and what is required to get there. In many instances, the work done in developing the strategy and business execution plan assists in establishing the foundation for achieving this. In essence, it covers the following key points:

- Definition of the training group's mission and purpose.
- Establishment of a governance culture.
- How the training group will hold itself to account.
- Implementation of an effective compliance programme.

Adopting and implementing a governance programme helps a training group, and specifically the management team, to achieve the following:

- Develop a vision that can be reviewed and assessed against internal and external factors.
- Improve overall performance.
- Assess the overall view of the business, separate from the operational view.
- Ensure that robust accountability and visibility of high-level operational activities have been established.
- Assist in managing risk.
- Find the right balance between achieving short-term gains and developing long-term objectives.

Governance report

A typical training group governance report is targeted at senior executives with stakeholder interest in the success and overall sponsorship of the group. This also includes an understanding of the value it contributes to the company overall. The report can be structured as:

1. Reference section
   a. Strategy document containing the strategic intent, marketplace knowledge, innovation focus and business design. This is reviewed annually and referenced as required.
   b. Organisational structure.
2. Performance and progress review section

Improving performance drives better results, which in turn puts more value into the training business. This is measured through increases in overall value in the financial and non-financial (such as customer satisfaction, student coverage, partner enablement) areas. The information and data provided enables senior executives to make business decisions based on clear and proven facts regarding current progress of the business. Standard training business-based KPIs form the basis of the review:

   a. Financial performance regarding training bookings, delivered revenue, sales pipeline and conversion rates, cost of sales, profit.
   b. Customer satisfaction.
   c. Classroom fill rates, instructor utilisation.
   d. Product coverage from the training offering perspective.
   e. Employee staffing levels.
   f. Marketing activities.
   g. Content development road maps.

    h. Legal and regulatory issues.

    i.   Industry trends.

Gaining senior executive feedback on KPIs provides an environment in which to identify opportunities and address issues in a positive and effective manner.

3. Risk management section

    a. Infrastructure and systems issues.

    b. Legal and compliance issues.

    c. Performance issues.

Governance plays a key part in assisting in the development of the business in a controlled and thoughtful manner. Being able to challenge and validate the results provides an insight into how the training group is progressing against the competition, dealing with industry trends and finding new ways of increasing overall training productivity.

FINANCIAL METRICS

Training managers or executives need to be able to measure financial metrics to justify and validate overall business effectiveness. The nature of the training service provided will define what is required to be monitored and reported to stakeholders. The key metrics are normally sales, revenue, costs and profit. To calculate profit, the following accounting principles apply:

- training revenues – operating (variable) expenses = gross profit (operating) margin
- gross profit margin – overhead (fixed expenses) = operating income
- operating income +/– other income or expense (non-operating) = net profit (before tax)

Operating variable expenses are often referred to as cost of goods sold (COGS) or cost of sales (COS) and defined as the expenses that rise or fall based on sales volume. The expenditures commonly included are:

- Sales commission.
- Specific costs related to the direct delivery of training:
  - payments to freelance instructors;
  - cost of training materials;
  - transportation costs;
  - rental costs for equipment.

In deciding whether an expense should be included in the COGS, if the expense occurs *only* when training is sold, then it should be included.

Operating income is calculated by subtracting the fixed costs of running the training business from the gross profit margin and typically includes:

- Salaries, often divided into:
  - delivery (instructors);
  - content development;
  - operational and administration;
  - sales;
  - marketing;
  - product management.
- Administration costs.
- Depreciation costs on capital equipment.
- Telecommunication costs.
- Facilities cost.

Net profit before taxation in some organisations is the same as operating income, depending upon whether other income or costs outside the normal mode of operation need to be factored in, for example interest based on income from monies deposited in a bank.

By monitoring the profit and loss account aligned with sales income, a training manager can obtain a view on how healthy the business is, and whether changes need to be implemented to maintain liquidity. For example:

- Is the profit growing in proportion to the size of the business and the training offering mix?
- Is the profit increasing or declining in terms of sales activity?
- Is the training business as profitable as other vendors in the technology training sector?

Other factors, such as:

- level of sales by training offering;
- sales to delivered revenue delay;
- value of training assets and their return on investment;
- number of employees;

all contribute to understanding the impact on overall profitability, allowing further modelling to be undertaken to aid in the decision-making process.

BUSINESS METRICS

Customer satisfaction and retention tends to be high when training organisations deliver on their commitments and provide expected quality. To be able to achieve this, training managers require access to informed and meaningful information about their business, which can only be achieved by using their knowledge to develop and implement effective metrics.

Metrics provide insights into how a training business can improve and where the focus of attention should be applied. The number of metrics can be many and varied, from mandatory and financial through to operational. The important lesson is that of simplicity. If there are too many and they are complex in nature, they will be ineffective.

Metrics tend to be more effective when aligned with the strategic direction and business design requirements of the training group. These typically include finance, marketing, sales, training delivery, content development, customer satisfaction and financial needs. The metrics need to monitor and support key critical task activities. This assists in allowing organisations to understand their business direction and whether goals have been achieved or issues or opportunities missed. Table 14.1 lists the steps that should be followed to develop effective training-related business metrics.

Table 14.1 Developing business metrics

Key steps	Description
Define the metric	Metrics should be specific, measurable, achievable, relevant and time-based, often referred to as the SMART model. Any metric that is set should be achievable and carefully thought through, otherwise it will be self-defeating and result in negative actions and lack of belief in what the training group is trying to achieve.
Obtain employee and executive buy-in	Metrics should be positioned and explained carefully to employees with linkage to how the training group will utilise them to achieve overall success. If possible, they should be aligned to a reward or bonus payment to aid and drive engagement.
	As with all metrics, obtaining buy-in and approval from senior managers will help to lead and drive change from the top.
Understand the data required to manage the business and how to collect it	List the metrics required to support and control the business and discard those that do not add discernible value. Ensure the metrics recorded are reliable and collected in a consistent manner.
	Ensure relevant tools and processes are in place to collect the data accurately. Note that manipulating results does not achieve positive progression; understanding the true position, be it positive or negative, aids decision making and reflects the true position of the organisation.

(Continued)

Table 14.1 (Continued)

Key steps	Description
Interpret the results and distribute accordingly	Analyse the results of the metrics and initiate actions. Where applicable, share the results with others; don't operate in isolation, as often they may be affected by additional factors outside training management control.
	There can be a tendency to set too many metrics, so keep them manageable.
Review the metrics and revise as required	The aim of setting metrics is to improve the business results of the training department. As time progresses, some metrics will be exceeded, and others may not have been achieved. Either way, it is important to revisit and revise them to ensure corrective or continuous progress can be made.
	Make sure the metrics still measure what they intended to measure. There is absolutely no point in retaining metrics that are out of date!

To ensure all training staff fully understand the importance and relevance of business metrics, it is important to actively engage everyone and communicate the results and interpretations to them on an ongoing basis.

TRAINING-SPECIFIC METRICS

Table 14.2 summarises the main metrics by training function that need to be considered when running a commercially based training business.

Table 14.2 Training-specific metrics

Training metrics (monthly)	Description
Financial management:	Financial metrics follow normal company financial guidelines.
Sales by offering	Sales by offering relates to the training modalities sold to customers in a specific month. A sale is a recognition of an intent to purchase training and is not classified as billable revenue because that occurs after service provision or delivery of the training.

(Continued)

227

Table 14.2 (Continued)

Training metrics (monthly)	Description
	Sales can be viewed as a required order rate, with the intention of supporting expected revenue streams in the future. Monitoring the monthly order rate and the delay between order placement and delivery can give an indication of future growth or decline. This provides sufficient time to address increased demand or to deal with low volumes by way of sales campaigns or reducing the number of offerings in a month to minimise costs and maximise profit.
Revenue by offering (including rateable and deferred)	Revenue is recognised once the training has been provided. In the case of a training subscription contract, the revenue is recognised rateably over the life of the subscription. So, when revenue needs to be recognised monthly, only a portion of the money is recorded as revenue.
	Attention should be given to deferred revenue. This is where the customer has paid the invoice, but the money can't be recognised as revenue because the training has not yet been provided to the customer. Yearly billing deals, such as training credits, tend to drive high deferred revenue.
	Monitoring, tracking and managing revenue is important as it has significant influence on the profit line. Assessing revenue forecasts over forthcoming months by offering type provides an insight into what actions need to be taken to capitalise on available resources and take advantage of growth opportunities.
Billing	Billing measures money collected following the delivery of training or the selling of a subscription. Note that billing will not always align with the monthly revenue amount, due to delayed or advanced payments. Normally, the finance department are more interested in this metric.
Cost of goods sold	Represent expenses that rise or fall based on sales volume. The expenditures commonly included are: • sales commission; • payments to training partners who sell or deliver training; • payments to freelancers that deliver the training;

(Continued)

Table 14.2 (Continued)

Training metrics (monthly)	Description
	• cost of training materials required to support the delivery of the training;
	• transportation costs to deliver the training;
	• rental costs for equipment required to deliver the training.
	For a training manager, these are controllable variable costs that represent a key metric to monitor. In situations where revenue was low for a month, the use of freelancers and training partners can be reviewed and minimised. Conversely, if revenue was strong, additional resources can be hired to support demand and increase overall profitability.
Gross profit	Represents the gross contribution after COGS has been factored in. Any challenges in the achievement of this metric requires attention to be focused on both the cost and the revenue lines.
Operational costs	These are the fixed costs of running the training business and typically include:
	• Salaries, often divided into:
	▪ delivery (instructors);
	▪ content development;
	▪ operational and administration;
	▪ sales;
	▪ marketing;
	▪ product management.
	• Administration costs.
	• Depreciation costs on capital equipment.
	• Telecommunication costs.
	• Facilities cost.
	For a training manager, this metric should remain constant and be monitored for unexpected variances. This metric is more important for year-end analysis and the following year planning cycle.
	Net profit will fluctuate as a consequence of gross profit and as per the operational cost metric, but is more meaningful for end-of-year planning.

(Continued)

Table 14.2 (Continued)

Training metrics (monthly)	Description
Training sales management:	As per the financial management metric.
Sales by offering Sales pipeline	While the sales by offering metric represents the closing of the sales negotiation process, the sales pipeline metric provides the training sales manager with a view on actual progress and an understanding of the probability of achieving the desired results. Selling is predominately a numbers game that requires certain stages to be attained. Key metrics regarding probability of closure within a month are indicators as to the level of success to be attained. Typical sales waterfall metrics are: • Number of unqualified opportunities to focus on and their value. • Number of qualified leads and potential value. • Number of deals and value in progress. • Number of deals and value committed to close. • Actual deals closed and their value.
Marketing management:	For a training executive to justify the cost of supporting a marketing department, they require metrics that measure lead and demand generation activities.
Lead generation	Measuring the number of new customer information profiles captured.
Demand generation	Measuring the number of qualified leads closed or passed to sales.
Content development:	Content development is guided by the technical training product management team in terms of what to build and by when.
Development road maps	Tracking of progress is via development road maps, which typically measure: • Target development completion times. • Required man-hours. • Commitment to alpha, beta and pre-post general product announcement (GPA) release date requirements.
Development time per modality	All modalities (ILT, VILT, labs, eLearning) have different target development times per hour of content, which will require agreed metrics to be defined.
Customer satisfaction	Student satisfaction with the quality and level of content provided while attending a completed course.

(Continued)

Table 14.2 (Continued)

Training metrics (monthly)	Description
Product management:	Product management is responsible for specifying what content should be developed for which target audience, and setting revenue, student and return on investment profiles.
Time to market	Metric aligned with the content development road maps.
Revenue and student attainment	Based on market analysis, each course or piece of content development will have an expected student volume and revenue target assigned to it.
ROI	Each course will be expected to generate revenue that delivers a return on investment over an agreed timeline.
Training delivery:	Training delivery is responsible for supporting training that has been sold in a responsive, cost-effective and efficient manner and that provides a high-quality student experience.
Utilisation	For a training delivery team to be efficient, it needs to achieve the following metrics: • Instructor utilisation (number of days an instructor is engaged in delivering training). • Classroom utilisation (number of days the classroom is fully utilised.
Fill rates	Fill rates measure the percentage of available seats (students) that have been filled by students attending a course. For example, nine students attending a 12-seater course is a fill rate of 75%.
Revenue per instructor	Revenue supported per instructor based on the student revenue delivered.
Students trained	Number of students trained, measured in terms of student days of attendance.
Customer satisfaction	Student satisfaction with the quality of instructional delivery and the physical training facilities.
Certification and exam development:	Certification and exam development is guided by the technical training product management team in terms of what to build and by when.
Time to market	Tracking of progress is via development road maps, which typically measure: • Target development completion times. • Required labour-hours. • Commitment to post GPA release date requirements.
Certification volumes	Number of students who undertook and successfully attained certification.

RETURN ON INVESTMENT

Training, like any other commercial business, needs to be able to show a ROI. For training, the product management team has the responsibility of assessing the market opportunity and deciding what content should be developed and delivered, including the level of investment allocated and over what period it is acceptable to recover costs and move to profit.

As a performance measure, ROI is used to evaluate the efficiency of a training investment and measures the amount of return relative to the cost. To calculate ROI, the following formula is used:

$$\text{ROI (\%)} = \frac{(\text{revenue earned}) - (\text{cost of development} + \text{delivery cost}) \times 100}{(\text{cost of development} + \text{delivery cost})}$$

and is normally monitored in terms of revenue contribution growth over an agreed lifecycle period.

The example shown in Table 14.3 is based on developing a five-day ILT course at a cost of £100,000 with run-time costs of £365 per attending student and a course price of £2,500.

Table 14.3 Investment and run-time costs

Course development costs	£100,000
Cost per course place delivery	£365
Course price (excluding discount)	£2,500
Unit increments (See Table 14.4)	5
BREAKEVEN POINT	47

Table 14.4 represents the profit and loss (P&L) and ROI based on student attendance and Figure 14.1 displays the breakeven point and the impact on ROI of increased sales and hence student attendance.

Table 14.4 P&L and ROI

Course places sold	Sales	Total costs	Profit/Loss	ROI
0	£0	£100,000	−£100,000	−100%
5	£12,500	£101,825	−£89,325	−88%
10	£25,000	£103,650	−£78,650	−76%
15	£37,500	£105,475	−£67,975	−64%
20	£50,000	£107,300	−£57,300	−53%

(Continued)

Table 14.4 (Continued)

Course places sold	Sales	Total costs	Profit/Loss	ROI
25	£62,500	£109,125	−£46,625	−43%
30	£75,000	£110,950	−£35,950	−32%
35	£87,500	£112,775	−£25,275	−22%
40	£100,000	£114,600	−£14,600	−13%
45	£112,500	£116,425	−£3,925	−3%
50	£125,000	£118,250	£6,750	6%
55	£137,500	£120,075	£17,425	15%
60	£150,000	£121,900	£28,100	23%
65	£162,500	£123,725	£38,775	31%
70	£175,000	£125,550	£49,450	39%
75	£187,500	£127,375	£60,125	47%
80	£200,000	£129,200	£70,800	55%
85	£212,500	£131,025	£81,475	62%
90	£225,000	£132,850	£92,150	69%

Figure 14.1 Breakeven and ROI

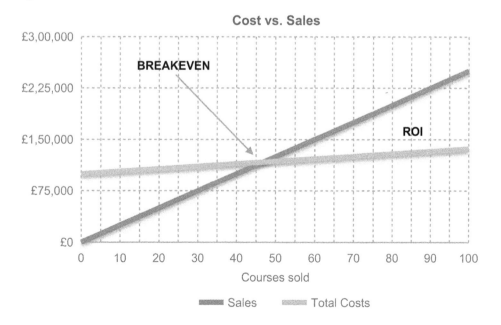

In certain situations, a vendor organisation may request a course to be developed that generates an indirect ROI rather than a direct one. An example of this is training developed for partners to assist in the selling of product. In these situations, the ROI is indirect because other components come into play regarding attainment of product revenue growth. The training investment in these types of situations provides a positive contribution to the company at large.

The ROI lifecycle can vary, depending on the frequency of content updates, and therefore care should be applied when deciding on the level and nature of investment to be made. For example, if the lifecycle of the course is expected to be 18 months or less, it is wise to develop seminar content rather than a comprehensive instructor-led course that normally would be targeted at high volumes and longer lifecycles.

SUMMARY

To ensure that a training business is operating to achieve its long- and short-term objectives, it must establish relevant controls to protect and steer the business, including the introduction and regular application of metrics management and governance control.

Irrespective of training organisation size or structure, it is good practice to implement a governance process to monitor, assess and control how the training group is run, including business and operational processes and systems used to protect and develop the training assets.

Establishing a training group governance policy requires the management team to be clear about the current state of the business, where it intends to go and what is required to get there. In many instances, the work done in developing the strategy and business execution plan assists in establishing the foundation for achieving this.

As governance plays a major part in assisting in the development of the business, being able to challenge and validate the results provides insight into how the training group is progressing and how it can excel.

Training managers need access to financial and business metrics in order to justify and validate overall business effectiveness. The key financial metrics are normally sales, revenue, costs and profit, which are granulated further according to the need and complexity of the business.

The business metrics, if chosen well and aligned with the strategic direction and business design requirements of the training group, enable managers to make informed and meaningful decisions about their business. While the metrics can be many and varied, the important lesson is that of simplicity. If there are too many metrics, and they are too complex in nature, they will be ineffective.

To ensure training staff fully understand the importance and relevance of business metrics, actively engage and communicate the results and interpretations to them on an ongoing basis.

15 FINANCIALS
Fiscal management and control

This chapter covers financial management, which is based on the planning, organising, directing and controlling of all relevant financial activities associated with the running of the training department. In some instances, this is undertaken in conjunction with a dedicated corporate finance department.

Typically, it covers investments regarding fixed assets known as capital budgeting, staffing and operational costs, with requirements to achieve one of the following:

- Generating an agreed level of profit through income generation, known as P&L management.

- Delivering an income stream from agreed internal and external resources that balances the costs, referred to as breakeven management (also referred to as cost recovery).

- Managing all costs to an agreed and defined budget, known as cost management (also referred to as a cost centre).

- Managing a combination of all of the above, depending on whether the training is targeted at internal employees, partner training or customer training (P&L management).

Finance departments work closely with training managers to exercise control over finances by way of providing insights into how the business is progressing. This is achieved by using techniques such as ratio analysis, financial forecasting and cost and profit control, all of which help the training team to model and analyse overall business progress.

The finance department will also ensure that funds are available to support the running of the training department, which includes monitoring that allocated funds are effectively utilised, managed and reported in accordance with country-specific legal requirements.

All companies are financially regulated, and in the US have to adhere to the Generally Accepted Accounting Principles (GAAP), which is a requirement of the US Federal Accounting Standards Advisory Board. This also aligns in principle with the International Accounting Standards Committee (IASC) requirements, which the European Union adheres to.

FINANCE IN A TECHNICAL TRAINING ENVIRONMENT

As covered in Chapter 14, training managers need to be able to measure financial metrics to justify and validate overall business effectiveness. The nature of the service provided will dictate what will be required to be monitored and delivered to stakeholders and sponsors, the key metrics being sales, revenue, costs and profit.

The main criteria with training, as it is in any business, is to understand what elements of the business need to be monitored, measured and managed. Typically, this falls into the following areas:

- sales;
- marketing;
- training product management;
- development;
- delivery;
- operational management.

All the above have costs requiring funding, monitoring and validation in relation to their overall contribution to the achievement of the required business model in operation at the time (for instance, cost recovery, breakeven, P&L). What differentiates one business from another, outside metrics management and the standard approach to measuring costs, revenue and profit, is that of ratio analysis. For training, the following can be used:

- **Sales:** revenue generated per cost of selling. Typical ratio range is 30:1 to 50:1, depending on the nature and size of deals.
- **Marketing:** revenue generated per cost of marketing. Typical ratio range is 90:1 to 150:1, depending on the number of sales staff and market opportunity.
- **Training product management:** revenue generated and supported per product manager cost. Typical ratio range is 5:1 to 8:1, depending on the nature and complexity of the training offering.
- **Development:** revenue generated per cost of development. Typical ratio range is 13:1 to 22:1+, depending on the nature and complexity of the training offering. It can be significantly lower if strategically important with low revenue expectations.
- **Delivery:** revenue delivered per cost of instructional delivery. Typical ratio range is 12:1 to 18:1, depending on complexity and maximum number of students per course.
- **Operational management:** revenue supported per cost of operational activity. Typical ratio is 70:1+, depending on training offering complexity and level of automation.

By monitoring key ratios aligned with sales income and working closely with the finance department, a training manager can obtain a view on how healthy the business is and whether changes need to be implemented to maintain liquidity. For example:

- Is the revenue and profit growing in proportion to the size of the business and the training offering mix?
- Is the revenue and profit increasing or declining in terms of sales activity?

Ratio analysis, in addition to the examples above, can be used in multiple ways to establish numerical or quantitative relationships between various training-based financial reference points. This enables assessment of strengths and weaknesses including historical performance. When looking to justify a position or investment decision, it helps to focus attention on specifics rather than high-level generic results. For example, the following is relevant for training managers:

- **Forecasting:** trends in costs, sales, profits and student numbers can be developed by calculating ratios of relevant figures over past months, quarters and years, which is helpful for forecasting and planning future business activities.

- **Operating efficiency:** granulating operational functional activity to analyse degrees of efficiency in the management and utilisation of training assets.

- **Inter-CEdMA company comparison:** comparison of the performance of multiple Customer Education Management Association companies to assist in understanding best practices.

Ratio analysis provides important relationships between various financial points that helps in understanding and interpreting financial statements more effectively.

FINANCIAL MODELS (P&L, COST, HYBRID)

Financial models provide training managers and executives with the ability to make decisions, plan, monitor and control their business. The first stage of modelling involves the assessment of the market conditions, opportunities and ability to service the need in accordance with corporate requirements. These corporate requirements will tend to define the nature of the financial model adopted. For example:

- Generating agreed levels of profit through income generation, known as a P&L account. P&L models are often adopted when companies are listed on the stock market, or value training as an independent contributor or as an important part of a chargeable professional services group.

- Delivering income from internal and external resources that balances the costs, known as a breakeven model. This model is adopted when a company needs to keep internal charges at cost and encourage engagement for the partner community, by way of charging them at non-commercial rates that do not inhibit them from working towards the common good of selling products.

- Managing costs to an agreed and defined budget, known as cost management, is typically applied when training is viewed as a cost of doing business in the same way that first line support, marketing or pre-sales support is viewed.

- Hybrid models, which are a combination of all of the above, are suitable when training is required to support multiple audiences in a specific manner. For example, internal employees (cost management), partner training (breakeven management) or customer training (P&L management).

Financial models are useful in the creation of projections, trends and forecasts. The example set out in Tables 15.1–15.3 highlights the main components that assists a training group to manage, monitor and assess its business progress.

Table 15.1 represents gross profit for an example training group, which is calculated by subtracting the variable cost of goods (also known as cost of sales) from the generated revenue. Table 15.2 represents the operating profit, calculated by subtracting the fixed operational costs from the gross profit. Table 15.3 represents the earnings before tax, calculated by subtracting the corporate charges from the operating profit.

Table 15.1 Gross profit

Fiscal year end 31/12	2015 Actual £	2016 Plan £	2015 to 2016 Variance %	2016 Forecast £	Forecast to budget variance %
Revenues:					
Public training courses	1,000,000	1,100,000	10	1,000,000	−9.1
Custom and tailored courses	400,000	460,000	15	460,000	0.0
eLearning	300,000	450,000	50	600,000	33.3
Certification	250,000	300,000	20	280,000	−6.7
Total revenues	**1,950,000**	**2,310,000**	**18.5**	**2,340,000**	**1.3**
Cost of goods:					
Public training courses – printing, external contractors	150,000	165,000	10	160,000	−3.0
Custom and tailored courses – printing, travel and expenses, external contractors	88,000	101,200	15	101,200	0.0
eLearning – distribution costs	15,000	15,750	5	16,000	1.6
Certification – examination fees	150,000	180,000	20	170,000	−5.6
Total cost of goods	**403,000**	**461,950**	**14.6**	**447,200**	**−3.2**
Gross profit £	**1,547,000**	**1,848,050**	**19.5**	**1,892,800**	**2.4**
Gross profit %	**79.3%**	**80.0%**		**80.9%**	

Table 15.2 Operating profit

	2015 Actual £	2016 Plan £	2015 to 2016 Variance %	2016 Forecast £	Forecast to budget variance %
Operating expenses:					
Sales and marketing costs	331,500	370,000	11.6	331,500	−10.4
Training delivery and administration costs	392,000	392,000	−0.0	392,000	0.0
Product management and development costs	390,000	390,000	0.0	390,000	0.0
Depreciation and amortisation	58,500	58,500	0.0	58,500	0.0
Other expenses	25,000	25,000	0.0	25,000	0.0
Total operating expenses	1,197,000	1,235,500	3.2	1,197,000	−3.1
Operating profit £	350,000	612,550	75.0	695,800	13.6
Operating profit %	17.9	26.5		29.7	

Table 15.3 Earnings before taxes

	2015 Actual	2016 Plan	2015 to 2016 Variance	2016 Forecast	Forecast to budget variance
Corporate charges:					
Finance, HR and space allocation charges	£97,500	£115,500	18.5%	£115,500	0.0%
Earnings before taxes	£252,500	£497,050	96.9%	£580,300	16.7%

With all three tables, it is possible to review the previous year's performance with the upcoming planned year. By granulating each main area into its constituent parts, variances can be observed that allow decisions and adjustments to be made regarding investment versus return.

Once the planned year is operational, variances to plan can be observed by comparing the forecast to the actual results. Any differences can then be discussed and appropriate action plans put in place to either address or capitalise on the findings.

Tables 15.1–15.3, when combined, form in this instance a typical P&L financial model, also referred to as an income statement. The other models, based around cost management and breakeven, are structured in a similar fashion. The breakeven model is based on balancing the costs versus the income received, whereas the cost management model is concerned with aligning actual costs with planned costs.

The majority of training managers or executives will be concerned primarily with satisfying one or more of the three financial models (P&L, breakeven, cost management). Whichever ones they are involved with, it is important that they are aware of how the models affect and support the overall financial results of the company.

Annual reporting

When a company provides its annual report showing its financial progress, there are three main components to it: the income statement, balance sheet and cash flow statement. Normally, the balance sheet and cash flow statement are the responsibility of the finance department, who will engage with training managers if any untoward issues arise that require any supporting interventions to be actioned.

The income statement, as mentioned previously, is the domain of the training manager. It reflects revenue, cost and profit, which the P&L fully aligns to, and represents performance for the current and previous years to enable comparisons, trends and forecasts to be observed and acted upon.

The balance sheet provides an overview of assets, liabilities and stockholders' equity. Any concerns the finance department has in terms of it affecting training will come under their remit and guidance regarding any issues to be discussed and addressed.

Similarly, the cash flow statement is under finance control and they use it to reconcile the income statement with the balance sheet, which enables decisions to be made regarding the financing of activities from debt and equity.

CREATING THE BUDGET

Budgeting is a key part of business planning and is the most effective way of keeping business finances on track. The budgeting process commences once the strategic and business alignment process has been completed, resulting in the business design being aligned with its critical tasks, including the objectives, financial forecasts and market focus (see Chapter 2).

The purpose and benefits of a budget plan are summarised in Table 15.4.

Initiating the budget process in good time is critical and is normally begun three to four months before the start of a new financial year.

Table 15.4 Purpose and benefits of a budget plan

Purpose	Benefits
Control and monitor financial spending.	Effective management of funds.
Provide an environment to make confident decisions.	Appropriate allocation of funds.
Report and capture financial progress against plan.	Ability to monitor performance.
Provide early indicators of performance issues.	Improves decision making.
Define a planned outcome.	Assists in identifying and analysing problems.
	Aids the forecasting process across all training-related fiscal components (revenue, development, marketing, delivery).

Based on the agreed business objectives and critical tasks that need to be achieved, the following considerations need to be investigated:

- Revenue requirements in terms of:
  - training modality;
  - geographic distribution.
- Costs of sales allocations in terms of:
  - costs of materials;
  - training subcontractors;
  - commissions.
- Fixed operational costs in terms of:
  - sales and marketing costs;
  - training delivery and administration costs;
  - product management and development costs;
  - depreciation and amortisation costs;
  - travel and expenses.
- Profit requirements in terms of:*
  - gross profit;
  - operational profit;
  - profit before taxes.

* Note: profit requirements only apply to P&L and breakeven models.

Once the initial figures for income and expenditure have been decided, data can be entered into a spreadsheet (see Tables 15.1–15.3) to allow further modelling to be undertaken to assess how costs can be better allocated or reduced. This ensures a maximum return on the cost allocation investment.

The key steps and best practices that should be considered when planning and creating a business budget are:

- Making time for budgeting and running *what if* scenarios.

- Using the previous year's figures and historical information as a guide and reference point.

- Creating realistic budgets and factoring in any changes in operational costs or priority positions that may affect the overall result.

- Ensuring the budget components contain sufficient information to monitor and control the key business drivers, such as sales, marketing, delivery, product management and development.

- Involving the right people with access to the right information and cross-checking against other departmental or corporate dependencies.

- Reviewing the budget plan with the finance department before final figures are agreed.

ANALYSING, MONITORING, TRACKING AND RECOMMENDING FINANCIAL ACTIONS FROM THE BUDGET PLAN

One of the advantages of a well-constructed and thought-out budget plan is its ability to assist in the measurement and control of business performance. The budget plan is, in essence, a targeted action plan that can assist in the following:

- Providing information on the relationship between costs and revenue per training modality.

- Analysing the effectiveness of cost allocations in generating or supporting revenue, for example marketing spend on demand generation activities related to public scheduled training.

- Monitoring and controlling the training business via the analysis of differences between budgeted and actual income.

- Benchmarking performance by comparing year on year variances across the revenue and cost components.

- Benchmarking training results against the company's product sales results, which can help in understanding lag time between product purchase and training demand.

- Comparing forecast revenue growth with authorised training partners in the same product offering sector.

Reviewing the budget on a regular basis provides an insight into how effectively the training group is performing against its financial income and expenditure goals. Analysing actual income versus the sales budget can assist in understanding why the results are higher or lower, resulting in recommendations for alternative actions to correct or capitalise on. Similarly, on the cost side, any overspending can be addressed by focusing attention on actions to reduce costs over the coming months to help address earlier issues.

A well thought-out budget, when combined with regular meetings to assess, monitor and address variances, forms an important part of the overall governance process to minimise problems and maximise opportunities.

FORECASTING

When running a cost centre, cost recovery centre or profit and loss centre, the responsibility to forecast the current or forthcoming financial period is a key aspect of the role. Senior executives right up to the managing director depend on forecasts to be accurate to make short- and long-term projections regarding cost and investment decisions.

Forecasts are, essentially, informed guesses based on using the right method and approach together with validated justifications. A number of methods can be used, depending on preference, and normally fall into two categories: qualitative or quantitative.

Qualitative

From the training perspective, this forecasting approach is based on opinions and general views regarding how the business is doing in relation to external market factors in force at the time. For example, following a significant cyber-attack, the training group could reasonably expect to see a surge in demand in the short term if it specialises in security training.

Qualitative data collection methods comprise a mix of structured and unstructured techniques such as focus groups, individual interviews and observations from market research and expert sampling, which could be enquiring into what trends a sales team is seeing.

Quantitative

This category uses data to generate statistics for analysis and computation to assess lagging indicators and turn them into effective leading indicators, and vice versa. For example, lagging indicators are output-based and easy to measure but hard to improve, whereas leading indicators are input-based and harder to measure but easier to influence. From a training perspective, this translates as follows:

- Training revenue, profit and costs are defined as lagging indicators because they are output-based; in other words, the results have already been achieved.

- At an operational level, the number of students trained is defined as a lagging indicator.
- Revenue and numbers of students trained are lagging indicators as a consequence of being related to a sales activity. However, when the background to a sale is analysed, a number of leading indicators come to the fore that allows further actions to be considered:
  - number of leads generated by marketing and sent to sales;
  - number of sales calls made;
  - number of deals progressed from qualified to closed.

Based on these leading indicators, and assessing their related success factors, two outcomes apply. The first is the ability to apply a conversion factor that can be used to forecast revenue, and the second is to assess what improvements or alternative actions can be considered to improve the leading indicator.

Other methods exist to assist in the forecasting process, such as time series, which refers to the collection of data from past events to forecast future events. For example, in Europe students do not attend courses during the summer vacation. This results in a predictable data point mapping to revenue reduction. Conversely, during the fiscal year-end period, companies have budget to be used up, which can result in a significant increase in revenue.

Forecasting plays an important part in assessing what financial results can be achieved over time. Of course, there is risk associated regarding accuracy; however, if the same process is consistently followed, the forecast will provide an informed and consistent reflection of expected results. A typical process that could be adopted is shown below:

- Data points are chosen to align with the training success measurement criteria and corporate need.
- Data point values are allocated that reflect known market conditions (internal and external) and mapped to monthly, quarterly and annual timelines.
- Data points are allocated acceptable variance tolerances based on known challenges and assumptions that may occur over the measurable timeline.
- Proposed forecast is reviewed for relevancy regarding financial control and achievement.
- Forecast model selected must support collection of the required data sets.
- Selected model data output is analysed and initial forecast made.
- Forecast is verified on an ongoing basis by assessing actual results over an agreed time period, and any variations addressed dynamically as required.

UNDERSTANDING VSOE AND REVENUE RECOGNITION

In principle, revenue recognition is reasonably easy to understand: basically, fulfil what has been sold and record the revenue. Where it tends to get complicated is when products and services are sold together.

An example of this is when a technology company sells a solution comprising hardware, software and services, which can all be delivered at different times. The hardware and software will normally be delivered first, followed by installation services, ongoing support and training over an agreed period.

Prior to 2008, accounting rules required revenue recognition for the entire solution to be deferred until all the components had been fully delivered. From a training point of view, this discouraged companies from selling training and services as part of an overall solution due to the restrictions regarding revenue recognition in the financial reporting period when it was sold. Consequently, financial reporting changes were introduced in 2008 by the Financial Accounting Standards Board (FASB), a US market regulator whose role is to establish and improve the GAAP within US-based organisations in support of the public's best interest. These reporting changes modified the way revenue from contracts with multiple deliverables was recorded and recognised. This also applies to American-owned companies operating in the UK and Europe.

The changes required companies to split solutions into separate parts, for example hardware, software and the various service-based components such as training. This allowed revenue to be recognised independently for each part and at different times, with the added advantage that, from a profit-based perspective, the costs could be allocated accordingly. The issue with these changes was the GAAP criteria requiring the selling price of a product or service to be fixed and determinable, which translates to being a fair value.

To achieve this, a methodology was established which defined a hierarchy that must be used to determine the monetary value of the separate components. The hierarchy is as follows:

1. **VSOE:** this effectively relates to what a company charges if training is sold separately; it is the responsibility of the training department to provide evidence of how the offering is priced if sold independently.

2. **Third-party evidence (TPE):** if VSOE evidence for the training offering is not available, then the finance department (revenue recognition team), working in conjunction with the training group, looks to third parties such as competitors to determine how they price a similar offering.

3. **Estimated selling price (ESP):** if neither VSOE nor TPE can be determined, agreement within the company must be obtained to provide the best estimate on what the training is worth based on market prices.

With individual selling prices being clearly defined using the methodology above, revenue can be more easily recognised or deferred. For training, it enables offerings to be included in a broader solution because it is less restrictive on overall revenue recognition. However, it can still inhibit the inclusion of training when sales teams do not get paid commissions on deferred revenue at point of sale.

CARVE OUT AND DISCOUNT POLICIES

Revenue and cost allocation go hand in hand regarding their impact on overall profit. The role of the finance department is to ensure that all financial components are recognised and allocated correctly. For publicly listed organisations, the importance around fiscal transparency is paramount.

While some sales staff are prepared to include training as part of an overall fixed price solution, the principle often applied is carve out, which effectively provides the training free of charge or, put another way, offers it at 100 per cent discount. Either way, it needs to be included on the balance sheet.

With that in mind, carve out is not beneficial to companies as it does not reflect or recognise the true value of training. In fact, it is often the case that the training department will not get any internal revenue recognition at all. Carve out also has the potential to affect the VSOE value over time, as does the support of excessive or uncontrolled discount policies. VSOE requires pricing to be fair and demonstrable. If it is constantly changing, then VSOE adjustments must be regularly implemented, which impairs the training group's ability to obtain correct revenue recognition over its reporting period.

The finance department, working with the training team, should agree on how the discount policy is implemented, monitored and approved. This ensures consistency of approach and defines sales interaction with the customer in a known and disciplined manner. Typically, sales teams can discount to a certain agreed level on deals above a particular value. Outside the defined level, a hierarchy of approval stages is supported, normally involving sales management working directly with the training team.

CROSS-BORDER REVENUE RECOGNITION AND TAX IMPLICATIONS

Cross-border business activities can be very lucrative and rewarding, but do come with challenges that need to be understood regarding revenue recognition and tax laws. The training team should work directly with their finance and accounting teams to ensure that they are trading correctly.

Finance and accounting teams typically consult with local country authorities, such as the Department for International Trade in the UK or via EU Council Directives, who provide advice on how and when to charge VAT, including the appropriate reporting.

Rules regarding VAT and cross-border recognition change constantly, and the training administration and billing teams need to be well versed in their application. For example, within the EU the rules regarding revenue recognition and VAT has changed in the last few years. Prior to 2015, VAT was payable based on the 'place of supply' rules. This stated that for digitally delivered content, such as eLearning, revenue and VAT would be based on the supplier country. Since then, the interpretation has changed to the location where the digital service is being consumed. The following list of training services come under the where the 'digital service is being consumed' rules:

- downloadable software licences, if provided to training partners;
- video tutorials;
- virtual instructor training, if it involves access to labs or digital content – if there is **only** instructor to student engagement, it comes under the place of supply rules;
- training content downloads;
- software as a service (SaaS), such as remote labs and training subscription services.

Instructor-led training, while recognised as a service, requires VAT to be paid by the attending student. Therefore, any student attending from another country pays local VAT.

If the course is sold by a sales representative from another country, the revenue is recognised in the country of delivery, not the country it is sold in. This can create difficulties within a company and may require a different compensation model to be put in place to ensure that the finance regulations do not impede the motivation to sell.

In terms of compliance, it is the responsibility of the training manager to ensure that the group is complying with the relevant regulations before any goods or services are shipped or delivered. These normally cover the following:

- customs duties;
- intra-country declarations;
- export licences;
- temporary export permits (to a trade fair, for instance);
- certificates and permissions;
- sanctions.

SUMMARY

Financial management is based on the planning, organising, directing and controlling of all relevant financial activities associated with the running of the training department. It encompasses capital budgeting, staffing and operational costs, with requirements to deliver an agreed fiscal result.

The role of the training manager is to be able to measure financial metrics to justify and validate overall business effectiveness, with the key metrics being sales, revenue, costs and profit.

Metrics management is a mix of reporting actual values and using ratio analysis. Ratio analysis enables numerical, or quantitative, relationships to be observed, which, in turn, allows for the assessment of strengths and weaknesses and historical performance to be taken into account in order to focus attention on specifics rather than high-level generic results. For example, the operational cost to support training revenue should typically represent a ratio of 70:1. Outside this, assessments can be undertaken to either capitalise on positive improvements or address negative variances.

In order to implement metrics management, financial models need to be agreed upon that provide training managers with the ability to make decisions, plan, monitor and control their business. There are three financial models typically used (P&L, breakeven, cost management), depending on the requirements of the company.

Once a financial model has been agreed, the budgeting process is initiated, normally three to four months before the start of a new financial year. This is then reviewed on a regular basis to provide an insight into how effectively the training group is performing against its financial income and expenditure goals.

Another important process is that of forecasting, which provides a view on the current quarter and future quarters' potential results. There are two common methods for forecasting: qualitative and quantitative. The first is based on opinions and general views of the business and the second based on the use of data to generate statistics for analysis.

Regulatory compliance can affect reported revenue results. For a training organisation, the situation gets complicated when products and services are sold together. From an accounting perspective, previous regulatory rules required revenue recognition for the entire solution sold to be deferred until all components had been fully delivered. In 2008 the Financial Accounting Standards Board (FASB) implemented changes requiring companies to split solutions into separate parts such as hardware, software and the various service-based components, which includes training. This required training revenue by offering to be fixed and determinable, which involves the use of vendor-specific objective evidence (VSOE) to be implemented and records kept on all sales in order to validate the revenue to be recognised.

A further complication regarding revenue recognition is that of cross-border business activities, which have to conform with local country authorities such as the Department for International Trade in the UK or via EU Council Directives.

16 STAFF MANAGEMENT AND DEVELOPMENT
Getting the best from your key assets – the training team

This chapter explains what is required to establish and maintain a team of employees to achieve business performance in line with agreed goals and expectations.

For any organisation to be successful, enablement models need to be established that align and monitor business performance through the combination of individual employee competencies. These models form the basis by which the business objectives can be mapped to a series of business activities, which can then be grouped into competencies, roles and responsibilities.

With job roles specified, competency and performance management can be undertaken to assist in the tracking, control and monitoring of both the overall team and individuals' contribution to the achievement of business goals and objectives.

Balancing the level of human resources required to support and grow a training business is an ongoing challenge for training managers. Implementing an employee and contractor recruitment policy provides the basis of an employment strategy to be defined.

Of equal importance is culture and climate, which have significant influence on employee behaviours and performance and require regular monitoring and development.

APPLYING ENABLEMENT MODELS TO DRIVE BUSINESS PERFORMANCE

Obtaining the best out of a training team requires a solid understanding of what the business objectives are, and what requirements there are on individual employees to collectively contribute to overall business performance and success.

To gain success, an enablement model needs to be established that forms the basis by which both management and employees can flourish. Among the many models that can be adopted, the business performance matrix shown in Figure 16.1 highlights the key principles that can be used to explain how to get the best from a training team.

How well a team performs can be evidenced by how well the business performance matches stated business objectives, and how well personal and team performances match the stated personnel objectives.

Figure 16.1 Business performance matrix

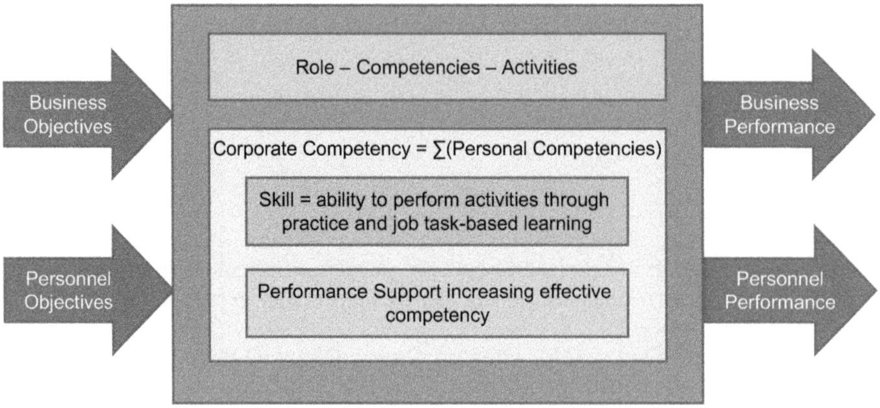

Achievement of business objectives requires a set of activities to be performed. These activities may be grouped into competencies and the competencies into roles and tasks.

The competency required to perform an activity is defined as:

access to information + knowledge + skills + experience = competency

Knowledge and skills generally increase through experience. The concept of performance support is to provide information in a structured form and at a time when it compensates for lack of knowledge, skill or experience, the application of which enables an individual to perform with a higher level of competency than they would otherwise possess.

Performance support may be provided by scripted procedures or job aids. Examples of job aids might be:

- Prepared technical briefs on course objectives and prerequisites for use by administration staff.
- Sales presentations and guidelines for prospective customers.
- Reference solution architectures for technical instructors to use during training sessions.

The closer that performance support can be incorporated into a business workflow, the more effective it will potentially be. Business workflow forms a key part in business performance success, through use of defined processes that assist in the execution of the individual and collective training roles to achieve overall training business objectives.

Being able to align and monitor business performance through the combined individual competencies provides the training department with a powerful way of assessing how well personal and team performances match stated objectives.

TRAINING STAFF JOB SPECIFICATIONS

Once the business objectives have been mapped to a series of business activities, they can then be grouped into competencies, roles and responsibilities.

For example: one of the business objectives could be to administer customer and partner instructor-led training requests in a professional and effective manner, leading to weekly billing on completion. The process would typically comprise:

- Defining the associated business activities:
  - receiving student bookings and billing them on course completion;
  - scheduling resources;
  - providing customer care and administration support.
- Defining the required responsibilities per individual or combined business activity (for example, *receiving student bookings and billing them on course completion*):
  - to answer incoming requests for training and provisionally book the student on the required course;
  - request student information and purchase order number;
  - monitor incoming receipt of purchase order and send out joining instructions;
  - on course completion, send course invoice to student.
- Defining the required competencies per business activity (for example, *receiving student bookings and billing them on course completion*):
  - Competency 1: ability to apply a friendly and professional tone and deal with all course requests in a knowledgeable and timely manner.
  - Competency 2: administer the training booking system in a proficient manner and in accordance with agreed service level requirements.
  - Competency 3: apply diligence when booking and billing students.

Once the competencies required have been assessed and aligned to job roles, a broader more-detailed job specification can be drawn up that can be structured as a career path based on required levels of performance and overall responsibility. Table 16.1 provides an example of a typical learning administrator role.

Job specifications provide the means to assess and guide training staff by focusing both the manager and the employee on the nature and scope of the role, along with the required competencies. Any shortfall in performance can be cross-checked against the competency criteria of ensuring that employees have:

access to information with sufficient **knowledge** to use the **skills** gained to apply their **experience** in a **competent manner**

which provides management with the ability to document progress, address shortfalls and instigate a proactive two-way communication with the employee. From the employee perspective, it provides them with a clear set of expectations and a reference

Table 16.1 Typical learning administrator job specification

	Job titles	
	Learning administrator	**Senior learning administrator**
Primary responsibilities	• Assisting in the planning, organisation and coordination of all training events.	• Planning, organising and management of all training events.
	• Maintaining up-to-date records and contacts databases.	• Managing training administration issues for ensuring database integrity and systems operations efficiency.
	• Using professional concepts and company policies and procedures to solve training administrative-related problems.	• Ensuring system interface requirements are defined and the interface with external training vendors runs properly.
	• Arranging appointments and the coordination of training events.	• Assisting in proofreading reports, documents and presentations.
	• Handling incoming and outgoing correspondence for the department.	• Researching and collating information on topics of interest and training needs.
	• Assisting with budget base administration, including recording and reporting.	• Liaising and communicating with other departments.
	• Undertaking general typing duties for the department and taking minutes in meetings as and when required.	• Actively promoting training courses via student database.
	• Recording student bookings and sending out joining instructions.	• Billing students and following up on bad debt payments.
Primary competencies	• Knowledge of approved instructors and training partners to enable proficient and effective scheduling.	• Knowledge of budget codes, allowable and non-allowable expenses, and budget types for the training department.
	• Shows ability to manage multiple conflicting priorities without loss of composure.	• Ability to administer departmental funds effectively and keep management well informed.
	• Determines the appropriate allocation of time.	• Demonstrates flexibility in the face of change.
	• Demonstrates the ability to foresee problems and prevents them by taking action.	

(Continued)

Table 16.1 (Continued)

	Job titles	
	Learning administrator	**Senior learning administrator**
	• Interacts professionally with customers and training staff at all times. • Works as a competent member of the team, willingly providing back-up support for co-workers when appropriate and actively supporting training group goals. • Displays proficiency using standard office equipment and training booking and LMS systems. • Demonstrates an awareness of fundamental training business principles as well as an understanding of the overall industry.	• Balances conflicting priorities in order to manage workflow, ensure the completion of essential projects and meet critical deadlines. • Utilises analytical skills and a broad understanding of the business to effectively interpret and anticipate needs. • Demonstrates advanced proficiency by quickly adapting to new technology and easily acquiring new technical skills.
Scope	Works on activities of moderate scope where analysis of needs, content and sources requires a review of identifiable factors. Exercises judgement within defined procedures and practices to determine appropriate action.	Works on all activities of administration where analysis of needs, content and sources requires constructive and positive action. Exercises judgement within defined procedures and practices to determine appropriate action.
Business impact	Contributes to the fulfilment of student bookings and training department objectives. Failure to achieve results or erroneous judgements may require the allocation of additional resources to correct and/or achieve training administration goals.	Contributes to the fulfilment of student bookings, billing, customer satisfaction and training department objectives. Failure to achieve results or erroneous judgements may require corrective action and possible loss of training bookings and/or achievement of training administration goals.
Success factors	• Customer centred. • Problem solving. • Peer relationships.	• Fiscal management. • Problem solving and resolution. • Peer relationships and development.

(Continued)

Table 16.1 (Continued)

	Job titles	
	Learning administrator	**Senior learning administrator**
Experience	1–2 years in a sales or training administration role.	2–3 years in a training administration and scheduling role.
Qualifications	GCSE English and Mathematics.	GCSE English and Mathematics.
Leadership and supervision	Normally receives general instructions on routine work, and detailed instructions on new assignments under general supervision. Follows established directions. Work is reviewed for accuracy and overall adequacy.	Receives guidance on weekly activities and priorities from the training delivery manager in order to interpret and action relevant activities in the fulfilment of the role. Follows established directions. Work is reviewed on a results basis.

point by which they can focus not just on the role, but also on their areas of development and future advancement.

TRAINING STAFF COMPETENCY MANAGEMENT

Competence is a combination of practical and thinking skills, experience and knowledge linked to a willingness to perform work activities in accordance with agreed standards, rules and procedures leading to the achievement of training business objectives.

Management is ensuring that staff understand the performance that is expected from them, and that they receive appropriate training, development and assessment with a commitment to maintaining or improving their competence over time.

Employee training and development teams (often part of a human resources group) will have the responsibility of working with technical training management to create a level of competence for both individuals and the team. Over time, as knowledge and practical experience grows, the performance of the training team will develop and strengthen.

As part of a shared services function, the employee training and development team should provide support and access to a competency management system (CMS). This provides a structure through which to assess, plan and implement the required training and development activities to ensure that both individual and team performance is being attained.

There are many CMS environments. The technical training manager needs to understand which one is available and how it can be used and applied to develop a strong relationship with employees and to ensure they can maximise its benefits and gain the all-important regular performance feedback from management.

PERFORMANCE MANAGEMENT

Business performance is based on delivering defined outcomes. For a training group, these outcomes typically comprise:

- Number of students trained.
- Fiscal achievement, which, depending on the company, can be cost control-based, profit and revenue contribution-based or bookings-related.
- Time to market with training offering availability.
- Customer satisfaction.
- Other factors, depending on levels of granulation required and audience type.

As discussed in the previous section on competency management, competence is a combination of practical and thinking skills, experience and knowledge applied to the achievement of business objectives leading to desired performance achievements.

To achieve a desired performance requires a solid understanding of all the factors that impinge on how the organisation operates. Having very competent staff but poor business processes, culture, pay scales, systems, organisational structures and communications hinders the organisation from achieving the required performance goals. The training management team must therefore establish a process for performance management that typically covers:

- A documented view on the overall training business strategy.
- Defined business goals and associated business activities to support the achievement of the goals.
- Defined training staff competencies to support required business activities and goals.
- A CMS to track and report on progress.
- Organisational mapping and dependencies defined at individual and team level.
- Access to learning and development to ensure required professional and organisational skills are catered for.
- Assessment of the training group's culture and effectiveness in undertaking its role within the organisation and customer base.
- Availability of appropriate systems and tools to deliver on the training group's business goals.
- A fair and appropriate compensation scheme.

As can be seen from these points, performance management is not simply about performance appraisal. It is much broader and entails having regular and informed dialogue with individuals and teams within the training group, including those within the company and its partners and customers.

An established process drives engagement throughout an organisation. It provides the training management team with an opportunity to assess all aspects that can impinge on the group's success and puts them in a position to address issues in an effective manner. When shared with individuals and teams, the process helps to drive positive and constructive actions.

For performance management to be effective it should have:

- A business strategy document that is clear in its intent, leading to an executable business plan with defined goals and related business activities.

- An organisational structure with defined competency and performance measurements.

- A CMS to track employee competencies, with performance appraisal included.

- Learning and development planning aligned to CMS employee and performance input.

- Regular culture review and feedback involving all of the training group's contact points.

- Regular system and tools review, factoring in any team or individual performance implications on successful delivery of desired business goals.

- Annual review of salary and benefits aligned to industry trends.

- A continuous cycle, because performance management is a process, not an event.

Performance management is a critical component in a training group's success that should encourage and involve individuals and teams to discuss in an open and meaningful way, not just their specific performance appraisal and pay, but the overall vision, goals, achievements and obstacles that enable them to move the group forward in a homogeneous manner.

EMPLOYEE AND CONTRACTOR RECRUITMENT

One of the many challenges facing the manager of a training function is how to balance the level of human resources required to support and grow their business. Depending on the nature of the training business, frequency of delivery and the ability to achieve fiscal objectives at the monthly, quarterly and annual level will decide the necessary employment strategy to be applied.

For example, if the nature of the training business is centred around eLearning with the RTM being distributor and reseller-based, there is a strong argument for hiring permanent staff. Product management, content development, marketing and channel sales functions can be streamlined to support planned and controllable growth. On the other hand, a training business based on the provision of multiple modalities and RTMs is faced with more complex challenges around the areas of development, delivery and sales. On the development side, some modalities may require specialist skills that cannot be utilised on a full-time basis. Delivery, in particular instructor-led, may be seasonal; for example, in some European countries employees take extended holidays, resulting in lowered demand at certain times of the year. On the sales front, while full country coverage is a requirement, the return on employee investment may not justify a full-time sales head.

It is factors like these that make the difference between success or failure of the training group when looking to balance overall costs, especially those related to headcount. To achieve the balance, it is important to define a strategy that blends the recruiting mix between permanent and contract staff. Understanding the difference between the two is vital.

Contract recruitment is based on hiring skilled training personnel for a short-term assignment. This helps to reduce the longer-term liability for both the training group and the parent company, because contract staff are not eligible for the same benefits as a full-time employee. Permanent recruitment requires full-time employees to be eligible for all the benefits the company is expected to provide by law, including tax liability, sick pay, pension entitlements, and to the development of ongoing skills and career prospects.

While contract staff will cost more on a daily basis, they are only paid until the job or contract is completed and of course provide increased degrees of flexibility to accommodate the variable demand and need of a training business. There are legal requirements associated with contractors, which can vary extensively depending upon the nature of the training service they are being requested to support. Working closely with the legal department will provide valuable insight into how to proceed.

When planning the training resource hiring strategy, the following points should be considered:

- What percentage of budget is being allocated to employment costs?
- Are there corporate headcount restrictions in place regarding the number of full-time equivalents that can be hired?
- What training functions can be contracted out without compromising security or confidentiality?
- Which staff positions can be fully utilised throughout the year and what is the impact on the profit or cost line if substituted with contract hire staff?
- Can more revenue and profit contribution be obtained by utilising contractors to accommodate variable market fluctuations?
- Can time to market be improved via the use of contractors?

Establishing a robust employment strategy provides the training leadership team with greater control, flexibility and leverage when dealing with corporate finance and business leaders.

CULTURE AND CLIMATE

Cultures evolve over time and represent the shared values and practices being adopted and implemented by a company. Normally, the culture with minor adaptations will be reflected in the way the training group is working collectively and individually.

Climate represents the way a company or group is operating at a moment in time, in terms of shared perceptions and attitudes. Typically, it is measured by how employees are being engaged and involved in the running of the company.

Both are important but very different in terms of impact on the way a company and its training group functions. Of the two, culture has a bigger effect on long-term sustainable success. If it is adaptive and progressive in nature, it can drive stronger employee responsibility and accountability in how they naturally deal with the problems, challenges and goals they are faced with. Climate provides an insight into how employees are engaged and communicated with, typically covering:

- Understanding what the training mission is and how it is implemented.
- Employee benefits and relevance within the marketplace.
- Management and employee interactions.
- Teamwork within the training group and the broader company organisation.
- Group effectiveness regarding change management.

By regular monitoring, the training management team and its employees can establish a positive and active channel of communication, allowing both parties to discuss and agree on appropriate actions to address issues and areas of concern.

To have a successful culture and achieve the required training group and company expectations, it is important to understand what that desired culture should be. As the group changes over time, with new and replacement employees, the culture will evolve but should strengthen and stabilise as it matures.

To establish a culture, the training management team needs to engage all staff in the process to ensure that the shared values and practices being recommended are understood, agreed and adopted by all. A typical process for the establishment of an employee training team culture covers the following steps:

1. Define or review the strategic intent and high-level business design objectives for the training group.
2. Identify the required behavioural strengths and highlight any weaknesses that the training team will need to address.
3. Cross-check recognised behavioural strengths and weaknesses with the rest of the company, trusted partners and suppliers to ensure broader alignment and relevance.
4. Align the reviewed behavioural strengths and weaknesses with agreed actions, timelines and owners, including combined management and employee support commitments and expectations.

5. Establish the use of feedback and prioritisation reviews to ensure training management and employees are sharing goals to determine if results are being achieved.

6. Maximise and encourage the use of open communications via meetings, email updates and social media postings to encourage formal and informal interactions.

7. Encourage ownership and accountability. If something is broken or not working, all staff should feel comfortable in addressing the problem.

If a culture is working well, no member of staff should feel inhibited or restricted in seeking support. All organisations experience positive and negative interactions regarding cultural expectations and achievements. It can help to drive forward thinking to achieve great results or to drive negative behaviour, minimising effectiveness. Either way, both should be taken into account and actioned to enhance or address the situation.

Culture is a strength that all successful training groups should be able to describe and display, with climate being a means to measure employee engagement and alignment at a specific point in time.

RESPONSIBILITY AND ACCOUNTABILITY

Responsibility and accountability are often misunderstood by many organisations and seen as being interchangeable. This can lead to inefficiencies, problems not being resolved and, ultimately, the training group failing. From a management perspective, this is an extremely important aspect of the overall business execution process, and a fundamental part of establishing and driving a strong culture and climate.

When a training manager assigns responsibility and allocates accountability, any confusion regarding its meaning needs to be addressed immediately. Failure to do this can be very damaging in terms of loss of reputation, revenue exposure and potential profit loss.

Responsibility can best be described as being in charge of a series of tasks in the performance of a role or function. For example, an instructor has responsibilities for imparting knowledge and developing the skills of students by following the course schedule.

Accountability is about taking ownership of situations someone is directly involved with, including seeing resulting actions through to completion and taking responsibility for what happens. For example, if an instructor recognises that course content is not correct or fit for purpose, they would address the situation immediately with the students, and contact the content development team to advise them of the problem and request corrective action.

Great teams led by great leaders ensure that all members of the team know their responsibilities and how they are accountable individually and collectively for joint success. Training management should define responsibilities and accountabilities for individuals and teams, but also engage the organisation as a whole to ensure that interdepartmental and interdependencies across the broader company and partner spectrum are factored in to the overall equation. This way, overall responsibility and accountability are understood by everyone and overall organisational effectiveness improved.

SUMMARY

Ensuring that a training team has a solid understanding of business objectives and their requirements as individual employees is crucial to the achievement of overall business performance and success.

Implementing an enablement model, such as the business performance matrix highlighted in Figure 16.1, provides a framework by which to map business objectives to required activities. The activities are grouped into competencies and then aligned with roles and tasks.

Each role should have a job specification defining the nature and scope of the role, responsibilities, required competencies, prior experience and qualification requirements.

Competence is a combination of skills, experience and knowledge linked to a willingness to undertake work activities in accordance with agreed standards, rules and procedures, leading to the achievement of training business objectives.

Employee training and development teams can provide support to technical training management to create programmes that enhance the competence of both the individual and the team.

Having competent employees is important; however, that alone does not guarantee overall business performance success. In addition, business processes, culture, pay scales, systems, organisational structures and communications need to be established and functioning correctly. All of these factors form the basis of performance management and provide a training management team with the ability to drive positive and constructive actions in the achievement of its business objectives.

Developing and expanding a training business requires human resources. Challenges associated with seasonal fluctuations, variable demand, language requirements and balancing budgets need a flexible approach to how personnel is used. By implementing an employee and contractor recruitment policy, training management can optimise and control resources in an efficient manner.

Departmental culture and climate also contribute to business performance success and need to be developed, nurtured and monitored on an ongoing basis. Culture evolves over time and represents shared values and practices, whereas climate reflects moments in time in terms of shared perceptions and attitudes.

17 LEGAL
Protecting the training business

This chapter introduces and explains the legal requirements that a training department needs to consider in order to protect itself, its partners and its customers. It looks into the various legal facets to be considered, including import and export restrictions and regulations, trademarks, indemnity and liability, intellectual property and data protection.

CONTRACTS VERSUS STANDARD TERMS AND CONDITIONS

When dealing with customers, training partners or suppliers, it is important to validate and protect the supply or purchase of the required goods and services. Normally, this takes the form of a contract, which provides legal protection for both supplier and purchaser.

A written agreement should be provided when supplying training, which includes standard terms and conditions. Purchasing sends their version, which will require consideration before acceptance. The complexity of the agreement will be dictated by whether the training group is part of a large corporation or small enterprise.

In some instances, both supplier and purchaser may request acceptance or modification of their terms and conditions. The process can appear complicated and time-consuming, which is why qualified legal representation should be engaged. From the training perspective, the key contribution to be made to this process is the development of standard terms and conditions. This allows the legal team to recommend their inclusion in a contract or sanction their use independently.

This raises the question as to when to use a contract versus terms and conditions. The training department needs to establish what the contracting policy is. A simple contracting policy may be more appropriate when selling scheduled public training, where standard terms and conditions can be used. If the training sold is more complex, perhaps involving customisation of content and multi-modalities, then a more detailed contracting policy needs to be enforced.

What is a contract?

In effect, a contract is an agreement between the training department to sell and the customer to buy training services on certain terms and conditions. Typically, a contract is drawn up when the training provision is complex in nature, requires additional terms and conditions and is of a large value.

What are standard terms and conditions?

These represent the training department's standard trading position relating to the sale of its training offerings and services via a formal written document. Typically, it includes price, payment and delivery terms, including protection for its intellectual property.

Using standard terms and conditions is a recognised way of contracting for several reasons:

- It minimises the time and expense of writing specific terms for each individual transaction.

- It enables more favourable terms to be established for the training department and negates lengthy negotiations for standard and repeatable offerings.

- It provides consistency regarding the training unit's policies and procedures, which in turn creates efficiencies.

- It provides standardisation of the training department's contracting procedures, allowing contracts to be handled and concluded by training operations and administrative staff.

As an example, Table 17.1 highlights the main sections that form a typical training organisation's standard terms and conditions.

Table 17.1 Sample description of standard terms and conditions

Main sections	Brief description
Definitions and interpretations	Explains what terms are referenced in the standard terms and conditions and their meaning (for example, joining instructions: the instructions provided to the client in relation to the services listed on the form).
Composition of agreement	Outlines the structure of the agreement and external reference support links.
Services	What services (training) are being provided.
Bundled provision	Inclusion of multiple offerings and guidance on access and distribution rights.
Fees	Fees payable excluding VAT.
Terms of payment	Method of payment and dates, including penalties for late settlement.
Cancellations	Policy relating to customer cancellation and that of the training organisation.
Intellectual property rights	Use of logos and distribution or copying restrictions that are in force.
Term and termination	Training organisation's actions to protect against customer insolvency.

(Continued)

Table 17.1 (Continued)

Main sections	Brief description
Liability	Covers joint legal liability and responsibilities.
Warranties and responsibilities	Commitment to provide the agreed training services without taking responsibility for mis-purchasing by the customer.
Modifications and third-party terms	Freedom for the training group to modify training content without prior notice, and engagement of third-party training providers.
Confidentiality	Outlines the levels of confidentiality, both written and oral.
Notices and contact details	Where customers can send written communications that will be recognised as being delivered officially.
Governing law and dispute resolution	Defines how the agreement will be governed, normally in accordance with the legal laws of the training organisation's home country.
Miscellaneous provisions	Covers such things as *force majeure*, data protection and export and compliance laws.

INDEMNITY AND LIABILITY

Whenever a company is involved in providing a service to others, it has a professional responsibility to provide a duty of care. The nature of that care is what differentiates indemnity from liability.

When providing training to customers, it is reasonable for them to consider instructors as being expert in their field and able to rely upon their professional knowledge and guidance. The duty of care responsibility is to ensure that any advice provided is accurate and complete. Any mistakes in the provision of this advice is protected by professional indemnity insurance.

Legal liability is primarily associated with personal injury or property damage as a result of attending or being involved with the training business. It is normal practice to cover this with public liability insurance.

Including a limited liability or indemnity clause in the contract or training terms and conditions may save a training department and its company from significant financial risk. However, the presence of a limited liability or indemnity clause does not always make it enforceable, so it is important to seek guidance from the legal department or an independent lawyer before finalising.

IMPORT/EXPORT REGULATIONS AND RESTRICTIONS

When establishing a presence in markets outside the country of operation, always seek advice when involved in exporting or importing training services, including regulations and intellectual property issues.

Countries tend to execute these in different ways, although the complexity can be simplified if they are trading under the World Trade Organization's (WTO) General Agreement on Trade in Services (GATS).

For those training groups operating within the EU, the EU Services Directive removes many of the barriers to service businesses being established in a member state. This allows training provision to be more easily established throughout the EU. In a similar fashion, the North American Free Trade Agreement (NAFTA) supports American, Canadian and Mexican service business-related interactions.

Many of the same basic rules apply for services as for trade in goods, and reference to the relevant agreement or country-specific regulation should always be undertaken. Below is a generic list of key points and issues that should be considered when trading in training services.

- Undertake thorough research and have a clear understanding of local culture before entering new markets.

- International services can be provided from within the country of origin, such as by using the internet to deliver a virtual training course, or in the customer's country, by sending an instructor. The important point here is that there is a difference between the two, which can have important legal and tax consequences if not clearly understood.

- Lack of a physical product has important implications for contracts, for example inability to use Incoterms (international commercial terms), which are a series of pre-defined commercial rules published by the International Chamber of Commerce (ICC). They are widely used in international commercial transactions and procurement processes.

- When trading in goods, the focus is on the responsibility for delivery as defined by the Incoterms regarding what is being supplied, which is normally easy to describe. However, when supplying training services it is more challenging to explain what is being delivered. This is where a service level agreement should be included in the contract, which helps to outline the agreed outcomes.

- Protecting intellectual property is a key issue (see later section in this chapter).

- Similar issues to exporting also apply to the importing of services, and therefore these are important to understand and address before completing a transaction.

- When trading internationally, different business cultures, legal environments and languages can increase the risk of confusion. It is therefore important to have a clear contract in place.

- Payment issues, such as choice of currency and protection against the risk of non-payment, need to be clearly defined.

- Delivering training services internationally is normally defined in one of four ways, depending upon the location of the supplier and the customer:

    1. **Cross-border trade:** both supplier and customer are in their own countries, while the service crosses the border. For example, training can be provided by phone and/or over the internet in the case of VILT.

2. **Consumption overseas:** the customer visits the supplier's country, where the supplier provides the service. For example, a student attends a course in another country.

3. **Setting up overseas:** the supplier establishes a presence in the customer's country. For example, opening and operating a training room at an overseas office.

4. **Movement of individuals:** individuals who will provide the service travel to the customer's country. For example, an instructor might travel overseas to teach a course at a customer's premises.

These methods of service delivery are defined in the WTO's GATS.

In 2010, the EU Services Directive removed many barriers from trading in services within the EU, effectively bringing member states closer to open trading.

The way services are supplied has important implications for which country's laws and taxes apply, especially when trading outside an established trading agreement, so it is important that appropriate government guidance is sought when considering trading as an importer or exporter. Some useful links are provided in Table 17.2.

Table 17.2 Useful import and export links

General description	Link
World Trade Organization	www.wto.org
EU Services Directive	https://ec.europa.eu/growth/single-market/services/services-directive/index_en.htm
North American Free Trade Agreement	www.cbp.gov/trade/nafta
General Agreement on Trade in Services	www.wto.org/english/tratop_e/serv_e/gatsqa_e.htm

CONTENT AND TRADEMARK INTELLECTUAL PROPERTY

Within the training world, intellectual property (IP) is an important part of what is offered, which differentiates it from grey market competition. As a consequence, most training providers will want to establish and protect a good reputation and brand name to ensure continued customer growth, which therefore requires courseware content to be protected.

When IP rights are granted, they cover trademarks, copyright, patents and industrial design. For most training providers, IP will predominately be based around content and hence come under the copyright designation. With IP laws varying from country to country, the basic principles are recognised internationally, and copyright filed in one country can offer legal protection in other countries under a collection of treaties administered by the World Intellectual Property Organization (WIPO),[1] which is an agency of the United Nations. As with any business activity, it is good practice to check which countries the training will be provided in, and whether WIPO jurisdiction applies. IP protection should also be included in employee contracts in case instructors or courseware developers move to training competitors.

When sharing content for the purposes of gaining feedback from potential suppliers or training partners, it is good practice to issue non-disclosure agreements (NDAs).

Copyright protects the form in which the content is recorded, and includes discussion forum posts, unless it is placed in the public domain or licenced environments such as Creative Commons.

Creative Commons

Creative Commons is a not-for-profit organisation offering copyright licences under six main categories. Licences allow digital content to be referenced, used or modified for commercial and non-commercial benefit to encourage controlled reuse and expansion.

From a training vendor perspective, this can encourage training partners to value add with their own material, which can enhance the content and reduce investment in additional modules. This effectively allows the partner to decide what additional training needs to be added, based on local requirements and industry specialisations.

The six categories of licences offered are:

- **Attribution:** allows distribution, remixing, tweaking and addition, even for commercial use, as long as the creator of the original work is credited.

- **Attribution-NoDerivs:** allows commercial and non-commercial redistribution, as long as the work is passed along unchanged and intact, crediting the creator.

- **Attribution-NonCommercial-ShareAlike:** allows remixing, tweaking and addition for non-commercial purposes, with the creator being credited and new creations licenced under identical terms.

- **Attribution-ShareAlike:** allows remixing, tweaking and addition for commercial and non-commercial purposes, with the creator being credited and new creations licenced under identical terms.

- **Attribution-NonCommercial:** allows remixing, tweaking and addition for non-commercial purposes, crediting the creator. Derivative works do not have to be licenced under the same terms.

- **Attribution-NonCommercial-NoDerivs:** allows work to be downloaded and shared as long as the creator is credited and the work is not used for commercial purposes.

---

1 WIPO is the global forum for intellectual property services (www.wipo.int/about-ip/en/), policy, information and cooperation. It is a self-funding agency of the United Nations (www.un.org/en/), with 191 member states.

Trademarks

As with content, trademarks also form part of IP rights. Trademarks should be registered in the training group's local country and individually in other countries where protection is required. To aid simplification, there are European and international application systems available.

European Union trademark protection is available by applying via the European Union Intellectual Property Office (EUIPO), based in Alicante, Spain. International trademark protection is covered by the 'Madrid Protocol', which is overseen by WIPO, based in Geneva, Switzerland. An international application has to be based on an existing trademark application or registration in one of the member countries. Once issued, the international trademark can be included and protects all training related documents, correspondence and promotions.

DATA PROTECTION

The right to privacy is a highly developed area of law in Europe, with the European Court of Human Rights applying a very broad interpretation in terms of its execution. Primarily, there are seven governing principles:[2]

1. **Notice–data subjects:** should be given notice when their data is being collected.

2. **Purpose–data:** should only be used for the purpose stated and not for any other purposes.

3. **Consent–data:** should not be disclosed without the data subject's consent.

4. **Security–collected data:** should be kept secure from any potential abuses.

5. **Disclosure–data subjects:** should be informed as to who is collecting their data.

6. **Access–data subjects:** should be allowed to access their data and make corrections to any inaccurate data.

7. **Accountability–data subjects:** should have a method available to them to hold data collectors accountable for not following the above principles.

In the EU, the General Data Protection Regulation (GDPR)[3] is used to regulate the processing of personal data, whereas in the USA there is no single law that matches that of the EU.

The USA does have a number of sectors that have acts of law protecting data, such as Video Privacy, Cable Television Protection and Competition, and Fair Credit Protection. But none as such apply to protecting data from a technical training perspective.

---

2 Provided by Wikipedia Foundation under Creative Commons Attribution-ShareAlike License.

3 The General Data Protection Regulation standardises data protection law across all 27 EU member states and imposes strict new rules on controlling and processing personally identifiable information (PII). It also extends the protection of personal data and data protection rights by giving control back to EU residents.

As many training organisations are part of multinational companies, it is prudent to adopt the seven EU principles. When considering the application of this fundamental level of privacy and protection, this helps in standardising across the company and simplifying the systems required to support the data captured.

CUSTOMER REFERENCES: IMPLICATIONS

Establishing a customer reference programme can have significant benefits (see Chapter 5); however, from a legal perspective, it is crucial to ensure that the training group and the customer follow the appropriate legal protocol.

The training group must always obtain written permission from target customers before publishing their names or brand. It is also vital that customers are given the opportunity to review any materials before proceeding, to ensure that information is not being disclosed that they consider as proprietary.

The golden rule is always to respect the customer's requests and publicity policies. This will protect the training group and its company from potential liabilities associated with disclosing customer information without permission.

SUMMARY

When a training group deals with customers, training partners or suppliers, validating and protecting the supply or purchase of required goods and services is crucial. This is normally undertaken in the form of a legally binding document.

Depending on the nature of the requirement, the document can be either a detailed contract or standard terms and conditions. Both include indemnity and liability sections. Whenever a company is involved in providing a service to others, it has a professional responsibility to provide a duty of care so that when advice is provided it is accurate and complete. This is covered by professional indemnity insurance. Legal liability is associated with personal injury or property damage, as a result of attending or being involved with the training business.

When operating in markets outside the country of origin, importing and exporting regulations and IP issues need to be considered and adhered to as well. These are covered by the World Trade Organization's (WTO) General Agreement on Trade in Services (GATS), and the EU Services Directive.

Intellectual property (IP) is an important part of what training departments offer and differentiates it from grey market competition; consequently, the content needs protecting. When IP rights are granted, they cover trademarks, copyright, patents and industrial design. The World Intellectual Property Organisation (WIPO), which is part of the United Nations, offers legal protection across all member countries.

Copyright protects the form in which the content is recorded and includes discussion forum posts, unless it is placed in the public domain or other licenced environments such as Creative Commons. Trademarks should be registered in the training group's local country and individually in other countries where protection is required.

The right to privacy is a highly developed area of law in Europe. In the EU, the General Data Protection Regulation (GDPR) is used to regulate the processing of personal data, whereas in the USA there is no single law that matches that of the EU.

Customer reference programmes can have significant marketing benefits; however, written permission from target customers must be obtained before publishing their names or brand.

18 INFRASTRUCTURE AND TOOLS
Introduction to the systems and technical needs required to run a training business

Training platforms have been constantly evolving over the past 30 years. In the early 1980s, the Silton-Bookman Systems Registrar application provided a degree of automation in the enrolling of students on courses, recording attendance and tracking their training. In the current era, learning portals provide an integrated environment for training administration, content publishing, authoring and delivery.

Coupled with changes in the way people now prefer to learn, these learning portals also provide access and engagement with social media, collaboration and ecommerce tools. With the current rate of change and demands now being placed on learning technologies, the infrastructure and associated development tools are rapidly moving towards being provided in a hosted software as a service (SaaS) model.

For a training provider, the SaaS model provides significant advantages in terms of minimising infrastructure investment costs, supporting scalability and providing access to functional tools such as authoring and on-demand labs. For the target learner audience, it provides access to formal and informal content via a web interface with the ability to self-promote, track and bill use as required.

This chapter provides an insight into the training infrastructure and associated tools to consider for the running of a successful training business. The decision to purchase, subscribe, operate independently or integrate a tool via a SaaS solution is one of choice driven by cost, management overhead, scalability and access considerations.

THE ABSOLUTE BASICS

All IT solutions require a structure based on what functions and features are required to ensure both the sponsor and the target audience are satisfied and serviced appropriately. The structure is often referred to as a technology stack, which primarily is a classification or categorisation of the main elements required to support the solution. For training, the stack could be referred to as a training or learning stack, with the categories referring to the main functions required to support the training business. Table 18.1 provides a generic example.

The basic requirements shown in Table 18.1 assist in the definition and formation of a learning infrastructure stack. Key to putting it together is understanding the nature of what is being provided and how the future of training is being visualised. The danger

Table 18.1 Training infrastructure basic requirements

Training stack category	Category description	Key functions	Function description
Training administration and management	Tools required to support the booking, bill tracking, planning and coordination of training requests and resources.	Reporting and analytics Standard office tools (word processor, spreadsheet) LMS covering: • registration; • booking and billing; • resource management; • scheduling.	Measuring and monitoring student attendance, cancellations, booking levels, revenue, expenses by course and training offering, and training resource utilisation. Producing documents and providing financial information. Environment that provides the ability to plan and schedule training courses, book and bill student attendance, and manage and control the required training resources.
Learning environment	The required environment to ensure the target student audience can access and participate in knowledge, skills and competency acquisition.	Learning portals Search Virtual classrooms	A dedicated environment where students log in to a portal that provides access to content, personal training schedules and other learning support activities. Facility to search the available learning environment for content, guidance or support information. Access to scheduled virtual classrooms, which often includes VoIP and chat functionality.

(Continued)

Table 18.1 (Continued)

Training stack category	Category description	Key functions	Function description
		Remote labs and sandboxes	Access to scheduled labs that can be undertaken remotely. Often aligned with virtual classrooms. Sandboxes are similar in principle to remote labs, but without a dedicated problem to solve. Basically, they are a place where students can try out or explore a software environment at their leisure independently of a specific course.
		VoIP and chat	VoIP is typically provided in conjunction with virtual classrooms to allow verbal communication between the student and instructor, but also independently with others.
		Performance support	Access to other training resources such as reference materials, and providing functionality that gives students the ability to ask questions that subject matter experts or instructors can respond to.
Content development and provision	The tools and systems required to aid the development, production and provision of content in the various required modalities, including practical lab-based activities.	Audio-visual production tools	Tools that provide the ability to develop graphical and audio-based content that can be included in course manuals, or be interactive in nature as standalone eLearning.

(Continued)

Table 18.1 (Continued)

Training stack category	Category description	Key functions	Function description
		eBooks	Tools that assist in the development and production of e-based content that can be downloaded from a portal and read as an ebook, such as on a Kindle, or be more complex in nature and include audio-visual techniques such as Articulate Storyline.
		Content libraries	A location that stores training assets such as pages, images, content, authoring and presentations for future reference, amendment or collation.
		Assessment software	Exam or question development requiring several tools to assist in item writing, validation and defensibility.
		eLearning and authoring tools	Similar tools to those used in the development and production of ebooks.
		LCMS	LCMSs provide authors and instructional designers with the ability to create content more efficiently by allowing the content to be developed in smaller units, such as learning objects, and be easily assembled for multiple uses.

(Continued)

Table 18.1 (Continued)

Training stack category	Category description	Key functions	Function description
Social and collaboration	An environment where students can interact and exchange ideas between themselves, subject matter experts and instructors to encourage the development of further skills and competencies.	Collaboration tools	Tools that provide students and training staff with access to those with common interests or needs.
		Online chat	Provides communication between members of the social group the students are involved with.
		Meetings and coaching	Dedicated environments, such as SharePoint, where specific events can be scheduled and supported to encourage the interchange of ideas, or dedicated locations set up to support the structures required for coaching.
		Social learning platform	The overall environment where all the elements required to support social learning and collaboration can be installed and configured.

is building a solution to the current need and not planning for scalability and future amendments.

A simple approach to defining a learning stack is to consider who the target user base is in terms of whether they are mobile or web-based. Mobile access is growing at significant rates, especially among non-commercial users. However, screen size can impact the effectiveness of training and the graphical interactivity that is included. Thought should therefore be given to building a responsive web interface that can accommodate all screen sizes and provide a user interface that is acceptable on a mobile screen. This is important if the training content contains rich material for SEO.

Another learning stack consideration when building from scratch is capitalising on existing tools that have been tried and tested within a training environment requiring strong technology integration.

Finally, making the decision on whether to build, buy or use a cloud provider is also an important consideration; more on this later.

TMS, LMS, LCMS, OTHER: WHAT IS RUNNING YOUR BUSINESS?

To run a training business, a defined process, procedure and structure is required to register, track, bill and monitor activity within the training department. Back in the 1980s it was known as a training management system (TMS). The TMS was initially a standalone application resident on a single PC providing administrative support regarding the enrolment of students on courses, recording attendance and tracking training programme progress.

As technology evolved and the needs of training managers grew, the TMS was eclipsed by a more comprehensive and responsive network-based management system, known as a learning management system. As many LMSs were web-based, they enabled the provision of access to eLearning content that could be downloaded and included within a personalised and trackable training programme. LMS functionality also included multi-administered resource management (including instructors, facilities, equipment), booking and billing management, assessments, student completion- and cancellation-rate reporting, collaboration, instructor course scheduling and statistical analysis.

Some LMS vendors include performance management support via employee appraisals, competency management, skills-gap analysis, succession planning and 360-degree reviews. For training vendors with responsibilities for internal training, this is a useful and a valuable addition.

As an LMS was focused primarily on the delivery of eLearning, student administration and training delivery management support, it did not provide any functionality to create and manage content. As a consequence, learning content management systems were developed to broaden the scope of the LMS to provide an environment where developers, authors and instructional designers could create, store, reuse, manage, publish and deliver eLearning content from a central learning object repository. When an LCMS and LMS are integrated within a broader training management system, it provides a rich environment to develop, manage and publish training content that is delivered and administered via the LMS.

An LCMS provides the ability for content to be modified and republished for various audiences, maintaining both version and history control. Table 18.2 highlights the key functional differences between an LMS and an LCMS.

With advancements in both LMS and LCMS development, common functionality will naturally occur. Care is therefore required when assessing the purchase of new generation systems to ensure training business suitability.

Since the advent of Web 2.0, integrated websites are being developed that mirror the functionality of both an LMS and an LCMS. They have additional functionality included for social media support, collaboration and ecommerce tools to provide an environment that can support a hosted SaaS training model, and they are more commonly referred to as learning portals. For today's learners and commercial training providers, the ability

Table 18.2 LMS and LCMS functional differences

LMS/LCMS	Functionality
LMS	• Content delivery.
	• Student registration, administration and attendance tracking.
	• Course scheduling.
	• Curriculum management.
	• Skills and competencies management.
	• Individual development plan support.
	• Reporting and assessment tools.
	• Training records management.
	• Resource management (instructors, training rooms; physical and virtual).
	• Performance management system integration.
LCMS	• Courseware authoring.
	• Collaborative content authoring and development.
	• Content management and version control.
	• Modality publishing.
	• LMS integration support.

to provide access to informal content, articles, case studies, books and other learning materials is a powerful new opportunity to consider in relation to the continuing change taking place in the way people prefer to learn.

CLOUD OR BUILD YOUR OWN?

Most technologies available today offer a cloud-based solution, and learning technologies are no different. From a training executive's perspective, cloud computing offers the potential to save capital cost investment, minimise headcount and provide better scalability and functionality.

In order to validate the potential of cloud versus owning and installing on-premise, it is important to understand the main differences. By way of definition, on-premise refers to training solutions deployed in the traditional manner where the technology infrastructure is acquired and the training LMS and LCMS are installed at the company's own premises. Irrespective of whether the IT service has been outsourced to a service integrator, the physical assets still remain on the training group's balance sheet.

Cloud computing refers to the delivery of on-demand computing resources such as a training LMS and LCMS via the internet on a pay-for-use basis, thus removing the requirement to provide the technology or be concerned with scalability or downtime issues. On the financial side, a cloud-based LMS solution no longer resides on the capital assets and therefore becomes a run-time cost of sale.

Making a decision about which solution should be chosen depends on some of the points listed below:

- employee expertise;
- resource availability;
- security or compliance requirements;
- budget availability;
- requirement for 24×7 access and technical support;
- scalability.

Table 18.3 provides some additional insight and suggestions regarding what to evaluate when deciding between an on-premise or cloud training solution.

Table 18.3 On-premise versus cloud

Considerations	On-premise	Cloud	Suggestion
Expertise	Employee costs can be high if the skill requirement is niche.	Staff specialise in specific offerings and cloud provider absorbs the costs.	Cloud
24×7 support and monitoring	Monitoring LMSs can run 24×7, but keeping staff around the clock can be very expensive.	Cloud service providers monitor 24×7, but may not monitor or provide relevant training support as required.	On-premise if service provision is specifically training related
Scale	Ability to scale and fund can be restrictive.	One of the major benefits is the ability to scale and pool resources, including access to broad and in-depth technical skills.	Cloud
Compliance	Legal and regulatory compliance can incur significant overhead and responsibility.	Will have teams devoted to compliance who can respond to issues quickly and efficiently.	Cloud

(Continued)

Table 18.3 (Continued)

Considerations	On-premise	Cloud	Suggestion
Service level agreements (SLAs)	When there's an outage, it will be up to the technical support team to get things back up and running.	Cloud service providers offer financially backed SLAs and provide full around the clock coverage.	Cloud
Understanding the training business	The training team will fully understand its business and know which customer or application is more important to focus on immediately.	Cloud services providers excel in generics and not the specific elements associated with training provision.	On-premise
Security	Security is critical, complex and expensive and must be maintained 24×7.	Cloud service providers leverage economies of scale and focus on providing high levels of security protection.	Cloud
Customisation	Maximum flexibility to customise and implement when required, including the inclusion of non-standard training applications.	Cloud-based service providers offer flexibility and many configurable options, but will be limited in what they can implement or support.	On-premise or cloud, depending on the levels of complexity required
Cost model	Requires capital expenditure, finance arrangements and longer-term investments.	Cloud solutions are subscription service-based and categorised as operational expenses.	Cloud

Choosing between on-premise and cloud is not mutually exclusive. Being able to pick and mix can be what is best for the business. For example, content development-based applications may be on-premise, with the lab and LMS cloud-based. One important factor to consider is that on-premise solutions represent large capital investments, whereas cloud-based solutions represent long-term subscription contracts. Weighing up the pros and cons of both options will assist in making a valid and balanced business decision.

SUMMARY

All IT solutions require a structure based on what functions and features are required to ensure both the sponsor and the target audience are satisfied and serviced appropriately. The structure typically needs to provide support for training administration and management, learning environment, content development and provision, and social and collaboration spaces.

When assessing the scope of the required structure, both scalability and the ability to implement future amendments need to be factored in. This is where the decision on whether to build, buy or use a cloud provider is also an important consideration.

Many of today's environments comprise network-based management systems, known as learning management systems (LMSs). As most LMSs are web-based, eLearning content can be downloaded and included within a personalised and trackable training programme, including multi-administered resource management, booking and billing management, assessments, student completion- and cancellation-rate reporting, collaboration, instructor course scheduling and statistical analysis.

LMSs can be integrated with learning content management systems (LCMSs) where developers, authors and instructional designers can create, store, reuse, manage, publish and deliver eLearning content from a central learning object repository. This provides a rich environment to develop, manage and publish training content that is delivered and administered via the LMS.

As the LMS and LCMS are feature rich environments, they lend themselves to being available as a cloud-based solution. This provides the potential to save capital cost investment, minimise headcount and provide better scalability and functionality.

Choosing between an on-premise or cloud solution is not mutually exclusive. The ability to pick and mix can be what is best for the business, and weighing up the pros and cons of both options assists in the making of valid and balanced business decisions.

APPENDIX

Chapter 2 concluded with a case study: the strategy to execution model. For clarity purposes, the stages associated with the development of the executable plan, with the exception of the critical tasks and interdependencies, were not described. In this appendix the details for the missing steps are covered as follows:

- talent;
- formal organisation;
- climate and culture.

The **talent** requirements for the training team and partner community needed to support the critical tasks are shown in Table A1.

Table A1 Talent requirements

Role	Responsibility	Accountability
Training delivery manager	Managing and monitoring all aspects of the fiscal year strategy and execution plan covering business performance, results and employees.	Fiscal results and achievement of all critical tasks defined with FYxx strategy document.
EMEA delivery management	Executing FYxx strategy within region and actioning/supporting cross-EMEA management critical tasks.	Fiscal results, quality of delivery and attainment of critical tasks within regions of control.
EMEA business programmes support manager	Providing and developing business support programmes aligned to regional business leaders' goal achievement. Key FYxx programme support will be communication, low/no touch route to market and partner programmes. Interim central region management.	All communication across company ensuring internal audiences know how to engage and use education services as per the FYxx strategy. Achievement of the low/no touch revenue objectives. Successful execution of partner enablement training programme and education partner programme (EPP).

(Continued)

Table A1 (Continued)

Role	Responsibility	Accountability
EMEA administration	Providing all administration services to the EMEA countries.	Delivery of all agreed service level agreement goals and objectives.
Global training partner manager	Establishing and managing reseller and delivery training partner channels to drive bookings and margin growth as per fiscal year requirements.	Enrolment of training partners to provide coverage as per agreed country plans. Achievement of agreed EMEA fiscal year bookings and margin plan.
Instructor	Delivering and teaching courses and modules across multiple modalities.	High-quality delivery and achieving agreed customer satisfaction scores.

The **formal organisation** required to support the business design requirements is shown in Figure A1. The organisation has three main departments to minimise management overhead, with a focus on training delivery, product management and training partner management. Through the use of service level agreements, finance, sales, accounting, legal, systems and infrastructure, and marketing are provided as part of a shared service function to assist in minimising staffing costs and overheads.

Further cost efficiencies are achieved by centralising training delivery with instructors and administration coming under local control for the Americas and EMEA regions. Streamlining training offering lifecycle management under the training product management team enables curriculum development, certification and publications to operate more efficiently.

Training partner management comes under centralised control and operates as a separate P&L from that of training delivery to ensure focus of attention on critical task requirements.

The final stage of **climate and culture** is equally important as the others in terms of steering employees towards the achievement of training group success. Via active engagement and involvement at all levels, the training group will focus on:

- discussing, understanding and defining what it is passionate about;
- discussing, recognising and agreeing what it can be the best in the world at;
- discussing and understanding what is driving the economic engine and how to control it, not the other way around;
- discussing and agreeing what they value and why;
- discussing and understanding how, individually and as a team, they are progressing towards financial, personal, career and teamwork goals;
- recognising success and their part in it.

At the end of each quarter, all members of the team will reflect on all six points in a candid and positive manner with a view to building a culture and climate for success.

Figure A1 Formal organisation example

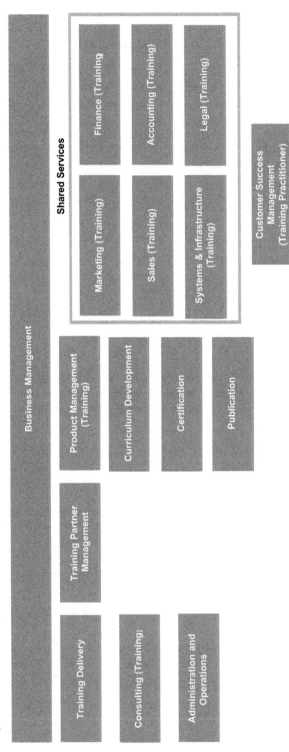

REFERENCES

Bandura, Albert (1977) *Social Learning Theory*. Englewood Cliffs, NJ: Prentice Hall.

Bandura, Albert and Walters, Richard H. (1963) *Social Learning and Personality Development*. New York: Holt, Rinehart & Winston.

Bloom, Benjamin S. (1956) *Taxonomy of Educational Objectives. Book I: Cognitive Domain*, 2nd edn. New York: Addison-Wesley Longman Ltd.

Branson, R.K., Rayner, G.T., Cox, J.L., Furman, J.P., King, F.J. and Hannum, W.H. (1975) *Interservice Procedures for Instructional Systems Development*, 5 vols (TRADOC Pam 350-30 NAVEDTRA 106A). Fort Monroe, VA: US Army Training and Doctrine Command, August 1975. (NTIS No. ADA 019 486 through ADA 019 490.)

Lombardo Michael M. and Eichinger, Robert A. (2000) *The Career Architect Development Planner*, 3rd edn. US: Lominger Limited.

Neibert, Jennifer (2013) *Agile instructional design: the big questions*. Learning Solutions. Available from www.learningsolutionsmag.com/articles/1262/agile-instructional-design-the-big-questions [28 January 2019].

OECD (2017) *G20/OECD principles of corporate governance*. OECD. Available from www.oecd.org/corporate/principles-corporate-governance.htm [28 January 2019].

Thorndike, Robert L., Angoff, William H. and Lindquist, E.F. (1971) *Educational Measurement*. Washington DC: American Council on Education.

Tuckman, B. (1965) 'Developmental sequence in small groups'. *Psychological Bulletin*, 63 (6). 384–399.

Watson, Russell (1981) 'Instructional systems development'. Paper presented to the International Congress for Individualized Instruction. EDRS publication ED 209 239.

World Bank (2017) *Governance*. The World Bank. Available from www.worldbank.org/en/topic/governance [28 January 2019].

FURTHER READING

PREFACE

CreativeDisplaysNow.com (n.d.), *History of communication from cave drawings to the web*. Creative Displays Now. Available from www.creativedisplaysnow.com/articles/history-of-communication-from-cave-drawings-to-the-web/ [28 January 2019].

CHAPTER 3

Accounting Tools (2017) *Selling, general and administrative expense*. Accounting Tools. Available from www.accountingtools.com/articles/what-is-the-selling-general-and-administrative-expense.htm [28 January 2019].

Aha! (2017) *Introduction to product management*. Aha! Available from www.aha.io/roadmapping/guide/product-management [28 January 2019].

Kovac, Mark, Ledingham, Dianne and Weinger, Lewis (2012) *Creating an adaptive go-to-market system*. Bain. Available from www.bain.com/publications/articles/creating-an-adaptive-go-to-market-system.aspx [28 January 2019].

Marketing MO (2017) *Return on investment – ROI – formula and use*. Marketing MO. Available from www.marketingmo.com/campaigns-execution/how-to-calculate-roi-return-on-investment [28 January 2019].

Marketing MO (2017) *Pricing strategy*. Marketing MO. Available from www.marketingmo.com/strategic-planning/how-to-develop-a-pricing-strategy/ [28 January 2019].

Schmidt, Marty (2017) *Total cost of ownership TCO for assets and other acquisitions*. Solution Matrix Ltd. Available from www.business-case-analysis.com/total-cost-of-ownership.html [28 January 2019].

Symetrics Group (2017) *A go-to-market strategy primer*. Symetrics Group. Available from http://symmetricsgroup.com/a-go-to-market-strategy-primer/ [28 January 2019].

Wikipedia (2017) Product management. Wikipedia. Available from https://en.wikipedia.org/wiki/Product_management [28 January 2019].

CHAPTER 4

Heathfield, Susan M. (2018) *Culture: your environment for people at work*. The Balance Careers. Available from www.thebalance.com/culture-your-environment-for-people-at-work-1918809 [28 January 2019].

iEduNote (2017) *6 elements of organizational structure*. iEduNote. Available from https://iedunote.com/organizational-structure-elements [28 January 2019].

Kuppler, Tim (2015) *Workplace culture vs climate: why most focus on climate and may suffer for it*. Human Synergistics International. Available from www.cultureuniversity.com/workplace-culture-vs-climate-why-most-focus-on-climate-and-may-suffer-for-it/ [28 January 2019].

OECD (2017) *Corporate governance*. OECD. Available from www.oecd.org/corporate/ [28 January 2019].

Schmidt, Marty (2017) *Return on investment (ROI) metric measures profitability*. Solution Matrix Ltd. Available from www.business-case-analysis.com/return-on-investment.html [28 January 2019].

CHAPTER 5

Accounting.com (2017) *What is GAAP?* Accounting.com. Available from www.accounting.com/resources/gaap/ [28 January 2019].

AICPA (2017) *AICPA mission and history*. AICPA. Available from www.aicpa.org/ABOUT/MISSIONANDHISTORY/Pages/default.aspx [28 January 2019].

Bradley, Anca (2017) *Two sides of content: lead generation vs demand generation*. Business.com. Available from www.business.com/articles/two-sides-of-content-lead-generation-vs-demand-generation/ [28 January 2019].

Ciotti, Gregory (2106) *Writing value propositions that work*. Help Scout. Available from www.helpscout.net/blog/value-proposition/ [28 January 2019].

Furgison, Lisa (2017) *How to create a unique value proposition*. Bplans. Available from http://articles.bplans.com/create-value-proposition/ [28 January 2019].

ICT Sector (2011) *What is demand generation?* ICT Sector. Available from www.ictsector.com/framework.html [28 January 2019].

Mccluskey, Heather (2015) *How to found a customer advisory board: best practices for product*. User Voice. Available from https://community.uservoice.com/blog/starting-customer-advisory-board-best-practices/ [28 January 2019].

Search Engine Land (2017) *What is SEO / search engine optimization?* Search Engine Land. Available from http://searchengineland.com/guide/what-is-seo [28 January 2019].

Selingo, Jeffrey J. (2014) 'Demystifying the MOOC'. *The New York Times*. Available from www.nytimes.com/2014/11/02/education/edlife/demystifying-the-mooc.html [28 January 2019].

Smart Insights (2013) *The push and pull product distribution model*. Smart Insights. Available from www.smartinsights.com/marketing-planning/marketing-models/push-pull-product-distribution-model/ [28 January 2019].

Wikipedia (2016) Vendor-specific objective evidence. Wikipedia. Available from https://en.wikipedia.org/wiki/Vendor-specific_objective_evidence [28 January 2019].

Wikipedia (2017) *Marketing management*. Wikipedia. Available from https://en.wikipedia.org/wiki/Marketing_management [28 January 2019].

CHAPTER 6

Adams-Mott, Ashle (n.d.) *Net vs gross revenue*. bizfluent. Available from www.ehow.com/info_8579058_net-vs-gross-revenue.html [28 January 2019].

The Customer Success Association (n.d.) *The definition of customer success*. The Customer Success Association. Available from www.customersuccessassociation.com/definition-customer-success-management/ [28 January 2019].

CHAPTER 7

Klipfolio (2017) *Sales metrics*. Klipfolio. Available from www.klipfolio.com/resources/kpi-examples/sales [28 January 2019].

Ready Ratios (2017) *Cost of sales*. Ready Ratios International Financial Reporting Tool. Available from www.readyratios.com/reference/accounting/cost_of_sales.html [28 January 2019].

Wikipedia (2016) *Spiff*. Wikipedia. Available from https://en.wikipedia.org/wiki/Spiff [28 January 2019].

CHAPTER 8

Reh, F. John (2016) *Understanding Pareto's Principle: the 80/20 rule*. The Balance Careers. Available from www.thebalance.com/pareto-s-principle-the-80-20-rule-2275148 [28 January 2019].

CHAPTER 9

Federal Trade Commission (n.d.) *Guide to antitrust laws*. Federal Trade Commission. Available from www.ftc.gov/tips-advice/competition-guidance/guide-antitrust-laws [28 January 2019].

Wikipedia (2017) *European Union competition law*. Wikipedia. Available from https://en.wikipedia.org/wiki/European_Union_competition_law [28 January 2019].

Wikipedia (2017) *ISO 9000*. Wikipedia. Available from https://en.wikipedia.org/wiki/ISO_9000#Contents_of_ISO_9001 [28 January 2019].

CHAPTER 10

Greenberg, Carl I. (2017) *How to conduct a training needs analysis*. XpertHR. Available from www.xperthr.com/how-to/how-to-conduct-a-training-needs-analysis/6716/ [28 January 2019].

hr-guide.com (2015) *Needs analysis: how to determine training needs*. hr-guide.com. Available from www.hr-guide.com/data/G510.htm [28 January 2019].

CHAPTER 11

Augment (2015) *Virtual reality vs augmented reality. Augment*. Available from www.augment.com/blog/virtual-reality-vs-augmented-reality/ [28 January 2019].

Faragher, J. (2014) *70:20:10 – a model approach for learning?* Personnel Today. Available from www.personneltoday.com/hr/702010-a-model-approach-for-learning/ [28 January 2019].

Gottfredson, Conrad (2013) *'What we got here is ... an EPSS'*. Learning Solutions. Available from www.learningsolutionsmag.com/articles/1228/what-we-got-here-is--an-epss [28 January 2019].

McLeod, Saul (2016) *Bandur: social learning theory*. Simplypsychology.org. Available from https://simplypsychology.org/bandura.html [28 January 2019].

Nelson, Brett (2013) *The 'Freemium' model: top flaws and potent fixes*. Forbes. Available from www.forbes.com/sites/brettnelson/2013/07/23/the-freemium-model-top-flaws-and-potent-fixes/#44a7dd0d3022 [28 January 2019].

Urban, Tim (2015) *The AI revolution: the road to superintelligence*. Wait But Why. Available from https://waitbutwhy.com/2015/01/artificial-intelligence-revolution-1.html [28 January 2019].

Urban, Tim (2015) *The AI revolution: our immortality or extinction*. Wait but Why. Available from https://waitbutwhy.com/2015/01/artificial-intelligence-revolution-2.html [28 January 2019].

Wikipedia (2017) *Gamification of learning*. Wikipedia. Available from https://en.wikipedia.org/wiki/Gamification_of_learning [28 January 2019].

CHAPTER 12

Gutierrez, Karla (2015) *The ins and outs of rapid prototyping for elearning*. Shift Disruptive eLearning. Available from http://info.shiftelearning.com/blog/rapid-prototyping-for-elearning [28 January 2019].

Huhn, Jake (2013) *What is Agile learning design?* Bottom Line Performance. Available from www.bottomlineperformance.com/what-is-agile-learning-design/ [28 January 2019].

Kurt, Serhal (2017) *ADDIE model: instructional design.* Educational Technology. Available from http://educationaltechnology.net/the-addie-model-instructional-design/ [28 January 2019].

Morgan, Ashanti (2015) *ADDIE vs AGILE model: an instructional designer's perspective.* Iddblog. Available from www.iddblog.org/?p=2184 [28 January 2019].

Pappas, Chrostoforos (2015) *The power of AGILE instructional design approach.* eLearning Industry. Available from https://elearningindustry.com/the-power-of-agile-instructional-design-approach [28 January 2019].

xAPI.com (2017) *What is experience API?* xAPI.com. Available from http://tincanapi.com/overview/ [28 January 2019].

CHAPTER 13

Althouse. Linda A. (n.d.) *Test development: ten steps to a valid and reliable certification exam.* Paper 244-25, Professional Development and User Support. SAS Institute Inc. Available from http://www2.sas.com/proceedings/sugi25/25/ps/25p244.pdf [28 January 2019].

ANSI (2017) *Product certification programs.* ANSI Accreditation. Available from www.ansi.org/accreditation/product-certification/Default [28 January 2019].

Badge Alliance (n.d.) *Open Badges infrastructure.* Badge Alliance. Available from www.badgealliance.org/open-badges-infrastructure/ [28 January 2019].

Florentine, Sharon (2014) *IT certifications: discover where the value lies.* CIO from IDG. Available from www.cio.com/article/2838187/careers-staffing/it-certifications-discover-where-the-value-lies.html [28 January 2019].

IAF (n.d.) *Home.* The International Accreditation Forum. Available from http://iaf.nu [28 January 2019].

Microsoft (n.d.) *Browse Microsoft certification exams.* Microsoft. Available from www.microsoft.com/en-us/learning/exam-list.aspx [28 January 2019].

O'Connell, Matthew (2017) *Proctored vs unproctored testing: does it really make a difference?* PSI. Available from www.selectinternational.com/proctored-vs.-unproctored-testing-does-it-really-make-a-difference [28 January 2019].

OpenBadges (n.d.) *Discover Open Badges.* Open Badges. Available from https://openbadges.org [28 January 2019].

PMI (n.d.) *PMI Agile Certified Practitioner.* Project Management Institute. Available from www.pmi.org/certifications/types/agile-acp

Prometric (n.d.) *Efficient test development and legal defensibility.* Prometric. Available from www.prometric.com/en-us/news-and-resources/reference-materials/Pages/Efficient-Test-Development-and-Legal-Defensibility.aspx [28 January 2019].

UKAS (n.d.) *Home.* The United Kingdom Accreditation Service. Available from www.ukas.com [28 January 2019].

Wikipedia (n.d.) *Blooms taxonomy.* Wikipedia. Available from https://en.wikipedia.org/wiki/Bloom%27s_taxonomy [28 January 2019].

Wikipedia (n.d.) *ISO IEC 17024*. Wikipedia. Available from https://en.wikipedia.org/wiki/ISO/IEC_17024 [28 January 2019].

Wikipedia (n.d.) *Standard-setting study*. Wikipedia. Available from https://en.wikipedia.org/wiki/Standard-setting_study [28 January 2019].

CHAPTER 14

BusinessBalls (2018) *Introduction to corporate governance*. BusinessBalls. Available from www.businessballs.com/corporate-governance.htm [28 January 2019].

Schmidt, Marty (2018) *Financial metrics: business ratios and cash flow metrics*. Solution Matrix Ltd. Available from www.business-case-analysis.com/financial-metrics.html [28 January 2019].

Schmidt, Marty (2019) *Break-even point analysis from fixed and variable costs*. Solution Matrix Ltd. Available from www.business-case-analysis.com/break-even-analysis.html [28 January 2019].

Schmidt, Marty (2019) *Income statement, profit & loss, statement of operations*. Solution Matrix Ltd. Available from www.business-case-analysis.com/income-statement.html [28 January 2019].

Schmidt, Marty (2019) *Return on investment ROI metric measures profitability*. Solution Matrix Ltd. Available from www.business-case-analysis.com/return-on-investment.html [28 January 2019].

CHAPTER 15

Accounting.com (2019) *What is GAAP?* Accounting.com. Available from www.accounting.com/resources/gaap [28 January 2019].

Averkamp, Harold (n.d.) *Financial ratios (explanation)*. Accounting Coach. Available from www.accountingcoach.com/financial-ratios/explanation [28 January 2019].

European Commission (2019) *VAT invoicing rules*. European Commission. Available from http://ec.europa.eu/taxation_customs/business/vat/eu-vat-rules-topic/vat-invoicing-rules_en [28 January 2019].

FASB (n.d.) *Home*. Financial Accounting Standards Board. Available from www.fasb.org/home [28 January 2019].

FASB (n.d.) *Revenue recognition*. Financial Accounting Standards Board. Available from www.fasb.org/jsp/FASB/Page/BridgePage%26cid=1351027207987 [28 January 2019].

GOV.UK (2019) *Department for International Trade*. Gov.UK. Available from www.gov.uk/government/organisations/department-for-international-trade [28 January 2019].

Learnyourcompany.com (n.d.) *Value based performance metrics*. Learnyourcompany.com. Available from www.learnyourcompany.com/methods/Value-based-performance-metrics.asp [28 January 2019].

Putra, Lie Dharma (n.d.) *Qualitative forecasting methods and techniques*. Accounting Financial & Tax. Available from http://accounting-financial-tax.com/2009/04/qualitative-forecasting-methods-and-techniques/ [28 January 2019].

Schmidt, Marty (2017) *Business growth metrics, cumulative average growth rate CAGR*. Solution Matrix Ltd. Available from www.business-case-analysis.com/growth-metrics.html [28 January 2019].

CHAPTER 16

Heathfield, Susan M. (2018) *Performance management*. The Balance Careers. Available from www.thebalance.com/performance-management-1918226 [28 January 2019].

Skousen, Tracy (2016) *Responsibility vs accountability*. Partners in Leadership. Available from www.partnersinleadership.com/insights-publications/responsibility-vs-accountability/ [28 January 2019].

Wikipedia (n.d.) *Competency management system*. Wikipedia. Available from https://en.wikipedia.org/wiki/Competency_management_system [28 January 2019].

CHAPTER 17

European Commission (n.d.) *Services directive*. European Commission. Available from https://ec.europa.eu/growth/single-market/services/services-directive/index_en.htm [28 January 2019].

freshbusinessthinking.com (2010) *What's the difference between public liability & professional indemnity insurance*. freshbusinessthinking.com. Available from https://www.freshbusinessthinking.com/whats-the-difference-between-public-liability-professional-indemnity-insurance.

Guardian Professional (2013) 'Setting out good terms and conditions for your small business'. *The Guardian*. Available from www.theguardian.com/small-business-network/2013/feb/06/terms-and-conditions-small-business [28 January 2019].

US Customers and Border Protection (n.d.) *North American Free Trade Agreement*. US Customs and Border Protection. Available from www.cbp.gov/trade/nafta [28 January 2019].

Wikipedia (n.d.) *Data Protective Directive*. Wikipedia. Available from https://en.wikipedia.org/wiki/Data_Protection_Directive [28 January 2019].

Wikipedia (n.d.) *Incoterms*. Wikipedia. Available from https://en.wikipedia.org/wiki/Incoterms [28 January 2019].

WIPO (2004) *WIPO intellectual property handbook: policy, law and use*. World Intellectual Property Organization. Available from www.wipo.int/about-ip/en/iprm/ [28 January 2019].

WTO (n.d.) *General Agreement on Trade in Services*. World Trade Organization. Available from www.wto.org/english/tratop_e/serv_e/gatsintr_e.htm [28 January 2019].

CHAPTER 18

CISCO (n.d.) *What is VoIP (Voice-over-IP)?* CISCO. Available from www.cisco.com/c/en/us/products/unified-communications/networking_solutions_products_genericcontent0900aecd804f00ce.html [28 January 2019].

Griffith, Eric (2016) *What Is Cloud computing?* PC Magazine. Available from http://uk.pcmag.com/networking-communications-software-products/16824/feature/what-is-cloud-computing [28 January 2019].

Kraft, Monica (n.d.) *Training Management System and Learning Management System differences*. Training Orchestra. Available from www.training-orchestra.com/en/tool-training-orchestra-blog-training-management-system-and-learning-management-system-differences-47-239-853.html [28 January 2019].

Mindflash (n.d.) *What is an LMS?* Mindflash. Available from www.mindflash.com/learning-management-systems/what-is-an-lms/ [28 January 2019].

Mindflash (n.d.) *LCMS and LMS*. Mindflash. Available from www.mindflash.com/learning-management-systems/lcms-and-lms/ [28 January 2019].

Rouse, Margaret (n.d.) *Software as a Service (SaaS)*. TechTarget. Available from http://searchcloudcomputing.techtarget.com/definition/Software-as-a-Service [28 January 2019].

Wikipedia (n.d.) *Registrar (software)*. Wikipedia. Available from https://en.wikipedia.org/wiki/Registrar_(software) [28 January 2019].

Wikipedia (n.d.) *Web 2.0*. Wikipedia. Available from https://en.wikipedia.org/wiki/Web_2.0 [28 January 2019].

GLOSSARY

accreditation: used to measure competency and efficiency of organisations such as channel and training partners to ensure they are adhering to agreed standards

ADDIE Model of Instructional Design: a framework used to develop training courses; it comprises five phases, namely: Analyse, Design, Development, Implementation and Evaluation

AGILE Instructional Design: a project-oriented iterative process that uses collaboration, feedback and iterations to improve the eLearning design and development process; it comprises five stages: Align, Get set, Iterate and implement, Leverage and Evaluate

American Institute of Certified Public Accountants (AICPA): develops standards for audits of private companies and other services including educational guidance

authorised training partner: an independent training provider that has been approved and authorised to provide technical training for an IT vendor in the use and application of its products

breakeven: delivering training income from both internal and external resources that balances the costs, known as a breakeven model

carve out: a way of ensuring training is included seamlessly within a sales transaction; the main issue is that no revenue is recorded as actual training, and hence delivery costs have to be absorbed, so it is important to gain corporate agreement on any carve out strategy regarding booking and revenue allocation before agreeing to this mode of operation

certification: used to validate the skills and competencies of an individual's level of proficiency; most IT companies implement certification programmes to validate their channel partners and to ensure customers have the skill required to be competent in their roles

cloud-based infrastructure: provides training organisations with access to third-party IT infrastructures, which can be configured to provide access to various applications in support of training delivery, content development and management

collaboration tool: interactive technology established to support and assist in the sharing of information, or activities specific to a group of students attending a course remotely

commercial training: for our purposes, this is an IT vendor training group established to provide training to its employees, partners and customers within an agreed financial framework and with an expected return on investment

cost centre: managing costs to an agreed and defined budget, known as cost management; often applied when training is viewed as a cost of doing business, in the same way that first line technical support, marketing or pre-sales support is viewed

cost of sales (COS): relates to the actual cost involved in selling the training; sometimes referred to as cost of goods sold (COGS)

course schedule: lists the courses on offer, available dates, locations and price in local currency

curriculum development: in training, a curriculum comprises a series of training activities that a student undertakes in order to gain knowledge, skills and proficiency in a particular product, so the development of the associated content and materials are collectively known as curriculum development

customer advisory meeting (CAM): provides an environment where customers and the training team can share ideas among themselves, and the customers can advise the training team on their needs, concerns and observations

customer reference programme: provides the training team with the ability to obtain customer testimonials that can be used to enhance sales and marketing activities, to assist in active demand generation

customer success management: a programme of internal activities to ensure a customer achieves the success they are looking for via the purchase of a company's product or service; this is accomplished by regular and meaningful interactions with all groups within a company, including the training department

demand generation: part of the marketing process and focused on shaping the target audience perspective on what they should consider buying, and, hence, is measured in terms of bookings or amount of revenue generated

eLearning: provides access to a training portal where students download subject matter content via the internet

electronic performance support system (EPSS): an application that provides on-demand, task-based training to help in the development of employees' skills and performance in the workplace, thus assisting in the improvement of productivity and employee development

estimated selling price (ESP): in relation to revenue recognition for bundled sales solutions, an agreement within the company of the best estimate on what the training is worth based on market prices

freemium: a play on the words free and premium; a pricing strategy where the product or service is free of charge and additional services are charged at a premium rate

gamification: uses the techniques of game design to aid student engagement, motivation and problem solving

general product announcement (GPA): release announcement and date for a new product following alpha and beta stages

Generally Accepted Accounting Principles (GAAP): principles adopted by the US Securities and Exchange Commission; the purpose of GAAP is to ensure financial reports reflect earnings in the period that they were delivered

go-to-market (GTM) strategy: focused on how a training offering will be placed into the market in order to reach market penetration, revenue and profitability requirements

governance: for a training group, this relates to being able to demonstrate how well-run and governed it is, in order to show that shareholder value is being maximised and protected

grey market: relates to non-authorised training partners who provide training without the approval of the vendor

gross domestic product (at purchasing power parity) per capita: commonly known as GDP (PPP); used to price training according to the economic performance and buying power per person in a country

gross revenue: the price charged before discounts and any applied reimbursements

inclusion rate: a measure of the number of deals, not the revenue value, that has been included with a sale

instructional systems design (ISD): a systematic approach to designing, developing and delivering instructional content and offerings in a consistent and reliable manner

instructor-led training (ILT): comprises an instructor, a classroom, lab equipment (dedicated or cloud-based) and catering

ISO 17024 standard: this standard addresses the definition of what is being examined (competencies), in terms of required knowledge and skills, and ensures the examinations are independent and provide a valid test of competence

ISO 9001 standard: defines quality practices for assuring organisations consistently understand and meet the needs of their customers

key performance indicators (KPI): used to assess and measure the performance of a specific business task. For example sales results in terms of order rates over a quarterly (3 month) period

kit sales: different from that of royalties, whereby the training partner purchases the training content (kit) upfront based on the number of course places sold; typical kit costs purchased from the vendor represent 15–18% of the student course fee

learning content management system (LCMS): an application allowing the creation and publishing of content in both print and web formats, and includes analytical tools to measure how students are interacting with the content

learning management system (LMS): systems designed to assign courses, training rooms and instructors, plus provide scoring and ability to manage student progress regarding eLearning content

managed training services: refers to any training activities that have been outsourced; this can be as simple as handling the printing of course material, or as comprehensive as managing the entire learning and development function

modified Angoff method: a study that test developers use in order to determine the passing percentage, or cutscore, for a test; it uses empirical data for validation

net promoter score (NPS): NPS is a management tool used to measure how an organisation is maintaining its customer relationships and loyalty; it is an alternative to traditional customer satisfaction research

net revenue: the price received after all discounts have been applied and the sale concluded

Organisation for Economic Co-operation and Development (OECD): OECD promotes policies that improve the economic and social well-being of people around the world

product management: a process that a training group implements to plan, design, build, operate and maintain a training offering; it can also be considered as a lifecycle management process

profit and loss: often abbreviated to P&L, this is about generating agreed levels of profit, through income generation, and minimising losses; collectively known as a profit and loss (P&L) account

quality assurance: guarantees that, during the training development, processes and administrative activities are implemented to monitor and control the training requirements and ensure goals are fulfilled

quality control: used to check that the training product or service being developed is in accordance with its specification

quality improvement: irrespective of the training development model being used, quality checks and assessment of development processes and tools should be regularly reviewed to check for and recommend improvements

quality management: important for a training group to adopt and undertake, as it ensures that the training product and service is consistent; this is achieved by implementing quality planning, quality assurance, quality control and quality improvement

quality planning: requires a training group to write and collect documentation that specifies the quality standards, practices, resources, specifications and content development models relevant to the training offering being developed

return on expectation (ROE): relates to the customer in terms of what level of behavioural or developmental change can be achieved at individual or group employee level

return on investment (ROI): the financial return on the committed and operational expenditure associated with the development and delivery of a particular training offering

revenue share: where the training partner purchases the content and shares the revenue obtained with the training group on a typical 35–45% basis

route to market (RTM): how the training offering reaches the end customer, which can comprise many channels: training partners, online sales, vendor sales staff and dedicated training sales staff

royalty-based income: where the training delivery partners purchase training content direct from the training group and print copies for consumption by the students who attend their courses; the partner reports the number of course places delivered and pays an agreed royalty amount, normally monthly

search engine optimisation (SEO): its main function is to increase website visibility. The main search engines use algorithms to rank a website's position and hence its overall position in the search results. In some instances it can be as simple as structuring the words on a website in a way the search engine operates

selling, general and administration (SG&A) costs: the actual cost of selling, which includes sales compensation, commissions, advertising and promotional materials

Shareable Content Object Reference Model (SCORM): a standard in eLearning that supports the tracking and tracing of student results in a learning management system (LMS); a course is SCORM compliant when the authoring tool produces a publishable version of student results and activities that can run on an LMS

social learning: extends formal training by providing an environment where students can discuss how they applied it in relation to their actual job, and the lessons they learned as a consequence; it also provides the opportunity to share experiences in a collaborative manner, reinforcing what students have learned, and assists in the better retention of information

social media: interactive technology allowing the creation and sharing of information; for a training organisation, it is typically in support of a course or curriculum

specialised product incentive fund (SPIFF): a specific form of incentive that results in an immediate bonus being paid for a sale; typically, they are paid by the training department to encourage product sales teams to include training as part of their overall deals

subject matter experts (SMEs): IT professionals within a vendor organisation who have expertise in their field and are often used by a training team to deliver advanced topics to students or assist in content development

technical training: covers the acquisition of knowledge, skills and competencies leading to overall individual or company performance in the use and application of technology

third-party evidence (TPE): in relation to revenue recognition for bundled sales solutions, the finance department and training group researches third parties, such as competitors, to determine how to price a similar offering

Tin Can: a standard that enables the collection of data related to the training experiences a student has both online and offline. It gathers data in a consistent format and is similar in principle to SCORM

total cost of ownership (TCO): includes the cost of buying a product and the additional costs associated in supporting, implementing and operating it; from a training perspective, TCO can be reduced by training and hence is a useful reference point for selling training to a customer

training attach rate: measures the relationship between product revenue and training revenue as a percentage rate in terms of the automatic inclusion of training in the sales discussion

training modality: primarily relates to learning style, which can be instructor-led training (ILT), virtual instructor-led training (VILT) or self-paced eLearning

training needs analysis (TNA): a process of activities regarding the identification of knowledge, skills, competencies or performance gaps that may exist when a new technology is being deployed to employees in a company, the output of which is used to help design and develop a training solution

training offering: can be categorised as a training product or service deliverable such as a course, seminar, practical lab session or subscription service

training partner advisory council (TPAC): provides an environment where selected training partners can share ideas, request new courses, discuss market conditions and debate new directions with the training group

value statement: informs a training group's employees and customers regarding its core beliefs and priorities

vendor: in the context of this book, the vendor is the IT manufacturer and supplier of products and services that the training organisation is supporting with relevant training offerings

vendor-specific objective evidence (VSOE): a revenue recognition mechanism used by companies that sell combined products and services such as training, in order to recognise a fair market value based on its individual sale value over a known period of time, rather than an allocated value

virtual instructor-led training (VILT): comprises an instructor who is remotely located and links up with students via conference phone or Voice over Internet Protocol (VoIP) and a virtual training lab with 24-hour access for the duration of the course

World Bank: provides funding for developing countries and has a common goal to reduce poverty, increase prosperity and promote sustainable development

INDEX

Lightning Source UK Ltd.
Milton Keynes UK
UKHW030616100120
356701UK00007B/513/P